Architecture for Rapid Change and Scarce Resources

Architects, development practitioners and designers are working in a global environment and issues such as environmental and cultural sustainability matter more than ever. Past interactions and interventions between developed and developing countries have often been unequal and inappropriate. We now need to embrace a new paradigm for architectural practice based on respect for diversity and equality, participation and empowerment.

This book explores what it means for development activists to practise architecture on a global scale, and provides a blueprint for developing architectural practices based on reciprocal working methods. It is essential reading for designers and architects with an interest in the developing world and for those involved in disaster planning and response. The content is based on real situations – through extended field research and contacts with architecture schools and architects, as well as participating NGOs. It demonstrates that the ability to produce appropriate and sustainable design is increasingly relevant, whether in the field of disaster relief, longer-term development or wider urban contexts, both in rich countries and poor countries.

Sumita Sinha is a practising architect and teacher, who has worked in India, France, Spain, Venezuela and the UK. Sumita is the founder of Architects for Change, the RIBA Equality & Diversity Forum. Sumita is the recipient of many awards including the UIA:UNESCO International Design Award and the Atkins Inspire Award 2008.

'This thought-provoking book links the structured world of buildings and design with the chaotic world of fluidity and diversity, bringing community participation in design into the centre of any planning process, even at a time of rapid change and resource scarcity. Reconciling the need for swift action with participatory processes is a challenge, but as Sinha shows, this brings about the most sustainable solution and creates the most value. The book provides practical tips and advice and provides a good overview for students of architecture, those engaged in urban planning, as well as the development activist.'

Nicole Kenton, *International Institute for Environment and Development, UK*

'This book identifies the need for cultural sensitivity in design and architecture, as well as wider development practice, as a result of the challenges of operating in an increasingly global environment. In an in-depth exploration of culture and perception, Sinha rightly acknowledges that respect and professionalism are central to effective working practice as development practitioners. This book helps readers to understand the challenges of operating in a different cultural context and through poignant recommendations asks us to examine our own preconceptions of ourselves and of others.'

Article 25

'At a time when modern architecture in the West has long since lost its social purpose and become the brand style of corporate capitalism, a now diminishing brand, this timely book offers a new prospect of an enlightened architectural future.'

Professor Mike McEvoy, *University of Brighton, UK*

'This will hopefully be a wake-up call for the architectural profession, and its education system, to re-establish its fundamental political, social and environmental responsibilities. More important perhaps, and more difficult, is the book's emphasis on the need to ask questions and create connections, to gain a deeper understanding of the inseparability of all life on this extraordinary planet. You may not agree with every sentence in the book but you must read it and at the very least begin to acknowledge some of the critical issues it raises about the future of human society.'

Roger Kelly, *former Director of the Centre for Alternate Technology*

Architecture for Rapid Change and Scarce Resources

Sumita Sinha

Routledge
Taylor & Francis Group

LONDON AND NEW YORK

First published 2012
by Routledge
2 Park Square, Milton Park, Abingdon, Oxon OX14 4RN

Simultaneously published in the USA and Canada
by Routledge
711 Third Avenue, New York, NY 10017

Routledge is an imprint of the Taylor & Francis Group, an informa business

British Library Cataloguing in Publication Data
A catalogue record for this book is available from the British Library

Library of Congress Cataloging in Publication Data
Sinha, Sumita.
Architecture for rapid change and scarce resources / Sumita Sinha.
p. cm.
Includes bibliographical references and index.
1. Architecture and society. 2. Architectural practice--Social aspects. 3. Architecture-
-Economic aspects. I. Title.
NA2543.S6S56 2012
720.1'03--dc23
2011032868

ISBN: 978-1-84971-115-9 (hbk)
ISBN: 978-1-84971-116-6 (pbk)
ISBN: 978-0-203-13518 -1 (ebk)

Typeset in Garamond
by GreenGate Publishing Service, Tonbridge, Kent

MIX
Paper from
responsible sources
FSC
www.fsc.org   FSC® C004839

Printed and bound in Great Britain by
TJ International Ltd, Padstow, Cornwall

Contents

Figures

Foreword

It is as impossible to be unaware of the challenge to house the world's ever-growing population, as it is to be unaware of the need to feed them. Similarly, the relentless demand on world resources – land, water, minerals and, of course, energy – is now part of the daily news. And yet in spite of our widespread awareness, there is no straightforward indication that any of these challenges are being met – either at governmental level or, at the other end of the spectrum, on a personal level. Cities grow, transport networks expand and industry produces and consumes more and more. Forests are cut, seas are fished to extinction. And in our personal lives we, in the richer countries at least, occupy more space, travel further, consume more and waste more food, day by day. And if that is not enough, the nations of the world squabble, on the one hand, over religious ideology and, on the other hand, over resources.

So it was with some curiosity mixed with a little foreboding that I embarked on reading this book. What is this rapid change? What *is* the impact of scarcity of resources? Are there some solutions to housing the world's poor to be found here, at last?

I remember attending a lecture three decades ago, along with a number of architecture students, by a highly motivated 'development activist' from Chile. It was little short of a rant, about the corruption, inequality and injustice that had led to generations of poor, minimally housed people. And his overriding message was that it was nothing to do with architecture. In fact, architects were almost vilified, deriding their (maybe well-intentioned but) inappropriate 'designer' shelters, or their promotion of government schemes that provide unaffordable housing displacing the deserving poor from their shanty towns. I remember at the time thinking, 'Oh dear, this is not the best way to motivate a room full of people – to tell them that the one thing that they are passionate about is irrelevant'!

So what has changed – if anything? Not, I think, the overall causes. Many of them will be found discussed in calmer and more informative terms, in this book. They sound depressingly familiar. So is there some new field in architectural design that by magic can in some way influence these non-architectural and powerful factors? Of course not. The only change is that the problem has grown in size; and perhaps (a small hint of a positive direction), in the development of world communication that brings these global problems more readily to the individual.

So, why is this topic located in the broad field of architecture?

If we forget about classical definitions of architecture and redefine it as the *field of the interaction between people and the built environment – how they respond to and influence it, and ultimately make it*, then we are immediately in territory in which architects, along with planners, urban designers, environmental engineers, social psychologists and economists might feel familiar (if not always comfortable). This too, is where we would find our 'development activist'. This broad list of disciplines gives a clue to where, if anywhere, solutions are likely to be found. And it is this field, rather than that of designing habitable structures, that this book addresses.

I would like to raise two particular issues. The first is resources. This is an ambiguous term – does it refer to the actual building materials and components, or does it mean the money to procure them? When we talk about resources on a global scale, and the current awareness of their diminishing reserves, we are almost certainly referring to the former. The relevance here being that if the world's homeless were to have their housing needs met to the standard that the rich countries enjoy, this would make demands on our dwindling reserves that could not be met. And exactly the same would apply to the increase in energy demand as for materials.

If, on the other hand, our meaning is the wealth to provide housing, then we are up against an even tougher problem. By all metrics, the gap between rich and poor grows steadily. Is this a surprise? No. The drive that makes primitive man gather food stocks, livestock, secure land and shelter around him has been evolving for thousands of generations and is demonstrably successful for the human species. The trouble is, we are now so good at it, and the richer we are, the better we are equipped to do it, that we can't stop. We have overshot our minimal needs manyfold – but the drive is insatiable.

So what is the future for the world's homeless?

I recently examined a PhD thesis.[1] The work studies the endeavour to achieve thermal comfort in three types of dwelling in Buenos Aires, designated as *incipient*, *consolidated* and *government*. These terms represent the three lowest rungs on the ladder from homelessness to 'good housing', and are defined as follows: (1) *Incipient* – built from waste materials and usually lightweight, (2) *consolidated* – often an improvement on (1) by the steady replacement and addition of conventional building materials, typically concrete, bricks and tiles, and (3) *government* – 'conventional' housing of a modest standard provided specifically to replace (1) or (2).

A summary conclusion was that in spite of the relatively poor thermal performance of the incipient and consolidated dwellings, the level of satisfaction was often greater than in the government housing. This was put down to the presence of greater *adaptive opportunity*[2] present in the informal housing types.

Detailed field reporting showed that behavioural and cultural issues, and the social structures within the shanty towns had a strongly supporting influence on this specific outcome.

As is so often reported, there is enormous creative energy present in these communities, and once the basic requirements of shelter, nutrition, hygiene and security are met, happiness quickly plateaus out. Maybe the light touch, insuring that only these basic needs are met, without damaging the fragile social structure, is the best way for development interventions to go. And maybe, as we, in the richer countries, are going to have to face global shortages, we should learn from these people who can already do so much with so little.

I have known Sumita Sinha since she studied for her MPhil at Cambridge in 1988. Passion is a much over-used word these days, but it is absolutely applicable to Sumita's love for this subject, and it shines through in her writing of this book.

Nick Baker
1 August 2011

Notes

1 Matthew French, Comfort, control and change: occupant control and socio-technical construction of thermal comfort in lower socio-economic Argentine dwellings. PhD Thesis presented Cambridge 2011.
2 Adaptive opportunity – a term usually used in comfort theory to describe the facility and freedom for a person to make small changes in the environment to improve their comfort.

Preface

This is a textbook aimed at students and professionals working in architecture, engineering, sociology, planning and any other subject where they are working in the field of rapid change and scarce resources, whether in the UK or abroad. Such students or architects have been called 'development activists' in the book (also called development practitioners by others, but I like the word 'active'). Development activism or practice is not a subject covered in architecture books. The reader will note that most of the reference books are not architectural, for much of this subject has never been written about in conventional architecture books. I have drawn from an electic range of sources, including Roget's *Thesaurus*, *The Dilbert Principle: A Cubicle's-Eye View of Bosses, Meetings, Management Fads & Other Workplace Afflictions* by Scott Adams (Harper Paperbacks, 1997) and an obscure but brilliant publication called 'Regeneration & Partnership Jargon' (Community & Voluntary Sector Network, 2003).

The book came about through my own research of about twenty years in this subject, having worked and lived in several countries. A conference I organized at London Metropolitan University called Inspire2Aspire in 2008 formed the backbone of this book along with lectures and ideas I have developed from it since. Each chapter is self-contained – thus, you can dip in and out. The subject area is so vast that chapters could only be introductions – perhaps each chapter is another book. The idea is that through reading each chapter and further discussing the points given at the end of each one, the student develops their own research and ideas, thus completing the chapter. The discerning reader will also see that I have avoided putting diagrams showing, for example, how a squatter settlement might work – there cannot be a system or diagram to show such complexities and uncertainties.

There are many issues – many of which are emotive – that are covered in this book, but even with 'facts' I found there are many answers to one question. I found strange paradoxes – errors in scholarly articles and truths in the *Daily Mail* – thus, in the end I had to make up my own mind (as you may have to do too).[1] I also depended upon what I saw and experienced – the 'documentary proof' is less important than actual proof. Although I had to use some – using statistics or figures which are often contested, cannot be practically useful (Darrell Huff's *How to Lie with Statistics*, Penguin, 1991 is brilliant). For example, it is pointless to argue whether the poor live on less than one dollar a day or one dollar and 25 cents – one recognizes abject poverty when one sees it. As I write this, Britain's biggest-selling newspaper has closed down, after more than a century of print – its downfall the result of phone hacking and other scandals. One truly does not know who or what to believe. So do write to me if you feel that there is something that needs to be updated or clarified.

Note

1 Many scholarly articles had factual errors, references to 'Third World' and spelling errors, especially of non-English names; one that sticks out particularly is 'Ghandi'. The *Daily Mail* has been carrying out a campaign for reduction of plastic bags (see 'Banish the plastic bags' and 'Plastic bag betrayal', 3 August 2011) as well as tackling issues on climate change.

Acknowledgements

I have to start by thanking my wonderful parents, Namita and Rasamay Sinha who, through their example, showed us how to live with love and compassion in a world of rapid change and scarce resources. My family was perhaps unconventional – a father who cycled to work, a home with no TV or fridge and an Uncle (affectionately called 'Meshai'), who made his own furniture and did all household repairs, including those on his car – all this in Delhi, more than thirty years ago was simply eccentric (as even now in India). My sisters and I joined in all this, not realizing how this would set me up to practise architecture of rapid change and scarce resources.

I have to thank the huge numbers of people all over the world who have welcomed me into their homes – with me travelling with my spices and cooking Indian food for them. Most of all, the people living and working in the slums and squatter settlements, ever cheerful, ever welcoming – some of whom have become great friends. Colleagues, teachers and students from the places I have studied or worked, especially the School of Planning and Architecture, Delhi, who continue to send their encouragement and help – some have supplied photographs, some their experiences. Some people have been kind enough to read draft chapters and send comments – David Satterthwaite from the International Institute for Environment and Development, Professor Teolinda Bolivar from Universidad Central de Venezuela and Diana Raby from University of Liverpool. Many thanks to London Metropolitan University, Royal Institute of British Architects and, in particular, The Centre for Education in the Built Environment who funded the research on participatory design. I would like to thank those people who have given great support through the years – Mike McEvoy, Robert Vint, Jacinta Garside, Wendy De Silva, Angela Brady, Virginia Newman, Cathy Stroemer (who heroically read many of the chapters and took out the jargon), Clare Crosland, Nicole Kenton, Robert Mull, Joel Valencia Paredes, Pamela Edwards, Suzanne Pritchard, Shrashtant Patara and the late Pratibha Patara, George Henderson, Ken Rorrison, Roger Kelly and Jane and Rod White. Many past and present students also helped by sending in photographs, case studies and comments – in particular, big thanks to Tatum Lau, Iain Smales, Stef Rhodes, James Lloyd-Mostyn, Bergur Finnbogason, Heather Stuart and Joao Wrobel; and especially Bara Safarova who took my painting of the *barrios* and designed a cover with it. My gratitude to my mentor in life, Daisaku Ikeda, Buddhist philosopher, whose quotes and work have deeply influenced me.

I have to acknowledge that I stand on the shoulders of giants – Nabeel Hamdi, Paul Oliver and Laurie Baker – with all of whom I have had the great good fortune to work. Nick Baker, who has written the foreword, not only taught me at the Martin Centre, Cambridge University, but also introduced me to croquet and *Blackadder* – big thanks to him! Thanks to my warm and encouraging commissioning editor, Nicki Dennis, and to wonderfully organized Alice Aldous and the team at Earthscan and GreenGate Publishing Services who have put up with delays from me and made a book out of what I gave them. Thanks to Daniel Rosbottom, who first encouraged me to write this book as did Sarah Wigglesworth, who also introduced me to the commissioning editor (who rather serendipitously just happened to be dining at the RIBA that night!).

A big thank you to James Jordan, for not only looking after our children when I was writing (and did not want to be disturbed!), but also for helping out with the photographs and technical issues. Chater and Catchik Paul Jordan, my children, have been wonderful – they have travelled to many of these places, with no fuss, perhaps with a lot of discomfort, but have never complained, and shown me the beauty and joy there. Yes, we can relax now – Mummy's book is done!

I dedicate this book to Chater and Catchik and the memories of baby Trets and to Kali Singha and all the children of the world who will inherit the arena of rapid change and scarce resources.

Part I

The world of the development activist

Chapter I

Introduction

Architecture for rapid change and scarce resources

If the nation is destroyed and people's homes are wiped out, then where can one flee for safety? If you care anything about your personal security, you should first of all pray for order and tranquility throughout the four quarters of the land, should you not?

(Nichiren, Japanese Buddhist monk, *Major Writings*, vol. 1, 16 July 1260)

On 10 April 2011, upon returning from work, I found that there was no electricity and, consequently, as a pump is used to feed water into our apartment block, there was no water either. I had become used to having both water and electricity all the time in London, despite having experienced shortages in both while living in India. I was feeling a bit smug because I had not been using a fridge or a freezer for almost two years[1] and so there was no food that would go off on this hot spring day. I could not use my computer, the Internet or telephone and I do not own a TV. So I turned on my solar radio and relaxed for a while. But then, I realised that I would not be able to cook because the hob uses an electrical spark to light the gas. I could water the plants with stored rainwater but would not be able to drink water myself. My supply of stored drinking water was running out and the shops were out of bottled water owing to local panic buying. The lease rules do not allow the use of fuel-based appliances such as barbecues or a 'storm kettle'. The electricity was eventually restored after two-and-a-half hours, just as I was thinking of going further to get food and water.

These two-and-a-half hours gave me a glimpse of a future and perhaps an ever-present reality for many of the world's poor. Despite progress in a technological sense, billions of people remain unfed, homeless or are dying of preventable diseases. According to Wateraid, 884 million people all over the world lack access to a safe water supply and 2.6 billion have no access to sanitation in 2011. They estimate that 4,000 children die daily from diarrhoea owing to lack of clean water and sanitation facilities.[2]

The Millennium Eco-system Assessment, prepared by 1,300 scientists from 95 countries, concluded in 2005 that the excessive exploitation of natural resources would be a cause of future poverty and hunger – not a solution.

Now, one in five people live on less than one dollar a day ($1.25 according to some).[3] Everyday, one in five of the world's population goes hungry while in richer countries, people are dying of obesity-related diseases. Half of deaths of children under five are associated with malnutrition (some six million annually worldwide). Some progress, indeed. As I write this, Britain, apparently the seventh largest economy and the home of the Industrial Revolution, is in the midst of a 'double dip' recession after just 300 years of industrialization. Its former colony, India, is now the third largest economy (while paradoxically, having the world's largest number of poor). However, we often find the paradox that the poor are happier than the rich (Figure 1.1). Amartya Sen, the eminent economist notes: 'Economic growth can make a very large contribution to improving people's lives; but single-minded emphasis on growth has limitations that need to be clearly understood'.[4]

We look at the practical impact of economic issues on the development activist's work in Chapter 2.

Architecture for scarcity

All these words – architecture, rapid, change, scarce and resources – are loaded with meanings that differ from time to time, place to place and culture to culture. Architecture is linked to our senses and social communication – a development of visual and cultural identities. It is an essential element in our spatial language using forms and voids, embedded within complex fields of urban and cultural discourses and specific context. Architectural practice today is a complex arena – ever changing and ever expanding. The idea of 'pure architecture' is perhaps a futile term – reductive and stagnant. In a lecture at the University of Westminster, the architect Ian Ritchie argued that the shift from an industrial reductivist to a post-industrial holistic approach required a complex enquiry that needs to instigate the social, political and philosophical criticism of design, 'if we are to re-define our work with any intelligent sense of value and meaning'.[5] Questions about the future of architects and the direction of their work are being raised all the time. The *Building Design Magazine*[6] reported that Michael Gove, the British Education Secretary, had told the then President of the Royal Institute of British Architects, Ruth Reed, that there were 'too many architects'. The Royal Society of Arts organized a competition in 2011 called 'The Resourceful Architect' in response to the intriguing questions about 'architects' ingenuity, strategic thinking and social role'. As jobs for life and patronage decline, architects have to re-educate themselves in the world of rapid change and scarce resources and create their own meaningful work. This aspect is discussed more extensively in Chapter 9. The nature of participatory work along with the clients and beneficiaries, which is increasingly becoming an important tool of design for the development activist, is described in Chapter 6 (Figure 1.2).

Figure 1.1 Proud mother from my village in West Bengal, India. Indeed my English husband remarked that he had seen the biggest smiles in this little remote village with no proper roads, water and electricity. For more on this paradox, see clinical psychologist Oliver James' book Affluenza (Vermilion, 2007).

Photo: James Jordan.

Figure 1.2 MA Architecture of Rapid Change and Scarce Resources students presenting their work to stakeholders in the 'real world' at a crit, November 2008, London Metropolitan University.

Photo: Author.

A quarter of the world's armed conflicts of recent years have involved a struggle for natural resources of one kind or the other. Scarcity of resources and rapid change started in earnest with the Industrial Revolution. As the Industrial Revolution spread around the world, raw materials were taken not only from industrialized countries but also from non-industrialized colonies. Thus, the legacy of the Industrial Revolution – scarce resources – is to be found in most countries, not just the economically backward countries or former colonies. The topic of scarcity in many forms is to be found in popular discussion today. The University of Westminster organized a series of lectures in 2011 called 'Scarcity exchanges' bringing together 'leading international thinkers to expound on one of the most pressing, but often avoided, issues of the day'. Our world is also a very unequal place and this inequality exists not only globally, but also within countries and people. This presents a dilemma that is not only linked to scarcity but also to cultural differences.

Climate change is part of the rapid change of our environment and society. Famines and water shortage, particularly those flamed by climate change and wars, are on the rise. This means that people are also on the move, because they need food and water; and to escape from danger. Petrol is reportedly the reason for wars and invasions now while food is used as a weapon of choice in conflicts by either restricting or withholding it. Demand in Europe and America for gold, diamonds and coltan (mineral used for making mobile phones and computers) from the Democratic Republic of Congo (DRC) has claimed an estimated three million lives since 1998.[7] Armies of Rwanda, Zimbabwe and Uganda have also plundered DRC's mineral wealth.[8] Water is another source of conflict, rapidly taking over from petrol, probably as it is absolutely essential to human survival. Some of the bitterest issues in the Israeli–Palestinian conflict stem from water allocation and use. According to Amnesty International, Israelis are supposed to be using four times as much water as the Palestinians (I saw many restrictions in place for water use imposed on the Palestinians for farming, sanitation and drinking during my visit there in 2011[9]).

Unfair trade restrictions are also a reason for strange paradoxes. While in the European Union (EU), owing to agricultural subsidies, farmers are literally paid not to farm; the African and Asian countries are struggling with food shortages. Every European cow is subsidized by $2.50 a day, that is 75 per cent more than most Africans live on. The EU is also importing food into Asia and Africa that can be grown locally. As another example, the EU practice of importing sugar has caused world sugar prices to fall by 17 per cent.[10] The EU even imports beet sugar to Mozambique, where sugar is a lucrative export crop. The rise of Fairtrade practices since the 1970s is trying to stem this tide of inequality but it has a long way to go, given that the richer nations have already made huge economic headway. For the development activist, Fairtrade is very important because it supports community and social well-being in the form of construction of schools, centres and other buildings in poor countries.

Today, the world's richest 1 per cent receives as much income as the poorest 57 per cent.[11] And of course, it is the world's richest that commission architects to design their homes, not the ones that are homeless. It is very difficult to estimate the numbers of homeless people in the world because countries have different legal definitions for homelessness. Natural disasters and civil unrest, where people move between places and countries, also complicate the picture of homelessness around the world. The best we have is a conservative estimate from the United Nations in 2005, which puts the number of homeless at 100 million. However, the UN report looked only at people who did not have any homes whatsoever. Not included were people who lived in poor quality housing such as slums and squatter settlements, or people who are on the move. Urban population growth has led to a DIY mentality where the poor moving into the city have taken possession of vacant land and buildings, even streets (Figure 1.3). They build their own homes using whatever materials they can purchase or find. We look at the complex issues of homelessness, squatter settlements and slums in Chapter 3.

Studying these areas of rapid change and scarce resources also presents problems of documentation. The ways to observe and record such fragile, varied and dense settlements, composed of people who may be immigrants, and are vulnerable, illiterate and mostly poor, can be a challenging task for those who have been versed in studying formal settlements and order (Figure 1.4). Informal settlements, refugee camps and slums present a chaotic visual

Figure 1.3 New migrants to Kolkata, India, from Bangladesh, living on the streets.

Photo: Author.

Figure 1.4 Old Delhi, once praised by foreign travellers for its beauty and cleanliness, now an urban mess, through past colonial policies, commercialization, overcrowding and insensitive planning.

Photo: Author.

experience that can be difficult to put down as drawings. In Chapter 8, I list the ways that my students, colleagues and I have used to observe and record participatively, along with examples of good and bad practices.

Urbanization and globalization of architecture

Ninety per cent of ancient Greeks lived in the countryside, but the 'polis' or the city defined how they lived and interacted. In 1800, only 2 per cent of the world's population was urbanized. In 1950, only 30 per cent of the world population was urban. In 2000, 47 per cent of the world population was urban. By 2030, it is expected that 60 per cent of the world population will live in urban areas. Venezuela is one of the countries that has already crossed this mark – 92 per cent of its population already live in urban centres. São Paolo, for example, grew 72 times its size in one decade until 2000. The phenomenon of the megacity where the population is more than 10 million is a relatively new development, which has not been seen before. Architects and planners are struggling to understand huge conurbations such as Tokyo-Yokohama (33 million) and Mexico city (22 million). Many of these cities also have densities not seen before – Mumbai, for example, with 20,482 persons per square kilometre (India has eighteen of the world's fifty densest urban conurbations[12]). Most of this urbanization happens without infrastructural support – without any water, electricity or sanitation in place (Figure 1.5). People who live in squatter settlements and slums in the poor nations improvise much of these. High densities, poverty and lack of facilities can be responsible for high crime rates – Juarez, in Mexico, is now the murder capital of the world (my visit there, even in 1995, was not easy tourism). Most planned cities are dependent upon the car and oil – and food. A city's food footprint can be more than 125 times its size (according to a 1998 report by the Centre for Sustainable Cities, Toronto impacts on an area 280 times its size[13]). How can this be sustained with resources that are rapidly becoming more scarce? Andrew Marr's series on Megacities on the BBC in June 2011 explored the dilemma of modern cities. Can modern urban centres ever be sustainable? We read more about this in Chapter 5, particularly whether traditional cities and technologies can have any lessons for us today.

Interestingly, the face of rapid urbanization also looks the same wherever we go – hot climate, cold climate, rich country or poor country (Figure 1.6). This was something I have long wondered about – why do city centres all over the world look or try to look the same? The insidious presence of modern architecture as a marker of progress is now seen in all capital cities of the world. The decision makers of our societies such as politicians often put architecture as a show element. In 2008, Ajay Maken, the Urban Development Minister for

Figure 1.5 Squatter camp, East Delhi, which lies uneasily next to a railway track. Many people have been run over while using the railways tracks as a toilet at dawn.

Photo: Author.

Figure 1.6 City centre, Singapore, but it could be anywhere.

Photo: Jason Jarrett.

India, declared his intention to turn Delhi into the New Manhattan for the 2010 Commonwealth Games. So for the sake of the Games, several thousand people from squatter settlements were evicted from Delhi – the city sanitized and globalized for the foreign visitors. 'Glocal' was a word coined after the Rio Environment summit in 1992, to combine local and global, and to emphasize that one influences the other. In my view, global architecture has now become local; thus, I say 'glocalization' of architecture instead of globalization of architecture.

Building technologies and materials are constantly being improved, yet many basic building materials and technologies remain inaccessible to most people on the planet. Traditional building materials and technology have been abandoned, even though engineers and architects have developed advanced versions of materials such as machine-rammed earth bricks and complex bamboo structures (even reinforced bamboo concrete). Within the megacities of the world are to be found the shanty towns of tin, bricks and cardboard. It remains a mystery as to why only a small palate of materials – cement, brick, concrete, steel and glass – continue to be used by most of the world's population, despite architects and engineers designing more eco-friendly buildings and technologies (Figure 1.7). The manufacture of many of these materials is energy intensive and polluting. We will examine this paradox in more detail in Chapter 4.

Figure 1.7 Structure designed using extruded earth and bricks, Delhi, by German architect, Gernot Minke, which remains unused.

Photo: Author.

Why do people (and governments) not think about the environmental consequences of their actions? I believe this comes down to three things. The first is the way our attention is taken by immediate happenings and the second by how we cater to our immediate needs. The third is about failing to make connections.

The immediate happenings

> We favour the sensational and the extremely visible. This affects the way we judge heroes. There is little room in our consciousness for heroes who do not deliver visible results – or those heroes who focus on process rather than results.
>
> (Nassim Nicholas Taleb, 2010[14])

Through the Internet and television, our awareness of events as they happen is almost immediate. The recent floods in Pakistan, the earthquake in Haiti, the tsunami in Japan and other images flood into our home via technology. People are able to donate money through the Internet and telephone; emergency supplies are flown in quickly. On the other hand, just as quickly this information or image is replaced by something else. For a week after the 2011 Japanese tsunami, one of the UK's popular tabloid newspapers continued to report on it in its front pages. By the eleventh day, the Japanese news had been relegated to page 23. The shocking news on 18 April 2011 that the nuclear disaster in Japan had been upgraded to Chernobyl scale and that it would take nine months to resolve it, was now on page 27. And this was only five weeks after the tsunami.

The Internet is also the home of many campaigns run through one's email box, social networking sites and websites of various organizations. The Internet is very popular in the richer countries. For example, Finland with a 5 million population has more Internet users than the whole of Latin America. The USA is home to one-third of all Internet users. There is hardly a day when some campaign does not come up, requiring donations or signatures. While this is a great tool and indeed many good things have been achieved through the Internet, it also has the danger of mobilizing support for many things that people might not have a complete picture of. According to Alex Wright, author of the book *Glut: Mastering Information through the Ages*,[15] today human beings produce 50,000 times the number of words stored in the library of Congress, or more than the total number of words ever spoken by human beings. Every year, data and statistics are growing by one-third – much of which is generated by self-serving individuals or organizations. Much of that comes via the Internet from social networking sites. Surprisingly, the Internet is also one of the most traceable and accountable forms of communication. Emails, searches and posts on the Internet can be traced back even if they are deleted. Most social networking sites do not claim to keep personal information private and many a prosecution has been brought up through the Internet. So the Internet has thrown up interesting new questions about privacy and ethics. The development activist has to check information thoroughly and make sure that privacy and ethical issues are not violated by their research, publications and work.

Public relations or PR is big business – in 2009, the biggest US companies generated $200 billion sales, but they spent only 14 per cent on research, compared to 31 per cent on marketing and administration. In the UK, more than £19 billion was spent on PR in 2008. There are 67,000 people employed to lobby elected members of US Congress – 125 for each. The EU has seven accredited lobbyists – including NGOs such as ActionAid who can lobby organizations and companies such as WHO, DaimlerChrysler, British Airways, Exxon Mobil and Shell. MP John Cryer reported that the UK has a £2 billion lobbying industry and said that those who try to influence parliament should be put on a register (as reported in all papers on 7th December, 2011). So with all the money spent on PR, it is difficult to believe who is right from information gathered from emails and the Internet. The economist Steven Levitt gives the example of Mitch Snyder, an advocate for the homeless, who claimed that there were three million homeless people in the USA in the 1980s and that every second, forty-five homeless persons were dying as a result of homelessness. People were startled by the huge figures – 'One in 100 homeless? 1.4 billion dead as a result of being homeless?' The USA population was just 225 million at that time and so eventually Snyder had to confess to fabricating these figures.[16]

Owing to the pressure of corporate social responsibility (CSR), the use of 'greenwash' or the unsubstantiated claims that various products are green are also getting very sophisticated. The number of products is also increasing – from baby powder, shaving cream to 'green SUVs'. These 'greenwashed' brands are among the 300,000 new products hitting the shelves worldwide every year. TerraChoice, a market research company, revealed the results of a study of 1,018 products randomly tested in 2010 to see whether they lived up to their claims. Of all the products surveyed, all but one failed. Some products advertized themselves as non-toxic but only replaced old toxins with ones that were banned years ago. Some products claimed so-called green status, but this could not be verified scientifically.[17] Building products are not free from 'greenwash' – as Tony Juniper, from Friends of the Earth, discovered during his trip to Ghana. He describes how wood taken from rainforests was being falsely certified in order to sell it in the UK market in his book *How Many Lightbulbs Does It Take to Change a Planet?*[18]

But perhaps the most convincing greenwash is the photograph of a real smiling person which is now found on many food (and some building) products in the UK, claiming that that person grew or made that particular product. According to Climate Change Action, Chinese workers quality testing iPhones are now taking pictures of themselves and leaving them in the photo library of the new phone. In a world where goods are made globally, the emotional impact of seeing a picture of the person or people who grew or assembled the product you may be holding in your hands, is the equivalent of pulling on one's heart-strings from a distance. It is also about playing on people's ethical stance to sell a product. Now, owing to pressure from the Advertising Standards Agency, if one cares to read the small print, some of these photographs state that these are 'representative' of the people, not the actual people!

Companies now own stadiums or buildings or sponsor events not for altruism but to generate publicity for themselves and use it as a 'trade-off' against other contentious activities. While looking at various banks that I could use for my charity account, I realized that the green credentials or humanitarian projects of various banks were a trade-off for other activities, for example investing in companies that manufacture weapons (perhaps an equivalent of carbon emission-trading). Dorothy Rowe's book *The Real Meaning of Money*[19] recounts the sinister ways in which our money is actually used. Even a prominent annual exhibition held in London for design and eco-building products has been criticized for its connection with arms manufacture companies. Often these issues need much investigation to uncover the truth. Connections are often tenuous – a football stadium in North London is now named after a Middle Eastern airlines company. An Indian web company has gone even further and 'adopted' an Indian village. The villagers have renamed the place 'snap.deal nagar' – a change from Shiv nagar, and have welcomed this web company, which among other things sells a well-known American brand of underwear to the middle classes. I suppose as the Indian god, Shiv, wore very few clothes, there might be a connection there. The company has now started providing water pumps for the villagers.[20] Of course, there has been Tatanagar in India – named after the Tata family who are prominent industrialists – and the UK has its Bourneville, from the Cadbury family. So, not all such actions are bad – after all, the bikes for public use in London are sponsored by a major bank.

Any campaign requires sufficient numbers of people who are well informed and sufficiently enthused about the project to effect any change. To do this, the development activist needs to ask the right questions, according to Anne Miller, author and inventor, echoing the need for a 'complex enquiry' from Ian Ritchie that I quoted earlier. Miller describes the case of Ann Pettifor, who is best known for her worldwide campaign to cancel approximately $100 billion of debts owed by forty-two of the poorest countries. She called this Jubilee 2000 (after the year 2000). Pettifor spent half the decade working in a draughty plastic shed, trying to find the right questions and finally succeeded in her mission by setting up the campaign, Jubilee 2000. In order to find a right way to resolve the other issues, the development activist can use Pettifor's method of 'complex enquiry' into issues.

Debt can have huge implications for a country's progress. Like Mathilde Loisel, in Guy de Maupassant's short story, *The Necklace*,[21] countries can keep paying debts and interest for years; and be unable to carry out any meaningful development work. Consider the example of Ghana, where false certification of timber is rampant. Timber is Ghana's third largest import and in order to repay its historic international debts, its rainforests are being cut down. By 2006, when Tony Juniper visited it, 250 square kilometres of rainforests had been cut to allow for 'economic liberalization policies'. Juniper comments: 'At least £30 million has been taken out of the country, and Ghana is deeper in debt than ever – only now it is missing another chunk of forest', which was in the UK, presumably being used for buildings and furniture.

Many development projects are plagued with misuse of money or corruption. Sometimes my students and I have gone into particular areas where we heard that non-governmental organizations (NGOs) were carrying out work but the people there appeared not to have heard about the NGOs or we could see nothing of the project described. NGOs have a difficult task to do and most work very hard to achieve their aims given the huge and sometimes almost hopeless scale of their tasks. However, the difference between the stated aims and what is actually achieved often makes me think that there are perhaps unreasonable expectations on both sides – from the NGOs who want to impress and succeed, to the funding organizations who want to see results rather quickly. So are the NGOs working towards the right goals at the right scale? Are they asking the 'right' questions? Is the money being used wisely? What are the 'right' questions about the project that the development activist needs to ask? Questions about ethics, corruption, resources, and environmental impact are just some that need to be considered. What kind of agreements need to be drawn up between organizations and countries that take into account ethics and equality?

What is acceptable culturally in one country or region may not be acceptable in another country or region (Figure 1.8). For example, in Kolkata, rather than going against the accepted culture of spitting the red betel nut juice, the Metro system has a groove along the tracks next to the platform to catch this where it can be washed away. Delhi's Metro system does not have this detail. As we work globally, ethical and cultural issues are becoming very complex, particularly for those working in areas of scarcity and poverty. Lack of literacy in the client and lack of knowledge of local language and culture from the development activist's side add to this complexity. A couple of sentences in a film about India made by my student caused concern in the mind of one of my colleagues in London regarding ethical violations, while we and an Indian human rights lawyer, Vinod Shetty, had found nothing wrong. We pointed out that he had not watched the film properly and got it wrong, and it showed me how hasty judgements can be dangerous and confusing. (Ironically, there was a potential real problem in the film – a statement which could appear to be derogatory to Muslims that this colleague had not picked upon. Shetty and I could clearly see that could be a huge problem if shown in Baroda, India, or

Figure 1.8 Children from a squatter settlement of West Delhi using a bus stop as a playground with swings – would this be acceptable in the UK with its 'culture of health and safety'? Appropriation and use of space depend upon the culture of a place.

Photo: Author.

even Bradford, UK, and we have now removed it). How can the development activist work in this complex cultural and ethical scenario? We explore some of these thorny issues in Chapter 7.

The immediacy of needs

Owing to pollution, the natural environment itself has become a scarce resource. Clean land, air and water are prized. So, many of us are willing to fly further afield to find holidays with pristine white sands, pure air and clear waters. Climate change has become a political issue, with not only some of the major polluters unwilling to engage in the debate but also dismissing the reality of climate change or global warming. Perhaps because the changes are subtle and sometimes appear to be faraway, environmental issues do not grab people's minds and hearts (or sell newspapers). Consider for example, the edition of a popular free newspaper that most people in the UK read on the way to work that was published on 18 April 2011. Most of the initial pages were devoted to the upcoming royal wedding, celebrity gossip and other matters. The more pressing and chilling environmental matters that may affect us personally one day were to be found later. On page 25, ran the headline 'Arctic coast crumbles at 30 m a year', page 27 was the report about the Japanese nuclear disaster and on page 29 towards the very end came the story '43 killed as tornadoes rip through US South'.

Countries such as the USA produce 25 per cent of the world's greenhouse gases although it has only 5 per cent of the world's population. However, the USA has consistently refused to do much about this. According to calculations by Architecture 2030, a non-profit organization supported by the American Institute of Architects and the US Green Building Council (USGBC),[22] among others, using environmental impact assessment (EIA) data, the building sector is responsible for almost half – 49 per cent – of all greenhouse gas emissions from the USA. They say that American buildings are the biggest contributor to climate change. Many of the world's poorer countries were suspicious of the USA's refusal to sign the Kyoto Protocol agreement on the environment, on the grounds that their economic progress would be impeded. Worse still, they suspected that such agreements were being foisted on them to keep them where they were. This suspicion would be natural, if we consider that two-thirds of the carbon emissions causing climate change now has been generated by the actions of the G8 countries (Canada, USA, France, Germany, Italy, Japan, UK and Russia), not the poorer countries.

Abraham Maslow's hierarchy of needs is often portrayed in the shape of a pyramid, with the largest and most fundamental levels of needs at the bottom, and the need for self-actualization at the top. The most fundamental and basic four layers of the pyramid contain what Maslow calls 'deficiency needs' – self-esteem, friendship and love, security and physical needs. Maslow's theory suggests that the most basic level of needs must be met before the individual will want to work on the higher-level needs. So, according to this theory, we can see that environmental issues are secondary to the world's poor, although they contribute very little to the pollution. Among the rich countries, it is the Scandinavian countries that are especially environmentally aware, as well as being high aid givers. Again in light of Maslow's theory, it is very interesting to consider that the world's richest nation, the USA, is also the world's biggest polluter and owes the UN the most in unpaid dues. We look at the financial matters, economy and aid programmes in Chapter 2.

Connections and contradictions

This book is also about examining connections and contradictions – and how we fail to make connections about how we live and what affect this may have on the environment. However, this is not entirely our fault. Gone are the days when someone down our street made or grew something that we could buy or sell (Figure 1.9). Production of modern goods, based on the assembly line, has become very complex and stretches through continents and countries. A product may be designed in California, some parts may be manufactured in Malaysia or China and then the whole product may be assembled in China, shipped to Ireland to a warehouse from where it is dispatched to various European countries. Places and people for each part of this 'design-to-delivery' service are selected on the basis of efficiency of labour and costs, not on environmental or ethical concerns. The net of interdependence, supported by

Figure 1.9 Small recycling centres such as this scrap merchant from West London have disappeared, and so has our understanding of connection between consumption and waste and the economic value of waste.

Photo: Author.

cheap labour, lax laws and easy transport, has become so complex, that hardly anyone can keep track of it.

Human beings have evolved with a sense of link causality to things near us – things we can see, touch or feel – not to something distant. According to the economist, Steven Levitt, most of the time such thinking works but when it comes to cause and effect, there is often a trap in such 'open and shut thinking' that disconnects us from the larger impact of our small actions. There is also the flip side to being completely engrossed with the world's problems – that is, being either ignorant or indifferent. Both extremes are unproductive and may lead to a subjective and emotional points of view. However, it is through exploring our doubts and discomforts that we can progress towards a solution.

By linking causation to effect, I do not refer to architectural determinism – a theory that claims that the built environment is the prime determinant of social behaviour. In its most extreme form, this position argues that the environment causes certain behaviours, denying any responsibility of the user. Winston Churchill famously said, 'We shape our buildings; thereafter they shape us'. The determinist belief was a contributory factor in the numerous slum clearances of the post-war industrialized world. Despite being a widely held belief, there has been no research to prove its validity. For example, George Elton Mayo's work on human behaviour carried out at the Hawthorne Works of the General Electric Company in Chicago between 1924 and 1927 shows that 'the need for recognition, security and sense of belonging is more important in determining workers' morale and productivity than the physical conditions under which he works'.[23] In *Freakonomics*,[24] the authors, Levitt and Dubner, quote research that showed that the location of a family home did not influence the child's future prospects. The determinist hypothesis as an explanation of behaviour, however, is still to be found as an argument for urban renewal (or the frenzied rush to buy homes in 'good areas' for the sake of children's education).

Many traditional cultures and philosophies have other ways of establishing connections between the individual and the environment without assigning power or value relationships. Buddhist philosophy has an interesting way of looking at the connections of the world – 'Esho Funi' – the principle that a person and the environment are 'two but not two' and through the theory of 'dependent originations', which seeks to make connections between the external environment and the individual. In African culture, particularly South African tribes, and in Malawi and Namibia, there is a beautiful phrase – 'I am because you are'.[25] This saying is part of the *Ubantu* Southern African humanist philosophy, often quoted by Nelson Mandela and Desmond Tutu. It may seem pointless to study economics, aid and women's issues in a book about architecture. However, this is precisely what the canny development activist should understand – how complex interconnections within society such as the status of women, economics or trade affect the built environment.

A good illustration of this interconnection would be the situation in Libya. The issues in Libya in 2011 appeared to be a political matter alone at first, nothing to do with the built environment. Soon, however, the connections became apparent when the UK-based architect Zaha Hadid had to make one-third of her staff redundant owing to projects being cancelled in Libya – an effect like that of the proverbial butterfly fluttering its wings. When thousands of fleeing Libyans landed in Italy and other parts of Europe, thought had to be given to how they needed to be accommodated. The then Libyan leader, Muammar Gaddaffi, used the perceived threat of invasion of Libyan refugees into Europe to try to deflect the armed action against his country. The then Italian Prime Minister, Silvio Berlusconi, on the other hand, tried to deflect attention from *his* political problems by saying that he would refuse to let Libyan refugees into Italy. Here, politics became entwined with scarcity of resources. Of course, when all political issues are resolved and the fighting and bombing stops there, building and infrastructural work will be one of the major aspects of the country's rehabilitation.

I was amused to read recently about a celebrity who said that she was exhausted with jetlag owing to the amount of flying she had to do in one month in order to campaign for climate change. Clearly she had not made the connection between carbon emissions and climate change. (The reader might be interested to know that I pay to offset my carbon emissions when I fly but I do take the train as much as I can – hopefully the above celebrity takes these actions as well.) Cheap air travel has made flying more popular than taking the train or other forms of mass transport. India, which has the world's second most extensive train connections, for example, now has one of the busiest internal flight networks. Recently, when trying to book a Eurostar train to Paris, I discovered that the cost of going by plane instead would be one-third the train fare. A Eurostar train can take 766 passengers while a typical plane to France from the UK, such as the 737-400 can transport around 200 passengers. Flying to Paris also generates ten times more carbon dioxide than trains through fuel use, so the train is a much greener and convenient option. However, unless serious consideration is given to carbon dioxide emissions, the cheaper and quicker option will always prevail, with dangerous health and environmental consequences of flying for all.

As part of the 1987 Montreal Protocol (revised several times since), 196 nations agreed to phase out the use of CFCs (chlorofluorocarbons, compounds of chlorine, fluorine and carbon) and nearly 100 other chemicals that break down the ozone molecules in the Earth's stratosphere. The ozone layer covers the entire planet at an altitude of around 15 to 30 kilometres and protects living organisms from harmful ultraviolet (UV) rays. However, the size of the hole is not closing and, reportedly, is even growing larger despite the phasing out of CFCs.[26] Some believe that this is owing to the lingering effects of earlier CFC use, illegal continued use of CFCs and increased use of methyl bromide-based pesticides particularly in the USA, while some experts blame climate change.[27] The climate change proponents believe that as the Earth's surface warms, the upper atmosphere gets colder in the Polar regions, creating just the right conditions for chemicals like CFCs and bromine to linger on and destroy the ozone. The increasing size of the hole in the ozone layer can be related to the increasing numbers of people suffering from skin cancer. There is another potential problem, even if CFCs are never used again and the hole above the Antarctic repairs itself in 50–60 years' time. As the hole closes up, this will mean a rise in global temperatures owing to residual global warming[28] with an increase in average air temperatures of around 3 °C and a reduction in sea ice by around one-third, leading to the flooding of low lying countries. This is an example of the interconnectedness of our individual and societal environment and health. Our health, environment and money can be seen as the three points of a triangle – any change in our environment will affect our health and finances. So for example, if we cycle to work, we can benefit the environment and our health, plus save money. On a societal level, as this shows, a small change in our individual habits can have a big effect.

Greenland, a self-governing dependency of Denmark, is one of the best places to examine the contradictions of our society.[29] Mainly a bare piece of land, which is mostly covered by ice sheet two miles thick, Greenland is warming twice as fast as the rest of the world. Its vast ice sheet holds 7 per cent of the world's fresh water and is melting by 50 cubic miles each year. When it melts and the seas rise by 24 per cent, it will inundate low-lying areas of the world. However, most Greenlanders are not worried about this. In fact it will do them good, even though their main export – fish – is shrinking fast. Greenland imports all its food, even fodder for cattle. So as the ice melts, farmers will be able to grow their own food for the first time. The melting ice will expose the areas where vast reserves of petroleum can be found. Exxon Mobil, Chevron and Cairn Energy have already acquired exploration rights. In what may be seen as even more ironic, the world's largest deposits of rare earth materials have been discovered under this melting ice. These are the same materials that are needed for green technologies such as hybrid car batteries, wind turbines and compact fluorescent light bulbs (for which China controls 95 per cent of the world's supply). The Lutheran Bishop of Greenland, Sofie Petersen, thinks this is a Faustian bargain:

> I think oil will change our way of living. Of course, everyone needs money but should we sell our souls? What will happen if we are millionaires, every one of us, and we can't deliver Greenland as we know it to our grandchildren?[30]

Scarcity of materials, energy and time

> There would be no poverty on earth if we made a sacred resolution that we would have no more than we need for our creature comforts.
>
> (M.K. Gandhi, public meeting, Switzerland, 8 December 1931)

Material progress has made 'economic growth' a necessity. However, all things we use need basic natural resources such as water, petroleum, coal and air, and cause pollution during the process of manufacture and disposal. Most of our manufacturing systems are not 'closed loop', where the waste can be reused quickly and without too much change. We are still using a linear system where the natural product is ultimately turned into a non-biodegradable waste and thrown into the vast waste bin called Planet Earth. Our extraction and manufacturing processes are also dirty and crude – the 2010 oil spill in the Gulf of Mexico is a reminder of that. We are also not using enough recycled materials or products, therefore not closing the loop. As a small illustration of this, I asked my students during one lecture whether they recycled their waste paper. All hands went up. Then I asked whether they bought recycled paper products such as toilet and writing paper. No hands came up this time. Recycling is just not enough; recycled goods need to be in the economic loop to make recycling workable. We are just using too much stuff and throwing it away too soon, contributing to waste mountains.

Our lifestyles are very dependent upon non-renewable natural resources such as petrol and coal. This is often termed the 'fossil-fuel lifestyle'. Peak oil is supposed to have happened – when the supplies of oil have peaked and are now on the dip. However, no one really knows that, simply because we do not know what really lies under the oceans and other places. I have read many reports that say peak oil has happened, others say it is due soon and some even predict we have a lot of oil that remains untapped; therefore peak oil is far away. The oil spill in the Gulf of Mexico, which will take British Petroleum years to clean up and from which the environment will take years to recover, is a reminder that exploration for oil carries a danger to human life and the environment. Similarly, the recent tsunami and the incidents in the Japanese nuclear reactor have made many countries, especially those in the seismic zones, rethink nuclear power.

At present, the lifestyles of people in the richer countries mean that more than one planet is needed to sustain them. Even an oil-rich but tiny country such as Qatar is consuming resources equivalent to nine earths.[31] Some countries protect their own resources while exploiting the world's poor. For example, charcoal made from Southern Somalia's dwindling forests is being imported to Saudi Arabia, which protects its own trees (Figure 1.10). Tony Juniper has called on us to carry out 'one-planet' living and to acknowledge the 'ecological debt' carried by the richer countries. However, now that other nations want to copy the material progress made by richer nations (Figure 1.11), it can be very hard to achieve this diplomatically. Juniper notes:

> If the pitch is 'do as I do', then you acquire some credibility. If, on the other hand, the message is 'Do as we say because we know what is best for you and the world', then quite a different reaction is forthcoming.[32]

Figure 1.10 Young trees cut down to make charcoal being sold in the market at Tétouan, a city in Northern Morocco. In many parts of Africa, deforestation has become a major problem with the cutting down of trees to make charcoal for internal use or for exporting.

Photo: Author.

Figure 1.11 Satellite dishes in a slum, Pune, India. The poor want to live like the rich, even when their houses are falling down.

Photo: Sebastian Anthony.

Also, people in the rich nations will have to do with less and this may not be acceptable to them as they are used to a certain standard of life now. So where we go from here is another dilemma.

Time is a resource that, although the same for everyone, is becoming scarce. We don't seem to have time for anything as we live in the fast lane now. So now there are movements and organizations to provide an antidote such as slow food, slow sex, tai chi, mindfulness, etc. For the architect and development activist, the need for quick designs, some of which come from architectural sweat shops in India, Taiwan and China, fast track, fast build, etc., could be something that needs to be examined in a critical way, questioning the need for 'fast designs'. Fast is good in disaster situations, where being fast is paramount for saving lives. But are hastily designed buildings (some shown in Chapter 4) that either collapse or become quickly unusable something we can really afford in times of scarcity and change? Gandhi said that a good thing moves with the speed of a snail. I was particularly impressed by this nature of true development work when visiting Ashish Muni Ganju's work in Delhi in 2010. Showing me around the village of Aya Nagar, he said, 'I have been working here for 20 years but you won't see anything'. Yet, looking at the village pond, which is now clean, and the people who are healthier and better informed about development policies and participating in them, I could see how real development is slow and almost invisible – with no bells or whistles.

Naming names

One of the reasons why many poor countries have failed to keep to their Millennium Development Goals may be because the goal posts are being moved all the time. Many of the development projects that a development activist may be interested in are part of these goals. From an article on the 'Failed States Index' from *National Geographic* September 2009, we learn that the reasons for failing are many and contradictory.[33] A country could be too large (Chad), too small (Syria), too crowded (Bangladesh), too sparsely populated (Micronesia), or have too much of every negative factor (Somalia). Nothing is predictable though and changes are rapid. Japan in 2009 was listed as among the countries least at risk, but this has changed in less than two years. According to Pauline H. Baker, the Millennium Development Goals Fund's president, such regimes in countries 'that are based on arbitrary and artificial separations made during colonial administration, devote more energy to consolidating authority than fostering national identities and robust government institutions'.[34] This is an interesting statement given that many of the failed nations lie in one continent – Africa – where power and tribalism prevail.

However, I find the term 'failed nations' rather strange – failed in what? Is the failure their fault alone or are other countries responsible? The terminologies – First, Second, Third World – continue their imposed cultural references of modernity and progress. None of these terms makes sense especially since the end of the 'Cold War', but they continue to be used (and most people I have spoken to, including professional and educated people, do not even know what these terms mean). In his book, *Planet of Slums*, written in 2006, Mike Davis refers to the 'Third World' almost everywhere in the text.[35] Out of all terms, 'Third World' rankles the most as it is often misused as a synonym for 'third rate' in popular parlance – for example, Britain's hospitals are referred to as 'third world'.[36] Other axis descriptors such as 'developed' and 'developing' and 'industrialized' and 'non-industrialized' can be crude and value-laden. Someone who is supervising students working in India has gone a step further by substituting the word 'country' with 'culture' – he has called India a 'developing culture'. In this book, I have simply used 'rich' and 'poor' nations only in the economic sense, and Western and non-Western when referring to cultural issues,[37] as that appears to be the biggest divider in a cultural sense. The geographic-based descriptors such as North and South; and Tropical and non-Tropical that are also quite popular in development books, have also been avoided here because, as I said before, rapid change and scarce resources are present everywhere (Figure 1.12). Also, these geographic terms are not strictly correct either – Australia, which is a rich country, for example, lies 'South' of the equator and Singapore, another rich country lies in the Tropics.

Sometimes artificial values are imposed upon us, through acts of history, judgements or by force – for example through colonialization. These then

Figure 1.12 Homeless man sleeping in a flowerbed by the river Seine, Paris. Poverty is ever-present in the G8 countries too.

Photo: Author.

become points of reference for the future. For example, in India the aspiration of a slum dweller is to live in a brick and concrete house, called a 'pukka', that is, denoting permanent and strong. Colonial legacies affect infrastructure too. A prominent shopping centre in the centre of New Delhi, designed by Lutyens and Baker, is based on the layout of Bath; this clearly does not work in that cultural and environmental context. Certain buildings are judged as architecture and some are not. Prizes are given to buildings in the annual beauty contests such as the Stirling prize. All these competitions are mostly held in Western countries, the buildings are located there and celebrate Western values. In the present system of architectural values, vernacular architecture, slums and squatter settlements do not feature in mainstream architectural theory and education.

The other terms used in this book such as slums, squatter settlements and informal settlements are also fuzzy. While Indians do not have qualms about translating the Hindi terms *bustees* and *jhuggi-jhompris* as slums in English, in the UK, my Western colleagues have often been horrified, even though I point out that the people who live there have no problems with that term. Squatter settlements are not lived in only by the poor – middle-class people may squat in rich countries, for other reasons such as political protest. Formal areas have informal areas or are used informally, as informal areas have formal parts and uses.

The UN description of poverty reads:

> Fundamentally, poverty is a denial of choices and opportunities, a violation of human dignity. It means lack of basic capacity to participate effectively in society. It means not having enough to feed and clothe a family, not having a school or clinic to go to, not having the land on which to grow one's food or a job to earn one's living, not having access to credit. It means insecurity, powerlessness and exclusion of individuals, households and communities. It means susceptibility to violence, and it often implies living on marginal or fragile environments, without access to clean water or sanitation.
>
> (UN Statement, June 1998)[38]

This rather general and extensive definition takes into account that poverty can be both absolute and relative, even in one country. Relative poverty means that conditions of poverty will vary from country to country – the poor in London may be considered rich in Pakistan, for example. In the above definition, 'denial of choices and opportunties' is perhaps the most universal feature of poverty.

Plato and Makiguchi: value systems in architecture

I feel I have to finish with some philosophical questions – in particular, what are wisdom, beauty, gain and benefit? The Platonic values of truth (honesty), goodness and beauty are prized in architecture. The Platonic values are considered absolute. However, truth may be complex and goodness may be relative. Beauty (or its opposite, ugliness) is also about a sensory response, relative to the observer and context. Kisho Kurukawa, the Japanese architect, says: 'Beauty is not solely created by the artist; it is completed by the citizens, users, and the spectators who, by doing so, contribute to its creation.'[39]

Tsunesaburo Makiguchi,[40] a philosopher of the early twentieth century, substituted honesty with gain or benefit because benefit was a better denominator of relative values common in society. Makiguchi's substitution was a sophisticated intellectual leap. Makiguchi differentiated between happiness and pleasure – the latter he said was temporary while the former was permanent. Examining different forms of value, Makiguchi concluded that happiness lay in three specific forms: 'beauty', an aesthetic value that enhanced specific aspects of the individual's life; 'gain', which enhanced the individual's life; and 'good', which enhanced the entire community or society. Thus, the three values – beauty, goodness and gain – 'create value'. Makiguchi's philosophy of value was an invitation to engage with and create beauty, gain and good. Makiguchi positioned the creation of value as the ultimate purpose of human existence, defining a happy life as one in which the capacity to discover and create value has been fully deployed. Thus, if we accept Makiguchi's theory, slums and squatter settlements, which may not have the usual 'Platonic qualities', can create value too, despite not being in the run for architectural prizes (Figure 1.13).

So I hope that this book will help you, the reader, avoid value judgements and enable you to become a discoverer of beauty, no matter where. I hope that the most likely outcome of reading this book is that you become a 'good asker' and ask lots of the right questions. This book is not meant to be a definitive account – there is much more to the topics I have written about. As I said to someone, this book is about all the things that a young architect needs to know that is not taught at university. The knowledge and the questions should give a person the right wisdom to take the right action. After all, even highly educated people can make terrible choices. Consider the case of Ted Kaczynski, otherwise known as the 'Unabomber' (University and Airline Bomber). He was a former student at Harvard University who scored 98.9 per cent marks on graduation, then became a Professor at the University of California, Berkeley. His last career as an anarchist and social critic spanned twenty years, with a bombing campaign which killed three people and injured twenty-three others. The trigger for his campaign was a development, taking

Figure 1.13 Beauty in a slum, Kalyanpuri, East Delhi.

Photo: Author.

place near his isolated cabin in Montana. He went out for a walk to one of his favourite wild spots, only to find that it had been replaced with a road. About this, he said: 'You just can't imagine how upset I was. It was from that point on I decided that, rather than trying to acquire further wilderness skills, I would work on getting back at the system. Revenge.'[41]

As Buddhist philosopher Daisaku Ikeda says: 'The more knowledge one gains, the more important becomes the question of what that knowledge will be used for. Knowledge without wisdom and philosophy produces nothing more than talented beasts.'[42] I hope this book will offer you a set of tools so that you can delve further into these issues (Figure 1.14). Although I have cautioned against reinventing the wheel or simply becoming a cynic, it should never be an excuse for sloppy and self-interested thinking and asking. According to Levitt, knowing what to measure and how to measure can make a complicated world much less so. So for the development activist, asking the right questions (and knowing when the right answer comes along), looking with curiosity and finding simple answers will help in finding the right archi-tecture for a world of rapid change and scarce resources.

Figure 1.14 London Metropolitan University students, listening to a lecture organised by the author at the offices of NGO Development Alternatives (India), 2007.

Photo: Author.

Discussion points

- Why do richer nations take less action for global environmental concerns although environmental issues are well publicized there and there is money to do more?
- Is it practically possible to achieve a one-planet living?
- With all our material and technological progress, why has it become so complex to design and build, instead of becoming simpler?
- Can you think of different ways of denoting countries or places of rapid change and scarce resources without putting value judgements on the terms?

Chapter 2

Big games and small money

I watched Comic Relief, the annual fundraising event staged by the BBC, this year (2011). A woman sang gospel songs while the camera lingered on the little faces in some faraway country in Africa. The child would die if we did not give money, we were told. As the evening drew to a close, a staggering £74,360,207 had been raised which is the highest total reached on the night in Red Nose Day's twenty-three-year history (note: the UK gives slightly less than ten billion in aid annually – about 0.4 per cent of its annual income). Much of this Comic Relief money came from the pockets of ordinary people in a country hit by the recession. My son was asked to wear a red garment to school, so that I could donate some money for Comic Relief as 'punishment' for not wearing the school uniform. I thought a lot about those little children, about the money raised and how it would get to them.

In January 2011, I received an email about Josh.[1] Josh is a Kenyan student in the Netherlands who sent money to his poverty stricken family in Africa and discovered that the international money transfer company took 20 per cent off Josh's money in fees (the World Bank recommends that transaction costs not exceed 5 per cent of the total). Awaaz, the campaigning organization, estimated that $44.3 billion worldwide was taken in transfer fees last year by various money transfer companies. Money transfer companies have never faced serious public pressure to lower their charges. I thought a lot about how money is transferred to the beneficiaries and how much goes into the pockets of unrelated organizations. Money, it appears, is big business internationally and environmentally, especially in the 'development' game.

GDP, GNI and GNH

> The GDP of Ladakh is among the lowest in the world, nearly nil per person. Yet Ladakh is considered by many to be one of the world's most balanced, sustainable and happy societies. Assessed by GDP, it is a basket-case.
>
> (Helena Norberg-Hodge)[2]

The economy has a role to play in the built environment and in the work of the development activist. Money – big or small – and how it is used, whether in big aid programmes or micro-credit, has an influential role to play in the construction industry. In an economic downturn, it is often the building industry that is the first to suffer. Conversely, in times of natural disasters, it is the building industry that is the first to show an upward trend in the stock exchange, as happened in the aftermath of the Japanese earthquake in 2011. Aid programmes also pose many problems – did the third largest economy in the world, Japan, need external aid after the 2011 tsunami and earthquake? Even more bizarrely, Japan now believes that it has a moral obligation to bid for the 2020 Olympics to recover from the tsunami damage (its failed bid for the 2016 Olympics cost Japan £118 billion).[3] Should international aid be stopped altogether and efforts switched to concentrating on fair trade, climate change issues and disaster mitigation?

Economics is not a science as is commonly believed – it depends on so many variables that there could not be an exact formula that succeeds each time and for each country or region. If it were so, then the economy would be in constant growth and there would be no recession and no stock markets. Rather than being a straight line, it could be depicted as an ever-expanding spiral with ups and downs – in other words, a complex geometry. The economy of a country consists of all its resources – people, natural and man-made – and the economic agents that produce, exchange and distribute the goods or resources of that particular part. An economy can be the result of a process that involves many aspects such as technology, culture, history and the environment. These factors give context and content, and set the conditions and parameters in which an economy functions. All kinds of professions, occupations or economic activities contribute to the economy of a region or communities (Figure 2.1). Some activities such as 'informal economy' (Figure 2.2), bringing up children and doing housework are not counted in the economy of the country and this can be an unfair representation of the economy. Regional economy can vary in one country. For example, the South of England is held to have a stronger economy than the North.

Countries are usually rated economically according to their gross domestic product (GDP), namely, what the country produces (including goods and services) and consumes internally. GNI is the country's gross national income. The GNI is the total value that is produced within a country, combining the gross domestic product along with the income obtained from other countries (such as dividends and interest). Although GNI and GDP sound similar, one of the main differences between the two is that the gross national income is based on location, while gross domestic product is based on ownership, instead of where the income is produced. It can also be said that GDP is the value produced within a country, whereas GNI is the value produced by all the citizens. The UK's Department for International Development (DfID), for example, prefers to use GNI, believing it gives a more accurate picture of the country's economy.

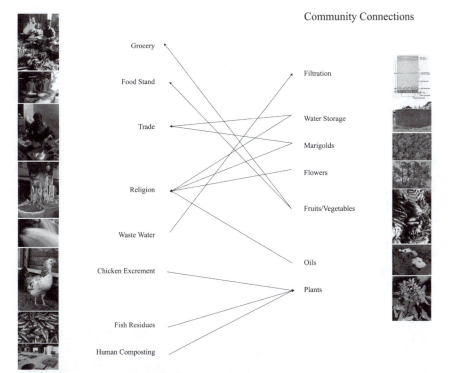

Grocery
Food Stand
Trade
Religion
Waste Water
Chicken Excrement
Fish Residues
Human Composting

Filtration
Water Storage
Marigolds
Flowers
Fruits/Vegetables
Oils
Plants

Figure 2.1 Project to join up different informal trades to form a 'closed loop economy' in Regharpura, Delhi by Heather Stuart, MA Architecture of Rapid Change and Scarce Resources, London Metropolitan University, 2009.

Figure 2.2 The formal economy does not include the economy created by small itinerant traders found in souks, bazaars and other informal markets, such as this display of natural cosmetics for the lips and face being sold by a Rifian woman from Northern Morocco in Tangiers.

Photo: Author.

However, neither of these values is real because they are not measures of the standard of living or the environment. They are both simply about the value of stuff going in and out of a country, whether negative or positive. Neither GDP nor GNI take into account voluntary and unpaid caring work such as looking after children and the elderly or working for free for charities. Thus 'women's' work at home is not counted as part of the GDP or GNI. The cost of cleaning up pollution and other environmental hazards does also not count in GDP or GNI, nor is the mental and physical well-being of the people counted. This can give rather strange indicators of a country's actual situation. For example, American life expectancy and literacy rates – key quality-of-life indicators – are only a few percentage points higher than those of the Indian state of Kerala, an area with GNP is less than $400 per capita, compared to more than $20,000 in the United States.[4] The former King of Bhutan, Jigme Singye Wangchuck, proposed a different way of comparing countries, which he called the 'gross national happiness' (GNH). The Centre for Bhutan Studies developed a sophisticated survey instrument to measure the population's general level of well-being. The Canadian health epidemiologist, Michael Pennock, then developed a 'de-Bhutanized' version of this tool.[5] People living with scarce resources often have high GNH (Figure 2.3).

Figure 2.3 These itinerant workers living in a peri-urban area of Agra, India, work with scraps of leather and live in tents, yet they are happy with their lives, they told me (2006).

Photo: Author.

Trade, colonialism and origins of global economy

Money has existed as a form of 'IOU' in various civilizations for thousands of years. Money and banking originated mostly from non-economic causes such as religious 'tithes', from blood money and dowry. Early money was anything from conch shells and feathers to cattle. Cattle are described as mankind's 'first working capital asset'. The English words 'capital', 'chattels' and 'cattle' have a common root. The Chinese reportedly invented paper money in 960 CE after a shortage of copper for making coins. Money instead of barter was a convenient form of exchange for goods and services. This was because it was conveniently stored, had high-value densities, namely gold and silver, and was portable and durable, being metal. These metals, being widely desired, were easy to exchange for others and therefore they came to be accepted as money. Banking originated in ancient Mesopotamia where royal palaces and temples provided secure places for the safekeeping of grain and other commodities. Receipts came to be used for transfers not only to the original depositors but also to third parties. The revival of banking in Western Europe, invigorated by the Crusades, with written instructions in the form of bills of exchange, came to be used as a means of transferring large sums of money, with the Knights Templar and Hospitallers acting as bankers.

Trade is an exchange involving goods, services or currency. A network that allows trade is called a 'market' – this may not be a physical place and could even be web-based. The original form of trade was barter, the direct exchange of goods and services. Trade exists owing to specialization and division of labour – most people specialize in a niche market and trade their skills or products for other skills and products. From as early as 2000 BCE onwards, there is evidence of trading between different empires using boats and ships, as water was the easiest method of transporting heavy goods. The first extensive trade routes were up and down the great rivers, which became the backbones of early civilizations – the Nile, the Tigris and Euphrates, the Indus and the Yellow River. As boats became sturdier, coastal routes extended human and trade boundaries. The Eastern Mediterranean was the first region to develop extensive maritime trade (Figure 2.4). In North Africa and Asia the camel became the most important beasts of burden, as it was well adapted to desert conditions. A tentative trade route became established along a string of oases North of the Himalayas. They were very exposed to the broad expanse of steppes – with their marauding bands of nomadic tribesmen – but protection by the Han Dynasty in China made it reasonably safe for merchants to send caravans into this region. In 106 BCE, for the first time, a caravan left China and travelled all the way to Persia without the goods changing hands on the way. The Silk Road was now open. By the first century BC the Romans had gained control of Syria and Palestine – the natural terminus of the Silk Road. Soon a special silk market was established in Rome.

Figure 2.4 A ship passes through the Bosphorus, Istanbul, carrying goods from China to Europe. Istanbul was part of the Silk Road. Turkey is now proposing that tankers that clog the Strait will be diverted into a 30-mile-long man-made waterway linking the Black Sea to the Sea of Marmara.

Photo: Author.

China at first wanted nothing that Rome had to offer and, thus, the Han rulers were unwilling to trade silk, either as thread or woven fabric. After a while they relented, but only in exchange for gold. It has been calculated that in the first century AD China had a hoard of some five million ounces of gold. In the meanwhile, in Rome the emperor Tiberius issued a decree against the wearing of silk owing to the drain on the empire's reserves of gold. The Silk Road, in this way, also introduced the globalization of economics (Figure 2.4).

Trade and exploration in the Middle Ages offered the possibility of conquering lands in the name of the explorer's king or queen, in return for sponsorship. For the first time, trade became less important than ruthless conquest. In the book, *Open Veins of Latin American*, Edward Galeano documents how the Spanish conquests literally drained the land not only of valuable minerals and metals but also of people. Most native peoples were murdered in acts of savagery that have seldom been seen since. Slave trade started when people were needed to work on plantations, mines and other places in the colonies as the natives had either died from disease, been killed or were not willing to work as slaves. In Latin America, where the Spanish and other invaders wiped out the entire native Carib population, the British brought in slaves from

Africa and Asia where this mixed race survives as the 'Caribbeans' of the West Indies. Portugal had a virtual monopoly on the African slave trade to the Americas until the mid-1650s, when Holland became a major competitor. In the period 1700–1800 Britain became the leading 'importer' of slaves. The slave trade was abolished by Britain in 1812, and subsequently by all other European countries. The practice of slavery and colonialism also brought in diseases such as the plague, smallpox, etc., which were not known in the 'New World' and wiped out the native population, flora and fauna. New peoples and plants were introduced in the new lands. Colonial culture including architecture was introduced and given preference in the conquered lands. This effectively brought in the globalization of architecture where architecture and building technology from imperial nations continues to be advanced in preference to native styles.

Bretton Woods, WTO and IMF

> We destroy the beauty of the countryside because the unappropriated splendours of nature have no economic value. We are capable of shutting off the sun and the stars because they do not pay a dividend.
>
> (John Maynard Keynes, 1933)[6]

The above quote by Keynes, the father of modern British economics, would have been crucial in the prevention of economic inequality today, had he won in the argument at Bretton Woods. The Bretton Woods conference held in July 1944 was the single most important point in the history of modern economics and international aid. The United Nations Monetary and Financial Conference, commonly known as the Bretton Woods conference as it was held there, was a gathering of 730 delegates from forty-four nations, mainly Allied (Western), which came together to decide how to regulate the international monetary and financial order after the conclusion of the Second World War. In 1940, an agreement with the USA pegged the pound to the US dollar at a rate of £1 = $4.03. This rate was maintained through the Second World War and became part of the Bretton Woods system, which governed post-war exchange rates instead of gold standards. All currencies became convertible and the dollar became the currency of choice for conversion purposes from that time.

The two most important organizations influencing aid and trade also originated from this conference – the General Agreement on Tariffs and Trade (GATT) and the International Monetary Fund (IMF). GATT was the result of an attempt to create an International Trade Organization. It lasted until 1993 when the World Trade Organization (WTO) replaced it. The original GATT agreement of 1947 is still in effect under the WTO framework, subject to the modifications of 1994. WTO has been criticized heavily because it is felt that many countries in the WTO wield little influence despite its stated aim of 'helping' the poorer countries. Martin Khor, the economist and director of the South Centre based in Switzerland, argues that the WTO does not manage the global economy impartially, but has a systematic bias towards rich countries and multinational corporations, thus harming poor countries, which have less negotiating power. The IMF describes itself as 'an organization of 187 countries (as of July 2010), working to foster global monetary cooperation, secure financial stability, facilitate international trade, promote high employment and sustainable economic growth, and reduce poverty'. It has been heavily criticized for its role in doing just the opposite owing to the presence of powerful countries that have an interest in maintaining a trade imbalance and financial insecurity that helps them maintain power. Interestingly, countries of the EU such as Greece, Romania and Hungary, along with Ukraine, are the largest borrowers from the IMF (as of August 2010).

Since the Bretton Woods conference, currencies have become the weapons of choice in trade and economic wars. On 29 November 2011, the *Evening Standard* reported on the growing currency wars as nations continue to devalue their currencies as a key mechanism for maintaining competitive costs and high levels of export. This model of growth, proposed by Germany and Japan, has been copied by emergent economies such as India and China. However, in countries such as Venezuela and Brazil, which have low growth and low exports, such models have proved to be a problem.[7] In today's world, the canny development activist has to be aware of such economic problems in different areas of rapid change and scarce resources and the effect they have on the construction and building industries.

Aid, not trade

The earliest form of foreign aid was military assistance designed to help warring parties that were in some way considered strategically important. Its use in the modern era began in the eighteenth century, when Prussia subsidized some of its allies. European powers in the nineteenth and twentieth centuries provided large amounts of money to their colonies, typically to improve infrastructure with the ultimate goal of increasing the colony's economic output. The origin of foreign aid today can be traced to two major developments following the Second World War:

- European Recovery Programme or the Marshall plan (after USA Secretary of State, George Marshall) – a USA-sponsored aid programme to rehabilitate the economies of seventeen European countries after the devastation of the war.
- The founding of significant international organizations, including the UN, IMF and World Bank. These international organizations have played a major role in allocating international funds, determining the qualifications for the receipt of aid and assessing its impact.

Contemporary foreign aid is distinguished not only because it is some-times humanitarian (with little or no self-interest by the donor country) but also by its size, amounting to trillions of dollars since the end of the Second World War, by the large number of governments providing it, and by the supposedly transparent nature of the transfers. Several non-European govern-ments also implemented their own aid programmes after the Second World War. For example, Japan developed an extensive foreign aid programme that provided assistance primarily to Asian countries. Much of Japan's aid came through procurement from Japanese companies, which helped fuel economic development in Japan. By the late twentieth century, Japan had become one of the world's two leading donor countries, and its aid programmes had extended to non-Asian countries, though much of the country's assistance was still directed towards Asia. Now, with the earthquake and tsunami of 2011, Japan has a bill of reportedly $200 billion dollars required for reconstruction; so, along with the economic status of a country, giving and receiving of aid is always a fluid situation.

'Odious debt' is a legal theory that holds that national debt incurred by a country for purposes that do not serve the best interests of the nation, such as wars of aggression, should not be enforceable.[8] Thus, there is a moral issue in paying such national debts. Such debts are considered by this doctrine to be the personal debts of the regime that incurred them and not debts of the state. The doctrine was formalized in a 1927 treatise by a Russian legal theorist, Alexander Nahum Sack, based on nineteenth-century precedents includ-ing Mexico's repudiation of debts incurred by Emperor Maximilian, and the denial by the USA of Cuba's liability for debts incurred by the Spanish colo-nial regime.

According to Sack, when a despotic regime contracts a debt to strengthen itself or to commit aggression on others, this debt is 'odious' for the people. Odious debts do not fulfil one of the conditions determining the lawfulness of state debts because the state debts must be incurred, and the proceeds used for the needs and in the interests of the state. Patricia Adams, executive director of Probe International (an environmental and public policy advocacy organi-zation in Canada) states that by giving creditors an incentive to lend only for purposes that are transparent and of public benefit, future tyrants will lose their ability to finance their armies, and 'thus the war on terror and the cause of world peace will be better served'.[9]

Types of aid

Understanding different types of foreign aid is crucial for the development activist. The term 'foreign aid' is a broad one. It refers to any money or resources that are transferred from one country to another without expecting full repayment. Official Development Assistance (ODA) includes all grants, and concessional or soft loans that are intended to transfer resources from more developed countries (MDCs) to less developed countries (LDCs) with the intention of fostering economic development. Concessional loans are those that have a grant element at 25 per cent or more. This does not include commercial or non-concessional loans, private foreign direct investment, nor does it include preferential tariff reductions offered by MDCs to LDCs.

To be considered aid, the funds should meet two simple criteria, in that they should be:

- non-commercial from the donor's point of view (this is an interesting point!);
- concessional, so that the interest and repayment is less stringent or softer than commercial terms (again, difficult to enforce and as Jubilee 2000's work shows, much misused).

In the 1970s the international community, through the United Nations, set 0.7 per cent of a country's GNI as the benchmark for foreign aid. However, only a small number of countries (Denmark, Luxembourg, the Netherlands, Norway and Sweden) reached that mark. Although the United States and Japan have been the world's two largest donors, their percentages of foreign aid compared to their GNI have fallen significantly short of the UN's goal. Despite the commitment to ODA of 0.7 per cent, the USA was bottom of several countries, with 0.15 per cent. In fact, the US owes the UN more than $1.3 billion in unpaid dues.[10] (The UN and its agencies operate on a budget of $10 billion a year, that is $1.70 per person – what the world spends on its military every five days.) Surveys in the United States, for example, consistently show that most Americans believe that foreign aid takes up 20 per cent of the country's budget – the actual figure is less than 1 per cent.

Humanitarian aid

Humanitarian aid or *emergency aid* is rapid assistance given to people in immediate distress by individuals, organizations or governments during and after man-made situations such as war or natural disasters. It is often distinguished from development aid by being focused on relieving suffering caused by natural disasters or conflict, rather than removing the root causes such as poverty or vulnerability (Figure 2.5).

Development aid

Development aid is aid given to support 'development' in general in poor countries. Development aid is held to be long term while humanitarian aid is short term. Individuals through organizations such as ActionAid and Oxfam, to name just two, distribute through individual countries' aid organizations and through international agencies such as the World Bank and ODA (Figure 2.6).

Figure 2.5 UN truck involved in aid, reconstruction and 'peace-keeping' in Hebron, Palestine.

Photo: Author.

Figure 2.6 Engineers outside a USAID project in West Bank, Palestine – part of a community infrastructure development programme that includes an engineers' job creation programme. This is an example of 'sector-wide' approach.

Photo: Ma'moun Abu Rayyan.

In 2011, the UK took a 'long and hard' look at its aid programme,[11] according to the Department for International Development (DfID) in its most radical shift since it was founded in 1997. This could be owing to the recession, or to the change in government. This has meant that aid will be decided in terms of impact and not cost. For example, Helmand province,

Afghanistan, which receives one-fifth of the UK funding of that country, will receive funding for non-traditional development such as council and court buildings and police stations. Dr Liam Fox, the then Defence Secretary, remarked controversially: 'We are not in Afghanistan for the sake of education policy in a broken thirteenth-century country.'[12] His statement came as the Taliban were targeting schools and teachers, especially schools for girls. Development agencies and NGOs are unhappy that Western governments are focusing too heavily on plans to complete a security handover from foreign forces at the end of 2014 without cementing gains for women such as 'safe' education.[13] India used to be the largest recipient of UK aid despite being the fourth largest economy in the world because the largest number of the world's poor live there. Now Ethiopia, followed closely by Bangladesh and Pakistan, will get most of the UK aid. There are countries losing direct aid from the UK – such as Angola, Bosnia, China, Indonesia, Iraq and Russia.

Specific types of development aid

- Project aid: aid is given for a specific purpose, e.g. building materials for a new school.
- Programme aid: aid is given for a specific sector such as education, e.g. funding of the education sector of a country.
- Budget support: a form of programme aid that is directly channelled into the national budget of the recipient country.
- Sector-wide approaches (SWAPs): this is a combination of project aid and programme aid/budget support; for example, support for the education sector in a country will include funding of education projects (such as school buildings) and also provide funds to maintain them (such as for school books).
- Food aid: food is given to countries in urgent need of food supplies in times of natural disasters, war and famine.
- Untied aid: the country receiving the aid can spend the money as they choose.
- Tied aid: the aid must be used to purchase products from the country that donated it or from a specified group of countries.
- Technical aid: professionals, such as architects or engineers, are moved into developing countries to assist with a programme of development.
- Multi and bilateral aid: bilateral aid is given by one country directly to another; multilateral aid is given through the intermediary of an international organization, such as the World Bank, which collects donations from several countries' governments and then distributes them to the recipients.

NPOs, charities and NGOs

A charitable organization is a type of NPO, that is non-profit organization. The term is relatively general and can technically refer to a public charity (also called 'charitable foundation', 'public foundation' or simply 'foundation' or a private foundation). It differs from other types of NPOs in that its focus is centred on goals of a general altruistic, religious, environmental or philanthropic nature. The legal definition of charitable organizations (and of charity) varies according to the country and in some instances the region of the country in which the charitable organization operates. The regulation, tax treatment and the way in which charity law affects charitable organizations also vary.

For development activists working with charities and non-governmental organizations (NGOs), it is essential to know how each organization works and what its focus is (Figure 2.7). For example, there are charities that work exclusively in disaster management while others carry out long-term development

Figure 2.7 Anil Sawan from Acorn Foundation (India), stands outside his modest offices in Dharavi, Mumbai. Many charities and NGOs operate under difficult conditions, both physical and financial; Acorn in Dharavi work with rag and waste pickers, among others.

Photo: Author.

work. Each organization will have particular beneficiaries and methodologies with which the development activist must work. Big international NGOs have been given an endearing acronym, BINGO, but they come with the usual red tape that hampers their work. In Gaza, for example, the work of Oxfam in water supply and that of other organizations building houses had to be stopped because cement had to come from 'accountable' sources, not from the underground tunnels leading to Egypt. One of my students writes in her essay:

> The head offices of these BINGOs are now so far removed from the activists on the ground that their rules are as, if not more, restrictive and unhelpful as some state laws, that this can get in the way of true participation.[14]

Fair trade, not aid

The fair trade movement advocates the payment of a 'fair' price to producers by buyers as well as improving their social and environmental standards. Fair trade is at present the fastest growing market – in 2008 it amounted to approximately US\$4.08 billion (€2.9 billion) worldwide, a 22 per cent year-to-year increase. While this represents a tiny fraction of world trade in physical merchandise, some fair trade products account for 20–50 per cent of all sales in their product categories in individual countries. Everything from bananas, chocolates, coffee to gold,[15] cut flowers and diamonds is now being traded fairly.

The current fair trade movement was shaped in Europe in the 1960s. Fair trade during that period was often seen as a political gesture against neo-imperialism. The slogan at the time, 'Trade not Aid', gained international recognition in 1968 when the United Nations Conference on Trade and Development (UNCTAD) adopted it. In 1965, Oxfam UK set up the 'helping by selling' programme, selling handicrafts from places such as South America and India in shops and by mail order. Throughout the 1960s and 1970s, thousands of volunteers in Western nations sold coffee from Nicaragua and Angola in 'Worldshops' based in churches, homes, street stalls, etc., to deliver their socio-political message attacking exploitation of poor workers abroad and domination of world trade. The alternative trade movement grew on both sides of the Atlantic with many Worldshops being set up in places such as California and London. Now many London Boroughs are proud to declare themselves 'Fairtrade Boroughs'. For the development activist, the fair trade economy is not only part of his or her ethical view but also important in terms of the projects they generate. In June 2008, Fairtrade Labeling Organizations International estimated that over 7.5 million producers and their families were benefiting from fair trade-funded infrastructure, technical assistance and community development projects.

As yet, building materials are not generally certified as fair trade or ethically sourced. The most that has been achieved has been with timber, which is Forest Stewardship Council (FSC) certified. In an emergency situation, the materials that a development activist uses might not be local or ethically sourced – however, the work needs to be done regardless. For long-term work, it might be ethical and cheaper to use local and traditional methods of building and construction. Reuse and recycling of building materials, although not part of fair trade, could be considered ethical and environmentally sustainable ways of building (Figure 2.8).

The informal economy

In any informal city, and indeed in any formal city, the informal economy exists as a very real presence despite not being part of the GDP as described earlier. The 'wanted' notes stuck in the shop windows, the advertisements on popular websites, buying and selling on the Internet, and the man with the advertisement board walking down a busy shopping street are all part of the informal economy (Figure 2.9). Bartering and haggling can been observed in any city, whether in the West or in the East. The informal economy provides an important economic exchange for the poor, whether through barter or sale. In India, Sharit K. Bhowmik wrote in *Economic Political Weekly* on 19 April 2003:

Figure 2.8 Timber, cardboard, metal, plastic, household goods and machines are sold along the main road, named the '60 feet road' in Dharavi, Mumbai. The informal economy (black or grey market) operates in the space and links provided by the pavements, alleys, streets and roads and determines the existence of the slum itself.

Photo: Author.

Figure 2.9 Market in Tétouan, Northern Morocco where anything could be sold in the informal part of the traditional market, the Souk. Here €1 coins picked from the streets or given by visitors are being sold for profit, amongst other odds and ends.

Photo: Author.

Street vendors across several Indian cities have generally been regarded as nuisance value, their presence seen as inimical to urban development. However, the range of goods and services they provide renders them useful to other sections of the urban poor and thus they form an important segment of the informal economy. A draft national policy on street vendors argues that needs of this section are vital for urban planning purposes. Regulation of vendors and hawking zones and granting vendors a voice in civic administration need to become definitive elements of urban development policy.

The black market exudes a more sinister or shadowy presence but it is also real. Whether it is exchange of goods or money, the black market exerts a powerful influence on the formal economy. The black market exists in a small way where the economic freedom is greater and in a larger way where corruption, regulation or legal monopolies restrict economic activity in various goods, services or trading groups.

For the development activist working in areas of rapid change and scarce resources, the presence of the informal economy could be a double-edged sword. My own experience has been that, generally, in the informal economies, it may be easier and quicker to obtain goods and materials for small projects. For larger projects, one has to have access via the formal economy and red tape, and it is generally much slower and many times more expensive. Again, recycling and reusing of building materials in places such as India operates very much in the informal economy and should become the first choice in building material selection by the development activist.

LETS

Local Exchange Trading Systems (LETS) also known as LET Systems are locally initiated, not-for-profit community enterprises that provide a community with various services and goods. Transactions of members exchanging goods and services are recorded using the currency of locally created LETS Credits. In some places, for example Toronto, the scheme has been called the Local Employment and Trading System. In New South Wales, Australia, it is known as Local Energy Transfer Systems. Michael Linton developed the 'Local Exchange Trading System' in 1983 in British Columbia, to work alongside the national currency, rather than as a replacement for it. Members in a LETS scheme do direct swaps using interest-free LETS credit and so like-for-like swaps for services or barter for goods need not be made. For instance, a member may earn credit by doing childcare for one person and spend it later on carpentry with another person in the same network. LETS is a fully fledged exchange system, unlike direct barter. Sometimes a small membership fee is paid to cover administration costs. Members maintain a directory of offers and wants to help facilitate trades. Upon trading, members may 'pay' each other with printed notes or log the transaction in logbooks or online, many times using humourous references such as 'Hammers' in Hammersmith.

For development activists, LETS is part of the formalized informal economy where social enterprise, bartering and local economy come together. However, it can be difficult to set up a payment for a professional service such as an architect, say, compared with a gardener, as I found out when I joined my loccal LETS. The imbedded cost of maintaining professional indemnity insurance, producing drawings and other expenses often mean that LETS is not a system for architects or professionals. It can work well, however, for informal consultation where advice maybe given without liability.

Micro-credit

Micro-credit is the extension of small loans (micro-loans) to those in need to set up their business. These individuals cannot meet even the most minimal qualifications to gain access to traditional credit or loans through banks or credit unions. The modern invention of micro-loans is credited to the St Louis entrepreneur, Menlo Smith. However, the modern form of micro-credit as a financial innovation is credited to Grameen Bank, literally 'rural bank', and Mohammed Yunas who started it. Yunas and the Grameen Bank received the Nobel Prize in 2008 for their innovation.

In the past few years, savings-led microfinance has gained recognition as an effective way to bring financing to very poor families. In India, the National Bank of Agriculture and Rural Development (NABARD) finances more than 500 banks that lend money to self-help groups (SHGs). SHGs comprise twenty or fewer members, of whom the majority are women from the poorest sections of society. Members save small amounts of money, as little as a few rupees a month in a group fund. Members may borrow from the group fund for a variety of purposes ranging from household emergencies to school fees. As SHGs prove capable of managing their funds well, they may borrow from a local bank to invest in small business or farm activities. Groups generally pay interest rates that range from 30 per cent to 70 per cent APR, or 12 per cent to 24 per cent a year. Nearly 1.4 million SHGs comprising approximately 20 million women now borrow from banks, which make the Indian SHG-Bank Linkage model the largest microfinance programme in the world.

According to Asian Development Bank,[16] since 2000, Indian women have been the major beneficiaries of its home workplace improvement sub-project (part of the Housing Finance Project II). It is estimated that 20–30 million people across India are home-based workers; 80 per cent of these are women. The creation of assets such as shops, carts, land or houses in women's names is crucial to improving low-income women's socio-economic status. I also observed micro-credit systems being set up by NGOs in India, in particular, the Self-Employed Women's Association (SEWA), which works with women (Figure 2.10). Small amounts of money are lent to women wanting to set up on

Figure 2.10 East Delhi woman helped by SEWA micro-credit sews clothes to be sold in the UK by Marks & Spencer.

Photo: Author.

their own. After getting formal training in running their business, SEWA also offers micro-insurance and micro-pension. Similar programmes are evolving in Africa and South-east Asia with the assistance of international organizations such as CARE and Oxfam. Micro-credit is not only provided in poor countries, but also in one of the world's richest countries, the USA, where 37 million people (12.6 per cent) live below the poverty line. Among other organizations that provide micro-loans in the United States, Grameen Bank started their operation in New York in April 2008. Richer countries[17] in which the micro-loan model is becoming popular include Israel, Russia, Ukraine and the UK. The Charity Bank in the UK offers loans to sustainable or social projects.

Even so, some have criticized the micro-credit movement as a privatization of public programmes that may induce cuts in health, welfare and education spending. Interest rates have been criticized as well. For example, Grameen Bank's statistics do not reflect the number of women who are repeat borrowers that have become dependent on loans for household expenditure rather than business ventures. Studies in recent years have shown that very poor people rely heavily on informal savings to manage risks such as sickness, natural disaster and debts. Many microfinance institutions are unable to provide safe, flexible savings services to the poor owing to their own connections with the formal banking economy and dependence upon external capital. The result is the poor are pushed further down the economic ladder.

In a BBC radio interview[18] with Professor Dean Karlan from Yale University, the results of a study between a group in Africa and one in the Philippines were discussed. He suggests that many micro-credit loans are in fact given to people with existing businesses, and not to those seeking to establish new ones. Many of those receiving micro-credit also used the loans to supplement their family income. The income that went up in business was true only for men, and not for women. This is striking because one of the supposed major beneficiaries of microfinance is supposed to be women. Professor Karlan's conclusion was that while micro-credit is not necessarily a bad idea and can generate some positive benefits, despite some lenders charging interest rates between 40 and 60 per cent, giving citizens in poor countries access to rudimentary and cheap savings accounts would be more efficient for poverty alleviation.

Criticism of aid programmes: teaching people to fish?

Poor people in rich countries giving money to rich people in poor countries.
(International aid defined by Anthony Horowitz, *Evening Standard*,
9 November 2008)

Aid is seldom given from motives of pure altruism; for instance it is often given as a means of supporting an ally in international politics. It may also be given with the intention of influencing the political process in the receiving nation. Whether one considers such aid helpful may depend on whether one agrees with the agenda being pursued by the donor nation in a particular case. Aid to underdeveloped countries has sometimes been criticized as being more in the interest of the donor than the recipient, or even a form of neocolonialism.

Some groups in donor countries have criticized foreign aid as ineffective and wasteful – and claimed that most recipients of foreign aid do not deserve it or do not use it wisely. Such criticisms have been bolstered by the generally disappointing results of foreign aid programmes in sub-Saharan Africa, where many countries remain mired in poverty, corruption and civil war despite the disbursement of significant foreign aid. It is interesting to note that in 2003 the US spent $396 billion on its military.[19] This is thirty-three times more than the combined military spending of the 'seven rogue states' (Cuba, Iran, Sudan, Syria, North Korea, Libya, Iraq and Afghanistan as of 2003 – although there are presently only five as Libya, Iraq and Afghanistan have recently been removed from the list). The people of the USA also spend the same on the porn industry as the government does on development aid – about 12 billion dollars.[20]

Criticisms have been levelled at both the donors and the recipients of foreign aid. Some groups in recipient countries have viewed foreign aid suspiciously as nothing more than tools of power – whether economic or social. The USA and former Soviet Union and their allies during the Cold War used foreign aid as a diplomatic tool to foster political alliances and strategic advantages. In addition to the Marshall Plan, in 1947 the United States provided assistance to Turkey and Greece to resist the spread of communism and, following the death of Stalin in 1953, communist-bloc countries donated increasing amounts of foreign aid to other countries and close allies as a means of gaining influence as well as promoting economic co-operation. Kuwait has donated many barrels of petroleum to the United States to help relieve high gas prices. In what must be a bizarre show of sympathy (or perhaps to gain political kudos), Bangladesh offered the United States $1 million in aid for Hurricane Katrina. Other countries affected by the 2004 tsunami such as Indonesia and Sri Lanka also offered aid to the USA for the hurricane.

Besides criticism of motive, aid may be criticized on economic grounds that it is not effective: that is, it did not do what it was intended to do or help the people it was intended to help. The economist William Easterly and others have argued that aid can often hinder self development and progress – and that teaching others how to fish can be more effective than giving them fish. Some technical aid has also been criticized as benefiting the donor nation more, such as the construction and building carried out in Iraq by the American companies. Reacting to the former British Defence Secretary's words about Britain's role in Afghanistan, the columnist Matthew d'Ancoma of the *Evening Standard* stated: 'Fox's abrasive remark about education policy in Afghanistan indicated where he stands: Britain is engaged in this conflict to protect its own interests, not to nation-build.'[21] However, it will also be clear to the reader from looking at the evidence around and from the photographs, that people living in extreme conditions are also extremely resourceful in how they use and create an efficient 'closed loop economy' without depending on foreign aid (Figures 2.1 and 2.11) (closed loop economy is discussed in Chapter 1).

Some funding has been criticized, owing to its use of conditions, despite being classified essentially as humanitarian aid. US aid and emergency funds from the International Monetary Fund (IMF) and World Bank, for instance, are linked to a wide range of free-market policy prescriptions that some argue interfere in a country's sovereignty. Policy prescriptions from outsiders can do more harm, as they might not fit the local environment or culture. The IMF can be good at helping countries over a short problematic financial period, but for poor countries with long-lasting issues it can cause harm. Aid giving also attracts a fair of amount of criticism in the way particular concerns are publicized or lobbied as described in Chapter 1.

Foreign aid is also affected by corruption. Ordinary people donating to foreign disasters have often asked for the money to be spent on projects in the UK. In a survey carried out by Harris Interactive in 2010 – the year in which Britons donated £60 million to Haiti earthquake victims – two-thirds of the respondents suggested that it would be better for the Britons to offer expertise instead of money; 62 per cent of those surveyed wanted the donated money to be spent on alleviating *domestic* poverty.[22] In Haiti, a month after

Figure 2.11 Tyre market, Old Delhi. Repair, reuse and recycling of materials is how the poor help themselves.

Photo: Author.

the earthquake of 2010, hundreds of protesters gathered to accuse the Mayor of Haiti of corruption and of hoarding food.[23] Aid has also been linked to even more sinister aims. In August 2010, the *Evening Standard*[24] reported that Pakistani militants were using 'food aid' from the USA to get support for their aims very simply. A charity linked to the militant group, Lashkar-e-Taiba, simply collected the food dropped by the US aeroplanes and distributed them from house to house by boat to the people, especially women and children, trapped in their homes.

Past colonial history and present economic inequalities continue to plague the issue of aid. Many believe that the wealth and even cultural wealth of richer nations is built upon plundering the resources of past colonies – whether people (slavery), resources (mineral or plant-based) or cultural artefacts such as jewellery or antiquities that were taken. Others believe that richer nations, particularly the USA, are continuing to plunder the planet and other countries in order to support their lifestyles. Many therefore believe that it is the responsibility of the world's rich to help the poor (perhaps in the way that Bill Gates is doing). In the words of Ann Pettifor, who started Jubilee 2000 to end the debt problems of poor countries:

> 280 million Americans bingeing on Toyota Land Cruisers, Sony video players and Cartier watches are doing so by raiding the piggy-bank savings of five billion people in developing countries. It's time the rich financed the poor, instead of filching from them.[25]

Many green campaigners and NGOs now believe that instead of giving money, giving more attention to issues such as climate change and fair trade will have more impact on people's lives in the poor and disaster-prone countries such as Bangladesh.[26] Oxfam UK, for example, has been running a well-known campaign on climate change and fair trade. For example, the one-metre sea level rise generally predicted due to global warming, will inundate more than 15 per cent of Bangladesh (among other countries), displacing more than 13 million people and killing thousands. Also, decreasing or writing off debts from poor countries will actually help people in need. In January 2010, the anarchist newspaper, *Freedom*, reported that NGOs such as Jubilee 2000 and One International have condemned the USA's plan to link its $100 million aid programme with conditions that link 'Western interests' permanently to the country. They have been campaigning for Haiti's $1.9 billion debts to be written off. As we can see, there are many issues to be considered in aid programmes and the development activist needs to be aware of these when working in the area of rapid change and scarce resources.

Discussion points

- 'NGOs are the new class middlemen who, with the benediction of foreign philanthropists, are usurping the authentic voices of the poor',[27] according to Gita Verma. What do you think?
- Can international aid ever stop? Should rich countries stop giving aid?
- Are programmes designed to combat climate change and promote fair trade better than development projects?
- During a BBC radio interview about military aid on 12 July 2011, I said all aid should be 'untied and unconditional'. This was dismissed by another interviewee who said, 'this will never happen'. What do you think?

Chapter 3

Gypsies, tramps and thieves
The story of cities and slums

For every immigrant, the city is a different dream. He comes to it in flight – from persecution, from economic drought, from the stifling tittle tattle of the home town – and enters in wonder and hope. The entry to a new city, even if it is made in the internationalized tedium of an airport lounge, is a dramatically heightened occasion.

(Jonathan Raban[1])

Gokul came to work in our house in Delhi in the late 1970s. His story is a poignant one and typical of migrants to the city. For over thirty years, Gokul, who hailed from a village in North India, was part of our lives with his cheerful manner and village songs. He and his family of wife, two girls and one boy, lived in a squatter settlement inside the Northern Ridge, a protected forest of West Delhi. The Ridge was walking distance from our house and the other houses where he and his wife worked; I went to see his house too. For years, the government turned a blind eye to the squatters in the protected environmental habitat, even as the settlement grew in size. Perhaps this was because, nearby, a huge 'illegal' *Gurudwara* (temple for the Sikhs) was being built slowly, and the middle-classes benefited from the squatters who worked in their homes. We heard daily from Gokul how the *dalal* or local mafia lord demanded ever-increasing rents and we helped him in every way we could, even though our own circumstances were extremely modest. The rape and murder of a rich schoolgirl and her brother in the Ridge changed the status quo for the squatters, even though it was committed by a runaway criminal, not by the community. All squatter settlements were removed from the Ridge (the pressure from various environmental groups was also an influence) but not the Sikh temple as it became a very sensitive issue, especially after the assassination of the Prime Minister of India by her Sikh bodyguards and the massacre of Sikh people that followed.

So Gokul and his family moved elsewhere in West Delhi, still nearby. But then he was moved again – because the land turned out to be government owned, illegally leased out by the *dalals*. So he moved *Jamna-par* (literally, across the Yamuna) to the less desirable land across the river Yamuna, where the middle classes did not go (snob values) in those days. Even Gokul complained about the ignominy of living *Jamna-par*. For years, he continued to commute to West Delhi, along with many of his friends. His timings became increasingly erratic – a sign of the increasing congestion across the single bridge that connected Delhi that time to its East. Sometimes he could not come at all but at no point did my family consider using anyone else – he was part of our family. As years went by he fell out with his children who had married, gone to live in better parts of Delhi and refused to support him. His wife died too and he could not afford to commute anymore but would turn up for visits and tea (chai), talking about returning to his village. He always wore a traditional *dhoti* and shirt – never the Western attire of trousers. We heard that he died two years ago in his village – a lonely and defeated man. This year, I noted that the new squatters are back in the Ridge.

My father is an economic migrant from a tiny village from one of the most backward districts of India in West Bengal, still without piped water or electricity and roads. Although he is infirm and in his eighties now, he dreams of going back to the village. My mother was Delhi-born in British India and does not feel the same. However, I have lived from time to time and worked in my village for more than half of my life and I feel the same drawing to my village as my father, even though I now live in London. My Uncle, whose grandfather was a judge in British India, was one of the people who remembers New Delhi being built and going to the 'inauguration' of the new city. His family lived six months in the summer capital of British India, Shimla, and the rest of the year in Delhi – this constant movement so much a part of his childhood that he hates travelling even now. Our house in Delhi was built by Sikh refugees from the divided Punjab in 1947, who then moved elsewhere. This feeling of being 'urban' or 'rural' even when choosing to migrate to the city or beyond, is deeply personal as these personal stories show. As the book *Arrival City* by Doug Saunders shows, migration is changing the face of the world.[2] The history of the city is always the story of movement and growth.

Slums all over the world

Slums, informal settlements and rundown areas have always existed in every city, like an ugly cousin or like a 'shadow city', a phrase borrowed from Robert Neuwirth.[3] As the standards of living have gone up, parts of the city, which may have been desirable once, become undesirable. Both Britain and the USA, which are two of the richest countries in the world, have had slums at various points in their history (and even now). Even at the height of British prosperity during Victorian times, there were areas that were classified as slums.[4] Much of Dickensian London and even later would have been classified as a 'slum' now. After the First World War, there were promises of better housing for returning soldiers – 'Homes Fit for Heroes' – in 1919 but the issue of slums and homelessness was not considered properly until the Housing Act of 1930. Throughout the 1920s and 1930s, several thousand homeless people organized protest 'hunger' marches, the largest being in 1932 with a million people. Through these and the efforts of trade unions, progress was achieved to alleviate homelessness and hunger before the Second World War began in 1939. The Great Depression, which started with the Wall Street crash of 1929, reverberated around the world, affecting countries that had economic relationships with the USA, including Latin America.

In the USA, 20,000 US veterans of the First World War and their supporters converged on the capital, Washington DC, to demand immediate encashment of their army service certificates in 1932. They built a camp that was burned down eventually but many squatter settlements emerged around the USA. The name 'Hooverville' for squatter settlements in the USA endures as a reminder that all this happened under President Hoover, who had promised better times. It was only in 1941 that the USA, which was by then relatively unaffected by the war in Europe, started pulling down these squatter settlements and new homes were built. Seattle's main Hooverville was the one of the largest (covering nine acres with about 1,200 people) and longest lasting, and is well documented. It has its own 'mayor', a 'vigilance committee' and remained there, owing to sympathetic public and officials, until the land was needed for war efforts.

It is not easy to define a slum – the UN-HABITAT document of 2003[5] found that the definition of slums varies from country to country and from time to time. Slums also transform and become 'gentrified' and absorbed into the formal city. William Chaitkin writes about the process of gentrification of slums using the example of *barriadas* of Peru:

> The barriadas were built by peasants coming to the cities, on whose outskirts they 'squatted' while trying to work into industrialized urban society, with all its material benefits. As these accrued, the original makeshift houses were improved until they achieved the desired image, and economic reality, of middle-class respectability; and the barriadas – once politically unified by community action – became new suburbs.[6]

Many names have been devised for areas with poor-quality housing and infrastructure. In India, they are called *bustees, Jhuggi jhompri* colonies and camps. In the USA, slums are referred to as 'disinvested areas' and in South Africa and the Philippines they are called squatter camps. *Imijondolo* are the squatter settlements of the Australian Aborigines. Venezuela calls them *barrios* and Brazil *favelas*. Peru has its *pueblos jovenes* or *barriadas*, Haiti its *bidonvilles*,[7] Jamaica, Trinidad and Tobago their squatter settlements. They are called *illas de emergencia* or *villas miseria* in Argentina, *asentamientos* in Guatemala, *gecekondular* in Turkey. These names point to desperation, poverty and emergency. A UN-HABITAT[8] document defines a slum household as a group of individuals living under the same roof in an urban area that lacks one or more of the following:

1   Durable housing of a permanent nature that protects against extreme climate conditions.
2   Sufficient living space, which means not more than three people sharing the same room.
3   Easy access to safe water in sufficient amounts at an affordable price.
4   Access to adequate sanitation in the form of a private or public toilet shared by a reasonable number of people.
5   Security of tenure that prevents forced evictions.

I prefer to use the terms 'slums' and squatter settlements. Some believe that the word slum should be applied to only dilapidated or poor housing, although many use these terms interchangeably, for example Dharavi, Mumbai, is usually referred to as a slum, rather than squatter settlement. Many consider the word 'slum' offensive (used commonly in India) and use the phrase 'low-income' or 'informal settlements' instead. I consider low-income settlements different from slums as these are by definition inhabited by people with low income (often from lower middle classes or blue-collar workers), not necessarily people in abject poverty or those who are homeless and such housing has sanitation, water and generally a better quality of construction and design. Informal settlements could be a good way to refer to such areas of poverty but it is not universally applicable as there are traditional or historical parts of the city which were designed in a formal manner but are now considered 'slums' (I have used the words 'formal and informal' in Chapter 8 as a measure of the level of design procedures and top-down intervention in the study of the architecture of the settlement). As for the term 'disinvested', I find that many residents of slums and squatter settlements take pride in keeping their homes as clean and beautiful as possible, even more so during festivities.

Squatter settlements start by occupation of buildings or land, that is, squatting or illegal occupation. Squatting is defined as the act of reclaiming and occupying abandoned or unoccupied spaces that the squatters do not own, rent or otherwise have permission to use. It includes land squats, squatter settlements, homes, social centres, gardens or protest sites. Squatter colonies through land or building appropriation in time become slums. Slums can go on to become 'authorized colonies' when they gain legal status, as happens in India. East Delhi located over the river Yamuna is an example where almost all of the land was originally under agriculture, and was purchased by private buyers and leased out to migrants or occupied by squatters (see also the issue of *lal dora* in Delhi, described later). As a child, I remember playing in the fields there and slowly saw the rise of these settlements over the years,[9] especially as my place of study was right across the river. In time, political pressure combined with the promise of votes has assured legitimacy and infrastructural support to these places, as described later.

India has a severe housing shortage; in the urban areas, the demand–supply gap is about seventeen million units. According to Asian Development Bank, over 90 per cent of the housing demand is from low-income families.[10] The slums prevalent in many Indian cities are evidence of the shortage of affordable housing – in Delhi, the capital, there are an estimated five million people living in slums according to the architect and planner Ashish Muni Ganju. With the number of slum residents increasing by between 9 per cent and 10 per cent each year, there is an urgent need to find a solution to this problem. Women and children, who proportionally spend more time at home, are the ones most adversely affected by poor living conditions caused by lack of safe water, lack of sanitation and waste disposal. More than 25 per cent of slum residents are home-based workers, mostly women. For these families, access to decent living conditions and basic urban infrastructure and services is important, not only for their health and welfare, but also to remain economically productive.[11]

The city: a way to belong

> By its form, as by the manner of its birth, the city has elements at once of biological procreation, organic evolution and aesthetic creation. It is both a natural object and a thing to be cultivated, something lived and something dreamed. It is the human invention par excellence.
>
> (Claude Levi-Strauss, *World on the Wane*, Chesham: Criterion Books, 1961, p. 127)

The large-scale urbanization and migration from the rural to urban centres is one of the biggest contributing factors to the rise of squatter settlements. This can be seen in countries such as Brazil and Venezuela. Venezuela in the 1960s is an example of rapid urbanization, when its population transformed from 30 per cent urban to 30 per cent rural in a decade – a huge leap. In India, I have seen a generational shift in family sizes now having fewer children than forty years ago. I have also observed that these slum children, when they grew up, understandably, move on to 'low-income housing' provided by the government, or to other 'better slums'. Slums are usually the densest part of the city and the place to which new migrants or immigrants head, with cheap accommodation and easy means of employment assured. The rise in densities of slums and squatter settlements, it appears, is not owing to internal population growth, but rather to migration, and occasionally immigration as in Kolkata (Figure 3.1). This is also borne out by other NGOs' research in Latin America, such as Mundo Real, working in Brazil.[12] Such migrations are happening all over the world, including Europe. Alain Tarrius in 'Europe without borders: Migration networks, transnational territories and informal activities'[13] notes how migratory patterns across Europe have changed and that there is a lack of economic, social and cultural integration for the newcomers to the city who have to find these supports themselves.

Figure 3.1   Newly arrived workers from Bihar, living in huts and using the polluted waters of this canal that leads to the river Hooghly (a tributary of the Ganges), North Kolkata. River banks are ideal for squatters – ownership is usually nebulous, water supply assured and the river provides for many types of informal sector activites.

Photo: Author.

In 2005, China, the world's most populous country, had 166 cities with a population of over one million compared to only nine in the USA (the figures remained unchanged in 2009). China will cease to be a rural country, with a landscape little imagined by Mao or, for that matter, Le Corbusier, according to Mike Davis.[14] However, slum growth has outpaced 'formal urbanization' in many cities of Asia, Africa and Latin America (Venezuela, for example, is 92 per cent urbanized). Etymologically, citizens – cosmopolitan, civil and civic – share a common origin. Most of these words arose from the thirteenth century onwards with the rise of cities and were assimilated from their ancient origins into everyday language and its cultural connotations. For example, civil is now taken to mean someone with grace and manners, not just an inhabitant of the city. Thus, belonging to a city had wider cultural, political and social connotations than just being from the city. In fact 'citizenship' is defined as the state of being a citizen of a particular social, political or national community. Thus, the attraction of the city is more than just economic – the newcomer to the city wants to belong too. In Mumbai, I met Mohammed Zahir, a taxi driver, who had left his village in North India to come and stay in the slum of Dharavi and drive a rented taxi by day. He felt he belonged to Dharavi, even though by his looks, language and origins he was an 'outsider'.

He even based his taxi runs around the slum, and in the twenty years that he had been in Mumbai, was not really familiar with other parts of the city. (I could see from his startlingly blue-green eyes and wheaten complexion, though weather-beaten now, that he must have been strikingly handsome at one stage and I did wonder if he came to Mumbai to be a movie star) (Figure 3.2).

Lewis Mumford who wrote about cities in the last century would have been amazed to see the cities of today, particularly the megacity and the migratory city. The megacity is a new iteration of the city, and had barely begun to arise out of the squatter settlements and suburbs around the time that Mumford was writing. A megacity is a true 'Black Swan' that urban theorists did not see coming. Today, the megacity is mega problem of the world, owing to the services, energy and other input needed for it. The megacities in countries such as Mexico and India put more pressure on the scarce resources, infrastructure and ecology of the city than a megacity based in a rich country like Japan.[15] Even smaller but denser cities are becoming chaotic with increased pressure on resources. Mumbai (about thirteen million people) for example, has more people than Mexico City.[16] What I call the migratory city is the 'moving city' of migrants who inhabit the city for some time (could be days or

Figure 3.2 Mohammed Zahir from North India who now sleeps rough in Western India (Dharavi, Mumbai). He talked about the language and cultural problems he had when he first moved here but he was also determined to earn enough money to go back home one day.

Photo: Author.

years), usually for work, and then leave (Figure 3.3). Jakarta is a good example of both the mega and the (temporary) migratory city. The usual population of the city is about ten million but during the day, the population rises by a further three million caused by the influx of people who come from the suburbs to work. However, it has reached its limits – the capital of Indonesia is now too chaotic to be a capital city, says its President, Susilo Bambang Yudhoyono. The city of ten million now has 6.7 million vehicles that move at speeds of less than 6 mph, homes that are overcrowded, with electrocution and flooding common in the rainy season.[17] The president wants a new capital.

The migratory city could also be the transitory city (sometimes called 'camps'), where refugees, immigrants and squatters settle. This transitory city can be in the city or on the periphery. These people are sometimes moving, sometimes being moved forcibly and occasionally, their stay may be legitimized by acquiring citizenships, visas or entry permits. These cities appear on the edges of cities, at frontiers, zones and camps – often made up of people being stopped at international and national borders for security or immigration purposes – such as the 'Jungle' in Calais, France. Sometimes these temporary cities are set up as a result of war and famine. Urban squatter settlements are appearing in various forms all over the world and this

Figure 3.3 An impromptu tailor shop, Delhi – the whole family gathers. Note the photo of Ganesh, the elephant god who wards off trouble, stuck on the tree. Religious items are often used to appropriate space.

Photo: Author.

development, along with the megacity, poses various new problems regarding sustainability and waste management (Figure 3.4).

Migration from the rural areas to urban areas (or even from a poor economy to a richer economy) is the biggest cause of the rise of squatter settlements. Kolkata is a good example of such a city, where people from outside the state of West Bengal, such as those from nearby Bihar, come to it for opportunities along with 'illegal immigrants' from Bangladesh. People move into the city to look for economic opportunities and in the hope of bettering their lives, especially as opportunities in the rural areas decline. These people who come to the city start on the housing ladder by either buying decaying properties, or by squatting on land or in buildings. Immigration is also a reason for squatter settlements; for example, some of the *bustees* of Kolkata and the *Colonias* along the USA/Mexico border where the illegal immigrants from Mexico live (see a student's account of her work in *Colonias* in Chapter 9). Some parts of the city become slums owing to lack of investment in the infrastructure, transport or even by middle-class people moving out, as was the case in Notting Hill in London in the 1950s.

Figure 3.4 Alexandra township, Johannesburg, South Africa (see case study in Chapter 9 on this).

Photo: Tatum Lau, University of the Witwatersrand, Johannesburg.

The city sanitized

> When my son grows up, how will I explain to him that we live behind a wall?
>
> (From the film *La Zona*)

As noted in the UN-HABITAT document of 2003:

> the number of cities that consider squatting, slums and informal hous-
> ing developments as a highly *undesirable and temporary* phenomenon to be
> dealt with various *window-dressing exercises*, rather than addressing the core
> issues of urban poverty, is perhaps indicative of the *general lack of under-
> standing* of the forces, trends and conditions that are causing the growth
> of informal urbanization.[18] (Emphasis my own.)

Colonialization and social segregation between the colonialists and the
native people have been used to disenfranchise the urban poor of their land
and houses. British colonial cities of Eastern and Southern Africa denied the
native population the right to tenure and permanent residency. In Rhodesia,
Africans had to wait until independence to acquire a legal right to land.
Ruthless colonial warfare in places such as Algeria displaced half of the rural
population from 1954 to 1962, and these people poured into the capital.
Most of the native Algerians lived in corrugated *bidonvilles* while the luckier
ones found themselves in the abandoned homes of the fleeing colonists. Many
remnants of these abandoned homes can be found in former colonies. In Delhi,
I interviewed some residents who were living in temporary barracks built for
the British army more than sixty years ago. These homes leak in the monsoon rains, some roofs have fallen in and the space is inadequate for families.
However, this is a good location for these residents to live in and they will
not move (Figure 3.5). In her book *Indigenous Modernities*, Jyoti Hosagrahar
documents how people living in traditional houses in areas of Delhi were classified as living in 'slums' in the 1930s of colonial India; large parts of the old
city were demolished and people moved into 'European-style' houses, many
of which are now derelict and lived in by squatters or classified as slums, only
sixty years after the British left.[19]

However, now that the colonialists have gone, the division of the city continues – with gated communities and armed guards coming up to protect the
rich from the urban poor. Nowhere is it more apparent than in Caracas, one of
the cities in the world with the greatest socio-economic divide. Gated housing schemes where the rich live are found in Venezuela and other countries,
often jostling with the *barrios* next to them as depicted in the film *La Zona*,
set in Mexico City. Such gated housing is often termed the 'architecture of
fear'. South Africa, Brazil, Venezuela and the USA are the other four countries where such 'city divided' can be seen. In Chapter 8, there is a reference

Figure 3.5 People living in the leaking army barracks abandoned by the British colonial army more than sixty-five years ago, New Delhi.

Photo: Author.

to the outrage caused by *favelas* in Rio being given prominence by Google maps – certainly most middle classes are embarrassed by slums and *favelas*, even though the people who live there work in middle-class homes or offices (Figure 3.6).

In the 1970s, the improvement of slums became more important than replacing them – this was called 'slum upgradation' or 'rehabilitation'. However, whether it was slum upgradation or slum clearance, often there was no consultation with the people, with 'improvements' imposed in a top-down approach – this could be sanitation, schools or healthcare centres, or whatever the government felt necessary politically. Participation in slum 'rehabilitation' was not common, especially in the poor nations, and was even considered an unnecessary expense and waste of time (there are many examples from India and Gokul's story as before). Raul Villenueva, the Venezuelan architect educated in Europe who declared that he felt out of place in Venezuela, designed many of Caracas' slum rehabilitation schemes (Figure 3.7) under the dictatorship of Perez Jimenez. The state housing institute, Branco Obrero, began to finance these housing schemes in order to get '*quick, visible results* (and not protracted, expensive research into [the people's] *social and economic issues*' (emphasis my own).[20] In any case, even now squatters are easily moved or removed – these people are mostly illiterate and powerless. Slum dwellers may not have the

Figure 3.6 Rio (and its ever visible *favelas*), the 'Wallpaper' city of the year, 2010.

Photo: Joao Wrobel.

Figure 3.7 Slum rehabilitation, Caracas – these housing blocks were designed and built in the 1950s after slum clearances. Originally named 2 December after the date of a coup by Marcos Perez Jimenez, these were renamed 23 Enero (23 January) after the date of the dictator's overthrow.

Photo: Author.

necessary documents and recourse to the legal help required to resist this move. Previous slum upgrading projects across the world have involved the demolition of entire neighbourhoods followed by the construction of repetitive social housing blocks or relocation of the communities to places far away from their source of income. This leads to uprooting of communities that have resided in the same location for decades, leading to loss of both livelihood and social security gained through kinship (or caste as in India).

City improvements for international events such as the Olympics or conferences mean that the city is sanitized to project an image of progress and 'beauty'. 'Haussmanisation', as Mike Davis calls it, has been used to clear slums in the wake of international events and projects. This invariably means that eyesores such as slums need to be removed. Dominican Republic's on-and-off President from the 1960s to the 1990s, Joaquín Antonio Balaguer Ricardo, was notorious as the 'Great Evictor'. He 'ordered' projects including schools, roads and hospitals during his twelve years in which slums were also cleared. In the 1990s Balaguer spent millions on conservation projects in the capital, Santo Domingo, for a visit by the Pope, including the construction of a grand new avenue lined with modern housing blocks. While visiting Istanbul, I found that in the wake of the city being declared the City of Culture 2010, its remaining *gecekondular* had been removed and people moved away. Belgrade similarly removed the Roma settlement in the city next to the river in 2009, as part of a regeneration scheme.

The 2010 Commonwealth Games in Delhi has seen the uprooting of thousands of people from various slums, reportedly more than 40,000. If the athletes could bear to look out of their new apartments overlooking the polluted river Yamuna, they would have hardly realized that the poor migrants, who worked the fields nearby, had been forced out in police operations only a month before. Some had farmed the land for nearly twenty years. As described by a visitor:

> the area comprised a chain of 22 small slums that gave shelter to 150,000 people and nurtured more than 40,000 homes. Till the year 2004, a world within a world existed in Yamuna Pushta [the name of the slum]. Schools, medical and healthcare centres, self-help groups, shops, restaurants, crèches, small businesses and various social organizations, worked closely with the community, bringing about immense positive change in the lives of the residents.[21]

The school attended by their children, run by a local NGO, was bulldozed in the slum clearance. Some of the displaced were resettled on the outskirts of Delhi while others were simply left to live on the streets or were forced to return to their homes in the villages. Around 3,000 beggars were 'removed'.[22] Those parts that could not be removed were simply hidden. On one of the main roads in from the airport likely to be used by many tourists and dignitaries, a row of hoardings now obscures these slums from traffic, as I observed on my visit in 2011.

Other countries have also dealt with slums in this way when preparing to host large-scale events. For example, in the lead up to the 2010 World Cup in South Africa, thousands of people were evicted. Many did not receive compensation or alternative residence, and those who were resettled lived in terrible conditions in slums outside the city. Before the 2008 Olympics in Beijing, China, 1.5 million people were displaced according to the Centre on Housing Rights and Evictions (COHRE). In the centre of Beijing, close to Tiananmen Square, the historic neighbourhood of Qianmen was partially demolished and replaced by a Disney-esque pedestrian tourist area – the main reason for demolition being that the area had fallen into disrepair and poverty, becoming an inner-city slum. Demolishing and making it into a tourist attraction seemed a smart solution but now these structures remain unused (Figure 3.8). Thousands of public housing units were destroyed before the 1996 Olympics in Atlanta and 30,000 residents were relocated elsewhere.

As land runs out in the crowded cities, governments take on the land upon which squatters sit, knowing that they are in a weak position with no papers to prove ownership or living in very poor conditions. Currently, Rio in Brazil is preparing to demolish some of its *favelas* in preparation for the 2014 World Cup. Rio's housing secretary, Jorge Bittar, said the demolition was part of a £285 million project to 'transform' the region around the Maracanã, previously the centre of a £330 million pre-World Cup refurbishment. Culture centres, tree-lined plazas and a cinema have been promised. 'This is a very poor

Figure 3.8 During the Olympics they were the pride of Beijing, but now these internationally acclaimed stadiums and other structures built on land appropriated from people stand forlornly behind gates and chains.

Photo: Arti Chari.

community, with very precarious homes [built] in an inappropriate area and we are offering these families dignity', he said. However, campaigners claim the demolition of Favela do Metrô which was built by railway workers in the 1970s is only the start of other cleansing and that other Brazilian cities would be affected by the infrastructure facelift. 'Between now and the 2014 World Cup, 1.5 million families will be removed from their homes across the whole of Brazil.'[23] Brazil was heavily criticized for sanitizing Rio de Janeiro during the 1992 Earth Summit and it remains to be seen what will happen in 2014.

New slum typology

> I am sure no one wants to live in a slum – given half a chance they will want to move out of there.
>
> (External critic at London Metropolitan University, 2011)

The sizes of slums vary from country to country as do the densities. The largest squatter settlement in Asia is Orangi town in Karachi (57 square kilometres) but Dharavi in Mumbai is much denser, with half-to-one million people packed into 2.23 square kilometres (about eleven times more dense than its surrounding city of Mumbai). Kibera, a slum in Nairobi, Kenya, which is of a similar size, has about one-fifth the density of Dharavi, while Khayelitsha in Cape Town, South Africa, has a density of about 1,000 persons per square kilometre spread out for miles next to a motorway. The 2003 UN report quoted earlier, gives an account of twenty-nine cities from all over the world, including Los Angeles, that are included in this definition of slums. However, as the author of the report points out, these qualities are not universally applicable, or comparable – as the UN-HABITAT document, State of the World's Cities 2006/7, notes: 'Not all slums are homogeneous and not all slum dwellers suffer from the same degree of deprivation'.[24] The residents of the *barrios* in Venezuela looked healthy, well-dressed and lived in much better quality homes than residents of the squatter settlements of Kolkata. According to the UN-HABITAT definition of slums, I was shocked to find out that I had lived in a slum for most of my life! Also, the ownership of lands is not a universal issue – many people in slums own the land or the house they live in. The house may be in poor condition or the area around it may have deteriorated.

India has a concept called *lal dora*, literally red line. The term was used for the first time in the year 1908 in British India. It denotes the habitable part of a village, the *abadi* around which can be drawn a red line. In 1957 and 1963, the Delhi Municipal Corporation allowed *lal dora* land to be exempt from the typical building bylaws and statutory regulations under the Delhi Municipal Act, especially if the building was for habitation. Initially a useful measure of the amount of habitable land, now this is used to flout various planning laws. As Delhi city has grown, it has enveloped village lands with *lal dora* land. Prime land inside the city with no veritable planning regulations is also extremely high value. Many *lal dora abadis* have secure electricity, water and sewage connections, with water from the Delhi Water board. There are at least 362 'villages' inside Delhi's National Capital Region (NCR), out of which 135 are urban villages and 227 are classified as rural. This has added to the problem of illegal housing and dangerous construction in an already precarious urban environment.

Mike Davies[25] defines slums according to historical, migratory and situational elements: formal and informal residency in both urban-core and peripheral locations. However, issues about tenure can be ambiguous. In Dharavi, for example, people settling there before 1995 have been given certain rights to tenure; however, proving tenure settlement before 1995 can be very difficult (people have been asked to provide voting papers and ration cards as a proof but that is not a conclusive proof of residency). There can be many 'favourable' circumstances for land encroachment that include natural disasters and political events such as elections, *coups d'état*, revolutions and end of colonial rule. So my own understanding and extension of slum typology includes only the contextual and social aspects, not the legal or material. You will see that some classifications are quite fluid and a particular slum could be a mixture of one or more types:

1 Peripheral
2 Boundary lines
3 Pocket
4 Historic
5 Occupied
6 Hippie
7 Transitional.

Peripheral

These are slums that enclose or form at the outskirts of the city – those found in most South American cities are like that.[26] Such areas easily become the 'Megaslums' when separate slums merge in continuous belts of informal housing and squatter communities. They are usually on undesirable land – hillsides, areas of seismic activity, flood plains or brownfields or even a combination of two or more of these. The *barrios* of Caracas, for example, lie on hills that have underground streams, seismic activity and unstable geology. Petare in Caracas (Figure 3.9) is the largest slum in Latin America. Although Rio's first *favela*, Morro de Providencia, started in the 1880s, most of the megaslums started in the 1950s and 1960s. Istanbul's *gecekondular*, which have sprung up on the periphery, are 'overnight cities' built quickly to avoid detection and displacement.

Figure 3.9 Caracas – the city disintegrated by *barrios*, roads and nature.

Photo: Alfredo Brillembourg.

The unauthorized colonies of East Delhi are now regularized but were initially built on flood plains. Starting off as small pockets, now these are interconnected forming a huge urban area with several names that were a testimony to their separate origins. Many of them took their names from existing middle-class areas in New Delhi, for example 'New Ashok Nagar', which took its name from Ashok Nagar in West Delhi. Some of these settlements take the names of powerful political figures such as Rajiv Gandhi camp and Sonia Camp to give themselves a political value in the hope perhaps that they will avoid eviction – but the word 'camp' betrays their origins even though now the houses are made of bricks and concrete.

Boundary lines

These are slums that are found in in-between areas, between formal and informal parts of the city and next to infrastructures or systems that lie between parts of a city (such as sewage pipes, railway lines or motorways). Dharavi in Mumbai is next to the city's main water supply pipe (Figure 3.10) while many of those in Kolkata are to be found next to railway lines – a precarious existence. Slums or squatter camps are also found on the boundaries between countries such as the refugee camps between Pakistan and Afghanistan, and Mexico and the USA.

Artificial boundary lines also create slums and reinforce superiority of one set of people over the other. In the building of New Delhi, for example, the Indian labourers building the city were given houses on the other side of a green ridge, which acted as a 'social divider' (where Gokul lived). Now these 'workers" homes and the area built in the 1920s and 30s are officially slums. In New Orleans, Pontchartrain Park was the first totally black settlement built in 1952 because even in the late 1950s black people were unable to buy property because the white landowners exercized their right not to sell it to them. Separated by an artificial 'industrial canal' was the whites-only Gentilly Woods area. Pontchartrain Park gradually fell into disrepair and became a disinvested area. It was devastated during the 2005 Hurricane Katrina, flooding first from the overtopping of a section of floodwall of the Industrial Canal caused by storm surge, then from major breaches sustained by floodwalls along the London Avenue Canal. In 2009, New Orleans topped the USA's list of cities with the highest proportion of empty homes. It was home to 65,888 vacant or unoccupied properties, down from 71,657 in 2008. Many people living in Pontchartrain Park are still awaiting reconstruction under the USA's first black president as I write this.[27]

Dharavi, bound by two main suburban railway lines and main roads, next to the city's main water supply pipes and an open sewage canal, is a perfect example of a 'boundary' slum. In the early nineteenth century a group of potters arrived from Gujarat and settled on the 1.7 square miles of mangrove swamp, which was then located outside the city. Dharavi was then an island in the marshland but due to the creation of a dam in the North, the water was drained from the land around it. Using their traditional knowledge of the earth plus the waste dumped into it, the potters and native fishermen created the solid land on which Dharavi stands today. Tanners and weavers

Figure 3.10 Dharavi, the slum built along the main water supply pipe to Mumbai city. For those in 'boundary conditions', living next to the water or electricity supplies allows them to siphon some off for their own use.

Photo: Author.

from Northern India joined the potters, creating a diverse group of people, united in their shared battles against poverty, hunger and disease. For those who criticize Dharavi's poor living conditions, one must remember that the settlement began during British rule (like Kibera in Kenya) and a blind eye was turned on these migrants who lived in precarious circumstances at that time (similar to Gokul's experience in Independent India). As Dharavi now lies sandwiched between North and South Mumbai, it is not only prime land but also an 'eye-sore'. Despite not being very pretty or salubrious, land prices are sky high in Dharavi, primarily owing to its location. Various urban regeneration schemes to remove this slum, made popular by award winning films (*Slumdog Millionaire* being a recent one) and books, have been planned but owing to the complexity of establishing residency and re-housing people, it remains a pipe dream.

Pocket

These are small slums that appear in the unused or 'unclaimed' parts of the city. They can appear in the unused open spaces (for example, squatter settlements of Kalyanpuri in Delhi which are in a park) and in inner-city land (for example, the 'pocket *barrios*' of Caracas) (Figure 3.11). The Indian architect and urban planner, Ashish Muni Ganju, refers to some of these city-centre slums as 'spontaneous' development. These squatter settlements are perhaps the most enviable of the lot as the land on which they sit is high value, politicians desire their

Figure 3.11 A pocket slum, Bella Campo, Caracas, near the posh areas of La Floresta.

Photo: Author.

votes and they are 'beautified' because they are in the city, and supplied with water and electricity. The squatter areas of East Delhi were 'illegal' settlements in the outskirts but now, owing to the expansion of the city, these are 'authorized' and are in the city proper.

In time, some of these inner-city slums are reclaimed back into the middle-class folds – usually called re-gentrification. An example would be that of Notting Hill in London, which became a notorious slum in the aftermath of the Second World War blitz. Peter Rachman bought housing from which he evicted white tenants and filled them with Afro-Caribbean people – vulnerable immigrants who did not complain about the appalling conditions they lived in. For example, Southam Street had 2,400 people living in 140 nine-roomed houses. Rachman even entered the English dictionary – as 'Rachmanism', defined as 'the exploitation and intimidation of tenants by landlords'. The dire housing conditions in Notting Hill led Bruce Kenrick, a social activist and Church Minister, to set up the Notting Hill Housing Trust in 1963. He also helped to drive through new housing legislation in the 1960s and founded the UK housing charity, Shelter, in 1966. The slums were finally cleared during the redevelopment of the 1960s and 1970s when the A40 (Westway flyover) cut through the area, and Trellick Tower designed by Erno Goldfinger was built to rehouse the people decanted from the slums. From the late 1980s middle-class white people began returning to the area, making this area one of the most expensive places to live in London. However, in other places in the UK, Rachmanism continues, according to Jon Snow.[28]

Historic

These are existing parts of the city, usually with traditional architecture, that have fallen into disrepair. Old Delhi would fall into this category, as would the historic parts of Cairo. In central Shanghai, the *nongtang* are traditional dwellings with a courtyard, enclosed by walls. Arranged in rows, they are easily accessible by sub-lanes connected to a main lane leading out to the city. The architecture and varied planning of the *nongtang* are reflections of the city's cosmopolitan traditions and evolving lifestyles of old. By 1940, a large majority of the population in Shanghai, nearly three million including many Westerners, lived in various types of *nongtang*. Physically dilapidated and densely populated by the working class, many areas with *nongtang* are now identified as slums. However, these areas provide the much needed accommodation and employment for unskilled workers and new migrants. The old city of Jerusalem could be classified as a slum, being threatened by overcrowding, lack of maintenance and poor infrastructure. These areas are also heavily commercialized. For example, Jerusalem's walled city is mostly a shopping and commercial area. Old Delhi or Shahjahanabad is also an extremely commercialized area with as many as 500 estimated different economic activities taking place in about 6 square kilometres (Figure 3.12).[29]

Figure 3.12 Shahjahanabad (Old Delhi) chicken market.

Photo: Author.

Besides overcrowding and over-commercialization, such areas can suffer from the 'out-migration' of people. Historic areas are blighted when people move out of these heavily commercialized areas – first the wealthy and then even the poor, leaving behind shops or worse still, empty shops. Many of the industrial and commercial activities carried out in these areas are often illegal, sometimes dangerous and polluting. In the mid-1980s I carried out a survey of industries in a certain part of Shahjahanabad (Old Delhi). The most dangerous ones were the plastics industries, which carried a fire risk – there have been several fires in the area. Illegal activities such as production of fake branded perfume, DVDs and books are all carried out here.[30]

Like Old Delhi, which has a railway station into which migrants come from all over the country, in Barcelona, Spain, the old city near the port, which is part of the medieval city, has become a magnet for immigrants. According to the UN report of 2003 quoted earlier, the 'old city' came to have very high housing densities in several neighbourhoods, such as the Barri Gòtic, Santa Caterina and Barceloneta. The highest concentration was found in the neigh-bourhood known as El Raval.[31] Its rundown housing provided inexpensive lodgings such as flats and dormitories to the incoming immigrants from the Philippines, Pakistan and Morocco. Low income and illegal activities and the highest levels of poverty in the city characterized this area. The buildings in this area vary in age – some are several centuries old – and the existence of slum lodgings in the area can be traced back at least to the mid-nineteenth century. El Raval, which is associated with drugs and prostitution, is now being gentrified with various urban regeneration schemes.

Occupied

'Occupied' includes squatted buildings or structures such as office buildings, motorways/underpasses, derelict or abandoned homes. For example, the Irish traveller community that has lived under the A40 motorway in West London for years is currently administered by two of London's richest boroughs – Kensington and Hammersmith. The most unusual example would be Cairo's city of the dead, where one million people use the Mameluke tombs as prefabricated housing, starting out in the eighteenth century as homes for the tomb keepers, and gradually for quarry workers and later refugees from the Sinai and Suez during the 1960s and 1970s. Now other people have taken on abandoned Jewish cemeteries, with families using the built-in shelving for clothes, cooking pots and a colour TV.[32]

In Venezuela, after the tragedy of the Vargas landslides in 1999 where reportedly 32,000 died and more than a million were made homeless, people moved into the nearest city, Caracas, and occupied empty office buildings (Figure 3.13). They still live there. In several other cities, people have moved into the smashed remains of unstable high-rise buildings and smaller homes all but destroyed in 1999. Others have built houses where previous homes were demolished by floods – a dangerous precedent to follow. After the recent floods in 2010, President Hugo Chavez moved homeless people into five-star hotels and resorts as a grand political gesture. It remains unclear how the present housing crisis triggered by natural disasters will be resolved.

Hippie (or pseudo slums)

> The slumming of London is something else.
>
> (Simon Jenkins, *Evening Standard*, 18 January 2011)

What I call 'hippie' or 'pseudo slums' are areas or buildings taken over by middle-class squatters in rich countries as a form of political protest (squatting has been a form of protest in many countries as exemplified in the American situation at the beginning of the chapter). Christiania, in Copenhagen (Figure 3.14), is a famous example where the informal city existed as a form of political and cultural protest. American communes, such as Drop city of the 1970s, were built by middle-class exiles from the cities, prepared to de-culture themselves through new environments, according to William Chaitkin.[33] Squatting is very common all over Europe. In London, squatters have become the centre of

Figure 3.13 Office building occupied by squatters since 1999 after the Vargas tragedy, Caracas. I named this the 'Squatter building'. The squatter building is the tallest one in the centre.

Photo: Author.

Figure 3.14 Christiania, Copenhagen, photographed in 1995.

Photo: Author.

new movements in education, political thought and culture. For example, one of the groups, calling itself the '84 Eastern Street, organized a sit-in to protect a work of art by the artist Banksy and to voice their protest against the 'gentrification' of the area. Other squatters have set up schools and art exhibitions. A massive amount of publicity is generated by these forms of protest because the buildings squatted in are in rich parts of London and owned by famous or rich people.

In the UK, squatting itself is not considered a criminal offence. It is illegal to get into a property by breaking in or damaging it and using the utilities. Ironically it is also illegal for the landlord to force their way in if someone is inside the property. The 'Democracy village' in London's Parliament Square, consisting of several tents, was described as a slum by Simon Jenkins. This land was right in front of the Houses of Parliament, seized in the year 2000 by a group of anarchists (Figure 3.15). It generated international publicity for various causes such as the Iraq war and green issues. The 'village' was finally removed in 2010 after a protracted legal battle. However, as I write, defiant 'villagers' continue to squat on the pavement surrounding the green square which is now fenced off. In Bristol, there was another form of protest using a squat. Nine people were arrested and eight police officers hurt after violent clashes sparked by a police raid on a property being used by squatters opposed to the opening of a Tesco store nearby.[34]

There are also groups of organized squatters who go around Europe, looking for free accommodation with publications such as 'squatter's handbooks'

Figure 3.15 Democracy village near the Houses of Parliament, London – note the central green area is now fenced off while the pavements are occupied by protesters.

Photo: Author.

to help them.[35] In London, legal publishers Sweet and Maxwell showed that squatting had risen threefold from 2009 to 2010 and was mainly affecting the priciest areas such as Chelsea, Belgravia and Mayfair. They attributed the rise of homelessness to the number of vacant properties and growing homelessness in the recession of 2010. However, a number of squatters were found to be middle-class backpackers from European countries such as Italy, looking for free accommodation in London.

Transitional

These squatter camps come up temporarily owing to various disruptions (mostly political) such as war, demolitions of existing squatter settlements by the authorities and transit camps between countries such as the 'Jungle' that came up in Calais, France. In the summer of 2009, 300 illegal immigrants, of which almost half were under sixteen, were detained by the French police, and the entire area, including a mosque, was bulldozed. Some refugee settlements become permanent such as Dharamsala in India where Tibetan refugees settled and Karol Bagh in Delhi, where Sikh regugees fleeing Partition in 1947 settled.

The gypsies and traveller community settlements present a unique view on the nature of transitional settlements because they regard themselves as travellers owing to their culture and ethnicity (Figure 3.16). Although their settlements are not 'slums', neighbours regard them as an eyesore, health hazard and encroachment. In May 2010, a group of villagers got together in the 'heart of England' in Meriden, West Midlands to 'preserve the tranquillity' of the area by forming a human wall to prevent a group of Roma from settling down.[36] Writing in defence of her people's culture on 13 May in the same paper, Mary-Louise Bishop said, 'We don't decide to become travellers, we are travellers. It's in our blood and in our beliefs'. There was an international outcry when France ordered large groups of gypsies from Romania to leave the country, however the status of Roma and traveller communities lies low in society.

Slums: the reality

> Housing as a verb.
>
> (John Turner)[37]

In 2005, the United Nations estimated that over one billion people reside in slums worldwide and that 94 per cent of these slums are found in the 'developing' world. Of the world's thirty largest megaslums, fifteen, including the largest five, are in Latin American cities, comprising a total population of over

Figure 3.16 Roma settlement in the dried river bed outside Belgrade, Serbia. These people were removed from central Belgrade.

Photo: Author.

fourteen million inhabitants. Security and safety compete with affordability and proximity to employment opportunities. The peripheral megaslums are the cheapest places to live and may offer the hope of future land ownership.[38] So these people will settle in areas of the city that are abandoned or undesirable. These, however, typically require long and expensive commutes to and from workplaces. In Belgrade, the Roma settlement lies on a dry river bed after having been evicted from the main city. When I visited this settlement, my Serbian taxi driver with a sense of irony and shame said to me, 'In the thirty years since the fall of communism, I have not seen any improvement in the lives of these people'. The urban poor have a difficult balance – housing, tenure, work, money, crime and family circumstances.

The people who are not able to find homes in the built-up areas then try to find land that appears to belong to no one and a squatter settlement starts (land owned by my grandmother in Delhi was taken over in this way). When new land is not available, people are forced to move into existing slums, which then start densifying. In Caracas, *barrios* are densifying at the rate of 2 per cent each year while in Mumbai, the *bustees* are densifying at an even faster rate of 9 per cent. Dharavi in Mumbai is the most crowded spot on earth – 18,000 persons per acre are packed into 10 by 15 foot rooms stacked on top of each other. The architects, Studio Mumbai, referred to this extremely claustrophobic context in a full-sized installation at the V&A museum in London in 2010. In Kolkata, an average of 13.4 people live in one small room. The architectural response to such tremendous density has been the verticalization of slums, that is, the stacking of rooms or storeys above each other. Sabine Bitter, an architect who has been working in Caracas calls them vertical *barrios* while the people who live in them call them 'vertical prisons'.

According to Aldo Rossi, the economy exerts a more physical and insidious presence in the city; he uses examples of Western cities – even to the extent of calling private landownership 'evil'.[39] He quotes the theories developed by Maurice Halbwachs and Hans Bernoulli to substantiate this. Halbwach's theory is about expropriation of spaces and how they are used by different groups of people through 'collective memories'.[40] Bernoulli's theory states that private landownership can be detrimental to the modern city and therefore land should be returned to collective ownership.[41] However, as Rossi concludes: 'behind and beyond economic forces and conditions lies the problem of choices; and these choices, which are political in nature, can only be understood in light of the total structure of the urban artifacts'.[42] Perhaps to make us think further or avoid pre-imagining the future, he understandably leaves open the delicate question about why either capitalism or socialism still does not discount land appropriation.

Speculation in urban land including those lands on which slums exist, is commonplace. 'Slum lords' or the mafia lords controlling the land can recoup their investments in months from the high rents charged – overcrowded poorly maintained slum dwellings are often more profitable per square metre than other types of real estate. The *dalals* in Mumbai are skilled businessmen in land speculation. Dharavi itself has become a target for land deals because the land it is sitting on is of high value and the *dalals* want to sell it at a huge profit. One shack we saw on the main road in Dharavi, measuring about 10 square metres, which passed off for someone's office, had a monthly rent of R25,000, that is, $550 per month (Figure 3.17).

As the poor who live in the slums do not own the land they live on, land tenure is an important issue in the slums. For example, three-quarters of the urban space is owned by 6 per cent of the people in Mumbai and just ninety-one people control most of the vacant land in Mumbai. In 1986, I carried out a survey for Intach, a conservation body in India at Nizamuddin, a very old settlement in Delhi, now classified as a slum. I was astounded to find out how much of the land was actually owned by a religious leader, the Mullah. The land around the mosque had been gradually leased out to people – Muslims and Hindus migrating from nearby states. In Caracas, Mumbai and Manila and many other slums, the people live on whatever land they find. In Caracas and Rio, these people live on steep slopes on the hills surrounding or located within the city. These homes are built right next to mountain streams or over them. How dangerous this practice is was revealed by the Vargas tragedy when a combination of heavy rains, cutting of terraces into hills and lack of vegetation, which contributed to land destabilization, along with seismic activity, led to the deaths of thousands,

Figure 3.17 The offices of Acorn India, a charity working with ragpickers and recycling projects, Dharavi, Mumbai – unbelievably, these types of spaces rent out at $550 per month.

Photo: Author.

left more than a million homeless and another 200,000 jobless. In 2010, heavy rains again claimed many casualties – about 2,000 houses collapsed in landslides and three people died in Barrio San Agustin where I was working at that time (Figure 3.18). The 2010 landslides and floods in Brazil killed more than 800 people, most of them living in crude shacks on hillsides. Daniel Salcedo, an engineering consultant in Caracas, began warning people about landslide risks in the late 1980s. However, the Vargas region was largely unprepared when disaster struck in 1999.

> Freedom to choose is important in any society, but some form of housing regulation is needed to avert foreseeable disaster. Every year the people are building and developing in the creeks and the hills, vulnerable to landslides and flows. It's easy to see that many people here could die. But nobody does anything. No central government authority goes to tell them 'You cannot live here'.[43]

Apart from the danger of living on such terrain, even without the bad weather, people face daily challenges. In Caracas, 2.5 million residents of the *barrios* climb an average of twenty-five storeys to reach their homes (*ranchos*) and walk for about thirty minutes to get to public transportation – Mike Davis calls this the mountaineering challenge of living in the *barrios* (Figure 3.19).[44] A system of ski cars (the Metrocable) has been installed in Barrio San Agustin, Caracas (Figure 3.20) and other cities of South America, such as Medellin

Figure 3.18 House collapse in Barrio San Agustin, Caracas, November 2010.

Photo: Adolfo Useche.

Figure 3.19 Transporting food and waste up the *barrio* stairways, Petare, Caracas.

Photo: Author.

Figure 3.20 Metrocable high above the Barrio San Agustin, Caracas (Architects: Urban Think Tank).

Photo: Author.

in Colombia. However, it benefits people who need to go from the top to the bottom and vice versa – people living in the middle still have to find their way to either top or bottom. Waste is not allowed to be carried in the Metrocable (I was told off for carrying an empty can that I meant to recycle and had to put in the bin before being let back in). So, even funerals also have to proceed down the hill. However, the Metrocable is an improvement to the people's lives, and the architects, Urban Think Tank, are working on other solutions for access.

Planning consultation and disaster warning is usually absent from the slums, with fire, landslides, earthquakes, floods and diseases (including obesity on the rise) accounting for many preventable deaths. There are many NGOs and charities working in slums and squatter settlements all over the world and they do admirable work in difficult circumstances. Lack of clear guidelines and agreements and differences in how each NGO operates in a country (especially 'non-democratic' countries such as Cambodia) plus the allegations of corruption and unethical practices make it difficult to see 'results'. And, sharp results may be difficult to see – results take years to manifest – something that funders do not understand. So, perhaps in desperation, international dignitaries may be taken to see projects beautified for that visit. As Gita Verma documents, overseas visitors attract the right attention from the government or NGOs but once the limelight is turned people may be abandoned, as this statement from a woman in the ODA-sponsored project in Delhi shows:

> When the English gentleman [British Prime minister, John Major] visited, officers were queued up here. The corporation had cleaned up all over. But after John Major left, no officer ever showed up again. Slum residents have been to the corporation several times but no one is listening to us.[45]

Crime is a natural consequence of living in such dire circumstances and high densities – the 'architecture of desperation'. Unequal social and economic situations cause people to aspire to material and social markers of wealth by begging, borrowing or stealing. According to International Labour Organization (ILO) research, urban poverty in Latin America rose by 50 per cent between 1980 and 1986, while average incomes of the working population fell by 40 per cent in Venezuela, 30 per cent in Argentina and 21 per cent in Brazil. In a place such as India where the prevailing culture is rooted in caste and religion, social mobility is not so easy and through the sheer disparity of wealth and social status, the poor remain desperately poor.[46] The most expensive house in the world, Antilla, which cost $1 billion to build ($2 billion according to some reports) is owned by Mukesh Ambani, the fifth richest man in the world and head of the Mumbai-based petrochemical giant, Reliance Industries. His home is a twenty-seven-storey skyscraper with the first six floors devoted to parking alone. There is a 'health level' which has a jacuzzi, yoga studio, dance studio, gyms, a juice bar and solarium, and an entertainment level that includes a fully sized theatre – there is almost 400,000 square feet of entertainment space (Figure 3.21). From the top floor, Ambani entertains guests with panoramic vistas over Mumbai, and possibly the slums – Dharavi, Garib Nagar and others (Figure 3.22).

Lack of papers proving tenure can easily become a reason for assumed criminality. Political and police powers may be used against people who may have lived on a land for centuries but have no 'modern' documentation to prove ownership. In a perverse move, Israel's State Attorney's Office is currently preparing a legal petition for more than NIS1 million (about $280,000 in 2011) against the residents of El Araqib, a Bedouin village in the Negev Desert.[47] This village has been demolished eighteen times since summer 2010. More than 150,000 Bedouin, the indigenous inhabitants of the Negev region, live in informal squatter settlements or 'unrecognized villages' in the South of the country. They account for around 12 per cent of the Palestinian population of the country, and yet discriminatory land and planning policies have made it virtually impossible for Bedouin to build legally where they live. Despite being unrecognized by Israel, the village of El Araqib has existed since before the creation of Israel in 1948. Bedouin residents were evicted by the newly

Figure 3.21 Antilla, the most expensive home in the world costing $2 billion, towers over Mumbai. Six people live in this buidling.

Photo: Chater Paul Jordan.

Figure 3.22 A few kilometres away, a man scavenges in Dharavi, Mumbai.

Photo: Author.

declared Israeli state in 1951, but returned to the land on which they live and where they cultivate. During my visit to Palestine, I saw many Bedouin settlements in insalubrious areas such as next to a motorway or a stone quarry (Figure 3.23).

Learning from slums: case studies

> It is frustrating to see groups of students travelling to … India's slum regions to help make their lives better by building new sewage systems or 'studying the community' to see what is needed to make the slum a better place to live. Instead they should be studying the slums to learn how to make London a better place to live.
>
> (From a student essay, London Metropolitan University, 2010)

The rich outsider views slums with pity and fear. Slums are the 'other' for these people but do they look in the mirror and recognize something? In the Mexican film, *La Zona*, the middle class living in the gated community hate the people of the *barrios* because they view all of them as criminals, and yet they descend into violence and murder themselves. During my visits to slums, I try to immerse myself there, looking for what I can learn. I think this is the way of the development activist. I have always been surprised by what I have learned. In Dharavi, I learned that the people had the money and resources to rebuild their houses themselves but were not doing so owing to the problems

Figure 3.23 Bedouin settlement in hills around Jerusalem, Palestine.

Photo: Author.

of tenure. In Caracas, I viewed the new multi-storeyed tenements given to people displaced by the building of the new Metrocable system. 'Did they like living in these shiny new apartments?' I asked them. These people said that they missed living in the *barrios* – the camaraderie and the life there. I have been amazed by the warmth and hospitality of these people, despite their difficult circumstances. I admire their creativity and resourcefulness.

I have come to believe that slums need a light touch from the development activist. This is not to deny the difficulties of living in a slum that I have already described, nor to close our eyes to the terrible filth, danger and disease that people there are exposed to. This is to say that the problems associated with slums can be resolved, using the same creativity and resourcefulness that already exists there, perhaps with a little help from the development activist. In the words of Kenneth Frampton, the rich can learn from the poor – and Western architects can learn from others:

> It is one of the ironies of the interrelationship between the so-called First and Third Worlds that Indian architects categorically demonstrated very comparable alternate land settlement patterns that could with minor adaptation have been employed equally effectively in both worlds. It is also significant and yet an understandably ironic fact that this remarkable production has also been largely ignored by the Western world.[48]

So what can we learn from slums? Many activities and initiatives have taken place in the slums and poorer parts of the world. There are many NGOs and charities working there on a long-term basis. It can be argued that many initiatives come from above and from richer, middle-class people, not from the slum dwellers themselves. That may be true. However, I have always argued that nothing will work if the people do not embrace the ideas themselves. Slums have been the subject of various urban experiments for many decades – from eradication to rehabilitation, and so on. And many of these experiments have not worked. Some inspirational ideas are described below. These are things that the 'Western' cities and the 'gentry' can learn from slums. Some ideas have been adapted for the city such as tape ball cricket from Pakistan slums to reduce youth crime and vagrancy in London. The Honey Bee Network is an idea started in the rural areas of India and has spread to slums in South America, documenting extraordinary creativity in an area of scarce resources, such as the invention of a stand on the front wheel of a cycle which is more stable, easier to vend from and has a portable bench. The inventions have been patented, manufactured and sold to rich and poor countries – thus leading to an international exchange of ideas and trade. I am not condoning the dangerous and unhealthy conditions of the slums and their 'micro-industries', lack of care towards the workers and their exploitation. I am hoping to show the positive side of slums and informal settlements while pointing out aspects that need to be improved. Slums demonstrate that high-density living is possible and can be life-enhancing. Certainly, most of my students have always left feeling good after working in the slums, moved by the courtesy and warmth shown by the people despite their own problems. The development activists as well as so-called experts can learn from the spirit of the slums.

Case study 1: slums and economy

Slums are a hive of economic activity, most of which is illegal, and some dangerous, as already described. However, these people who are not covered by welfare schemes and are mostly illiterate manage to eke out a living somehow. This is usually through low-skilled or blue collar work. In Caracas and Delhi, slum dwellers carry out various forms of cleaning, housekeeping and other such work in homes, offices and hotels. I met people in Caracas who kept the Metrocable working and in Delhi, the auto-rickshaw drivers keep the city moving – these people live in the slums and low-income settlements.

In Dharavi, we saw various forms of cottage industries, many of them based on recycling paper, plastic and metal; 200 varieties of plastic were being sorted out and recycled as future crockery and cups. Waste pickers collected 85 per cent of the waste in Dharavi and delivered it to the local businesses that recycled them (Figure 3.24). We interviewed a paper recycler whose annual turnover was $4 million dollars. He said that if he did not pay taxes, as some others were doing, his turnover would be larger. Surely he would have received several awards for his profitable 'green' business employing local people if he lived in the UK, I told him. I did note that the work carried out in Dharavi would fall below even the basic health and safety requirements. Further, the exploitation of women and children, who are the waste pickers, sorters and even sellers of the recycled goods, needs to be stopped. However, cities can learn from Dharavi that recycling using local resources can be a productive business.

In post-apartheid South Africa, the shack dwellers are as aspirational as their counterparts on the other side of Table Mountain. 'Things have changed since '94 [when the first democratic elections were held],' says Mandla Mnyakama, a photo-journalist.

> The government has brought changes and opportunities for people. Crime is lower. People are no longer angry like they used to be. There are high levels of unemployment but people are inspired to get on and do things on their own.
>
> (quoted in *Icon* magazine)[49]

The kind of informal creative economy represented by entrepreneurs who have set up shop in the Capetown slums – among them furniture makers,

Figure 3.24 Recycling is a profitable and vibrant business that engages new migrants in Dharavi, especially those with no literacy. It is estimated that between $500–700 million worth of products made from recycled materials are manufactured in Dharavi.

Photo: Author.

hairdressers and portrait photographers – is common to all poor countries and is, according to design writer John Thackara, a valuable resource. Following a visit to India, Thackara writes on his doorsofperception.com website:

> A majority of the population in many Asian cities lives in squatter settlements which makes urban planners anxious. Although perceived as problem areas by bureaucrats, these areas are also sites of intense social and business innovation ... they play a crucial role in keeping the city and its economy running.[50]

Thackara adds with a sense of irony:

> The irony is this: many bureaucrats (and property profiteers) in Asia want to get rid of these so-called suitcase entrepreneurs; but in the North, proponents of 'creative cities' are desperate to foster a comparable level of small-scale industries and street-level productivity.[51]

Case study 2: games and slums

A tape ball is a tennis ball wrapped in electrical tape that is used in play-ing cricket in the streets and slums of India, Pakistan and Bangladesh (Figure 3.25). This modification of the tennis ball gives it greater weight, speed and distance while still being easier to play with than the conventional cricket ball, especially for children. The increasing popularity of the tape ball in informal, local cricket has transformed the way games are played in cricket-loving nations of the Indian subcontinent. The innovation of tape ball cricket was started in Pakistan in the 1980s. Although not recognized by official cricket bodies, tape ball cricket is receiving widespread popular, media and commercial support, especially in Pakistan. During festive seasons and the cricket-playing months of winter and spring, major tournaments are organ-ized, often featuring as many as 200 teams representing corporations, clubs and neighbourhoods.

In 2005, hoping to capitalize on the enthusiasm created by England's win in the Ashes, the London Community Cricket Association began organizing tape ball cricket teams for children on estates in inner-city London, where a lack of playing fields has led to a decline in popularity of traditional cricket. The matches use a variant of the twenty rules designed to make matches last a half-hour or less. The street cricket programme, StreetChance, has 'broken down barriers between children from different estates and religions, encour-aged them to take part in a sport, and improved relations between teenagers and police', a study from Loughborough University found, according to the *Evening Standard* (20 September 2010). 'It helped to bowl out youth crime in 15 London boroughs. This programme has been running since 2008 and more than 13,000 children and 94 schools have been involved in it'. Sports has been shown to direct youthful energy away from violence and drugs. Reportedly there has been a 30 per cent decrease in violence after the vertical gym was opened in Caracas' pocket slum, La Cruz (Figure 3.26) according to a survey conducted by the Municipality of Chacao, Caracas.

Case study 3: science and the poor, Honey Bee Network

Since 1990 in India, the Honey Bee Network under the leadership of Professor Anil Gupta and the Society for Research and Initiatives for Sustainable Technologies and Institutions (SRISTI) have been scouting innovations by farmers, artisans, women, etc., at the grassroots level (Figure 3.27). The Honey Bee has a database of 10,000 innovations, collected and documented by SRISTI. Unlike the more privileged segments of urban society, the creativity of knowl-edge-rich but poor people goes largely unseen because they lack the channels for sharing their ideas with a wider audience, according to Professor Gupta, and the Honey Bee Network addresses this imbalance. To do this, SRISTI organ-izes eight- to ten-day treks to remote villages to tap into the innovative spirit

Figure 3.25 My son plays tape ball cricket in Kalyanpuri, Delhi, 2006.

Photo: Author.

Figure 3.26 A vertical gym with areas for basketball, etc. stacked up on top of each other, designed by Urban Think Tank next to pocket Barrio La Cruz, Caracas.

Photo: Author.

Figure 3.27 Woman selling herbal medicines in Kalyanpuri, East Delhi. Such knowledge of traditional medecine is not documented and the practice unregulated.

Photo: Author.

of local experts. These trips serve as a way to showcase and cultivate indigenous human capital, while also engaging remote communities in a participatory development process. Many a time, the executives of well-known brands such as Sony are known to join these trips in order to get ideas themselves.

Although SRISTI continues to provide institutional support, the Honey Bee Network's strength lies in its network of volunteers from over seventy-seven countries around the world. Using newsletters based on local language and cultural inputs, volunteers throughout the world help to cultivate the knowledge and creativity of marginalized societies. It began producing sixty-minute Positive News Radio Shows in Spanish, distributing them free to more than 100 community radios in countries of Latin America. Many inventions have been sold to rich countries such as the coconut tree climber to the USA and Australia; as well as to poorer countries such as the Maldives, Sri Lanka, Brazil, Mexico and the West Indies.

I feel that the Honey Bee idea can be applied to slums and squatter settlements. I have seen many examples of such traditional knowledge being brought into slums by migrating villagers. In 1921, M.K. Gandhi inaugurated the then new building of Tibia College (public university) in Karol Bagh, Delhi, located near slums and Old Delhi (Figure 3.28). Tibia College, which started in 1882, specializes in Ayurvedic and Unani medicine – for both Hindus and Muslims – and provides free medical care for the poor while the middle class pay a small fee (I have had treatment there). To this day, this facility not only provides care for the poor but offers Bachelor degrees in Ayurvedic Medicine and Surgery and Unani Medicine and Surgery as well. There is a herb garden and research facilities. Collections of folk tales, music and culture are also worth documenting to reinforce their cultural heritage and give dignity to the homeless or squatters. This idea was used by a student working with homeless Sansi women in Delhi.

Figure 3.28 Tibia College in Karol Bagh, New Delhi.

Photo: Author.

Case study 4: women and slums, the hidden players

> Women do two-thirds of the world's work, receive ten percent of the world's income and own one percent of the means of production.
>
> (Barber B. Conable Jnr, former President of the World Bank)[52]

Although women could appear to take a back seat in community matters, in reality, they are very influential within communities and homes (Figure 3.29). The average hours spent doing domestic or unpaid work is higher for women than for men in every region in the world. The biggest difference in time spent working in the home is in Central Africa where women work an average of 7 hours and 6 minutes, and men work 1 hour and 30 minutes every day. The most home-hours are worked by women in Northern Africa – they spend an average of 7 hours and 12 minutes daily on domestic work. On average, Japanese women spend the least time doing domestic work – 3 hours and 43 minutes every day.

At present no country has as good opportunities for women as there are for men. The territories where women have the most opportunities are in Western Europe. Yet, in the construction and design professions, women take a back seat. For example, at present, female architects constitute only 17 per cent of UK architects (in Greece and Croatia women form more than

Figure 3.29 Women talking about community projects, Barrio San Agustin, Caracas.

Photo: Natalya Critchley.

50 per cent of the architects). The fewest opportunities for women are in the Middle Eastern territories of Yemen and Saudi Arabia. Women cultivate more than half of all the food that is grown in the world. In sub-Saharan Africa and the Caribbean, they produce up to 80 per cent of basic food eaten. In Asia, they account for around 50 per cent of food production. In Latin America, they are mainly engaged in subsistence farming, horticulture, poultry and raising small livestock.[53]

In community groups in the slums, women have taken on extraordinary leadership despite the violence and problems around them. Taking on the roles of a mother, wife and community leader, I have observed how these women juggle their roles in such difficult circumstances (Figure 3.30). Sarita Kaur, for example, in Kalyanpuri, East Delhi, used the Right to Information Act 2005 to find out why toilets in her squatter settlement were demolished and not reinstated (Figure 6.1). Now they are to be rebuilt. In a project in Venezuela, my entire construction team was made up of women. Compare this with the statistics from Women and Manual Trades (WAMT) of the UK, which states that women form 1 per cent of the manual trades industry. In an extraordinary project, Freehouse, documented in Chapter 6, in a rundown

Figure 3.30 Archana Toppo from SEWA facilitates women's workshops and training, East Delhi. Here women are making samples meant for the UK market

Photo: Author.

part of Rotterdam, the Netherlands, with mostly refugee and recent immigrants, women are running and managing small businesses. Thus women from rich Western countries can learn from women of the slums.

Case study 5: music and slums

Like sports, music can also improve lives of young people. For more than thirty years an extraordinary music project has been running in Venezuela in an attempt to transform the lives of the children of the *barrios*. The Fundación del Estado para el Sistema de Orquestas Juveniles e Infantiles de Venezuela – the rather more catchy 'Sistema' in short – has been using classical music to tackle the social problems of the *barrios*. By offering free instruments and tuition through a network of after-school centres all over the country, the Sistema keeps thousands of children away from drugs-, alcohol- and gang-related violence. It has led to the creation of thirty professional orchestras in a country that had only two before. Currently, around 275,000 children attend the Sistema's schools and many of them play in one of the 125 youth orchestras.

The Simón Bolívar Youth Orchestra of Venezuela under its music director Gustavo Dudamel who is himself a product of the Sistema, has played many times in London including in the BBC proms. The Sistema's success has attracted the attention of the likes of international conductors such as Sir Simon Rattle who have been to Venezuela to work with young musicians. In a similar manner, local architects have also played a part. A scheme designed by Lab.Pro. Fab, architects based in Caracas, has turned a piece of land and some shipping containers into a theatre, art, computing and graphic studios for youngsters from the Barrio El Valle next to which it is located (Figure 3.31). I have watched not just classical music performances but also rap music and plays being performed by young people from the *barrios* and the exuberance is infectious. Although the architect created the form, the people of the *barrios* have taken it upon themselves to run it and look after it as a valuable community resource and turn it into a source of further inspiration.

Figure 3.31 Lab.Pro.Fab's container theatre, computer centre and youth centre, Barrio El Valle, Caracas.

Photo: Author.

Discussion points

1   Can slums be eradicated entirely from the world?
2   Is it morally acceptable for people to say that we can learn from slums when these people live in such abject poverty and disease?
3   How can issues of drugs, crime and violence be resolved in such areas?
4   How can the development activist work in slums without being swayed by politics or emotion?
5   Can you find other ways of classifying slums and squatter settlements?

Part II

The hard city and the development activist

Chapter 4

Materials and technology

Is the true spirit of contemporary Cape Town to be found in the neo-modernist villas that line the Atlantic seaboard, or in the tin shacks lining the N2?

(Marcus Fairs[1])

I first met Judith in one of the *barrios* of Venezuela in December 2009. She is a single mother with four boys and a girl ranging in age from late teens to under ten. Her home could not be more different to a single mother in London. The shack she had built of tin, timber pieces and cardboard was falling down the hill. She had put up a Christmas tree and nativity scene at the place where the shack threatened to fall over so that the children would not step near the sloping floor. The 'bedroom' had three beds that were shared by the family and she had hung teddy bears from the ceiling to stop the rain from coming in. Near the elaborate altar, there was a telephone and in the narrow passage that led to the bedroom, a fridge had somehow been squashed in. When I visited the year later, parts of the house stood at various angles and the Christmas tree had finally fallen into a crevice. Judith told me that she needed BsF30,000 (Bolivares Fuerte; about $3,600) to buy a better home. Judith's dream home will be of a concrete frame house with hollow brick walls. Like her counterparts all over the world, she aspires to the kind of building that the middle classes live in.

As I left her house that afternoon, a violent storm descended on the hill. I was soaked to the skin and wondered how Judith's house was doing. As far as I know, she is still waiting for that BsF30,000. Since I last saw Judith, the rate of inflation in Venezuela has reached 30 per cent,[2] who knows for how long Judith will wait? Judith's story is typical of the poor who live by the skin of their teeth in the *barrios*. According to the way the homeless are classified by the UN, she does not even feature in the billion people supposed to be homeless around the world. Thankfully for her, the children are doing well at school, looked healthy and I hope she will find a way out of her difficulties (Figure 4.1).

What one aspires to in a home is a personal and cultural issue. It is one of choices and priorities too. I could say to Judith, 'Get rid of the refrigerator

Figure 4.1 From left to right: Belkis Moncada, community leader from Centro Ciudades De la Gente (see Chapter 6), the author and her boys with Judith and two of her boys, August 2011, Barrio Julian Blanco, Caracas.

Photo: Jose Luis.

and the telephone' and save instead to buy the house and she might not agree with me. She might not imagine filling with earth the hundreds of tyres that I have seen in the *barrios* to create the kind of homes that Mike Reynolds likes to design for the rich in New Mexico. I have seen people living in the most decrepit homes in slums and squatter settlements, yet they have air conditioners, cable TVs, computers, etc. In a series of photographs taken after the 2010 landslides in Caracas, a man is shown carrying his refrigerator on his back while escaping from his collapsed home. The choices many make are based not just on individual preferences but to conform to their particular society, especially in a collectivist nation. Preferences for building materials and technology also take this view. This has been termed 'sociosemitics' by Paul Oliver, who notes that similar to spoken language, there operates an architectural language consisting of form and materials of what is acceptable to a certain society.[3]

Building materials: choices and change

While architects are trying to find ways and means to solve the housing crisis, the homeless appear to have a singular image of a home – that made of bricks and concrete. The photographer Craig Fraser invented the phrase 'shack chic' in 2002 as a reference to 'the style and innovation of Cape Town's shack dwellers'. Shack chic embraces everything from newspapers, tyres, plastic bottles and tin sheets. This makes for a nice coffee table book but what do its creators want? It would seem that the homeless and the poor do not want to be associated with shack chic. 'People aspire to be part of the mainstream economy and they express that through their houses,' says Matthew Barac, an architect and teacher from South Africa. 'For example, people who work as domestic cleaners in the affluent suburbs will try to imitate that suburban look in their shacks.'[4]

So, the most important points here are those of our aspiration and our choices. The middle classes and the rich have many more choices – if they want to live in shack chic tin homes, at worst it might be assumed that they are eccentric and at best, benign eco-hippies. India and Australia may have posh hotels and homes built of earth, Sweden has its ice hotel and there are other examples of buildings made of straw, lime and other 'alternate' and 'shack-chic' materials. However, these are not the materials of choice for people who live in squatter settlements or are homeless.

The cultural history of the material is also important (Figure 4.2). Using what is generally acknowledged as strong and long lasting for building is also a step upwards for social mobility. The British left their cultural imprint on building materials of India classifying earth and timber including bamboo as *kutcha* or weak/temporary, while brick, stone and concrete are *pukka* or strong/permanent. There has been an interesting reverse association too – the bungalow, which is the most coveted type of residential building in the UK. 'Bungalow' is the corruption of the Bengali *Bangla* home – a humble one-storeyed earthen structure surrounded by a covered walkway, the *verandha* (called 'verandah' in English).[5] My observation has been that the people who may need houses and who have easy access to materials such as mud or bamboo do not aspire to such materials and aesthetic. They may live in houses made of such materials temporarily, but once they have money they will move into *pukka* homes. This appears to be universal. For example, in the *barrios* of Venezuela, one can see a strata of buildings signifying the owner's financial and social status – the shacks of the poor made of bits of wood and corrugated tin while the richer residents live in brick and concrete homes.

The deterministic attitude of many 'experts' that alternate materials and technology can be foisted on the homeless and the voiceless appears to be a hypocritical move by those who themselves would not live in such environments. I remember being taken around in an air-conditioned SUV by an architect in his home country to look at his projects. The same architect was trying to build eco-friendly homes in London without using air

Figure 4.2 The ultimate in alternate materials? A door made of human excrement exhibited at the Museum of Toilets, New Delhi, in order to change people's minds about human waste. Will you change yours?

Photo: Author.

conditioning and proposing cycle-to-work schemes. The poor aspire to shiny new homes as anyone, eschewing recycling or reuse. During his visit to the N2 squatter settlements in Cape Town in 2005, Marcus Fairs described a shack-building enterprise set up in a street in the Brown's Farm shack settlement. Entrepreneur Judas Njengenja builds takeaway dwellings from new, as opposed to recycled, steel and timber: a crucial difference for his aspirational clients. 'Business appears to be booming,'[6] Fairs noted then. In a squatter settlements in Delhi and Mumbai, I saw dismantled doors and parts of buildings neatly stacked together – not for reuse as building materials but to be reincarnated as furniture (Figure 4.3).

Attitude to waste

There have been attempts to manufacture commonly used objects to give them a secondary use as building materials – these are called 'secondary use capability', such as bottles and bags that could have a second life as building materials. The most famous experiment that demonstrated people's dislike of using 'secondary use capability' for building is probably the WoBo or the World Bottle. In 1963, beer brewer Alfred Heineken who was holidaying in the Caribbean was concerned about the empty beer bottles on the beach and wondered if the beer bottle could be reused for building. A young Dutch architect, Jon Habraken, who was then working on prefabricated housing, submitted various schemes. A bottle with an afterlife as a brick, the World

Figure 4.3 Recycling of building materials at Sonia Camp, squatter settlement in East Delhi. However, in India, only about 25 per cent of recycled building materials are used out of 14.5 megatons of waste building materials.

Photo: Author.

Bottle, aka WoBo, was finally designed and a small shed was constructed using 100,000 bottles in Noordwijk, the Netherlands.

While Habraken went on to achieve fame in a different way, the shed at the Heineken estate and a wall made of WoBo at the Heineken Museum in Amsterdam are the only structures where the 'beer brick' has been used. For 'marketing reasons', beer-filled WoBos were never sold either. Designers and architects have not given up on the idea of 'secondary use capability' – a search on the Internet reveals many uses for plastic bags and bottles for buildings – there even exists a manual on how to fold and use plastic bags to make shelter. However, in another part of the world, a more literal shrine to beer bottles now exists. Holy men in Sisaket province, Thailand, collected a million green Heineken and brown Chang beer bottles to build the Wat Pa Maha Chedi Kaew temple. Even the washrooms and the crematorium are built of bottles but these are the usual beer bottles, not the beer brick.

The other main problem with this kind of thinking is that it accepted levels of conspicuous consumption and waste, perhaps even encouraged them. When Martin Pawley's *Garbage Housing* came out in 1975, it was the time of the first petrol crisis in the world and also a time of renewed ecological thinking with E.F. Schumacher and T.C. Boyle's *Drop City*, and various types of solar housing in the news.[7] Using waste for building appeared to be an innovative ecological idea then. But now with scarce resources and a different way of thinking, manufacturers have now moved away from 'wasteful packaging' to reduction and eco-friendly or biodegradable packaging (with some even offering incentives to encourage reuse of bags). Writing in the *Royal Institute of British Architects (RIBA) Journal* in August 2009, Gillian Horn, partner at architects Penoyre & Prasad, talking about her experience of working with Sarah Wigglesworth on her house in North London (Figure 4.4), wrote 'it's not an enormous surprise that straw-bale building hasn't taken off a storm, but then neither has any other building technology … onsite bricks are still bricks and still laid by brickies.'

Assimilation of technology

Paul Oliver argues that technological advance is ideally not a 'transfer' but diffusion – the dissemination and assimilation of cultural phenomena.[8] Thus, he differentiates between what he refers to as intervention, tradition and diffusion. He gives the example of the potter's wheel, which has been used since 3000 BCE and will continue to be used – this is a tradition. The history of the introduction and the continued use of bricks in England owing to royal patronage, fashion, assimilation of skills and influence is what he calls 'diffusion'. Intervention is something that is forced upon people. Appropriate

Figure 4.4 Home of Sarah Wigglesworth and Jeremy Till, North London, made of straw bales and recycled concrete, sandbags containing lime, sand and cement.

Photo: Author.

technology is what Practical Action, an NGO working internationally, calls work to demonstrate that the simplest ideas can have profound, life-changing effects on poor people across the world. They say:

> We do not start with technology, but with people. The tools may be simple or sophisticated, but to provide long-term, appropriate and practical answers, they must be firmly in the hands of local people: people who shape technology and control it for themselves.[9]

I prefer to call the process technology transfer or acceptance of certain materials as 'osmosis' because of how the use of a certain technology or material could be absorbed in time. Certain technologies or materials remain impervious to osmosis owing to a lack of external pressure while certain technologies become obsolete or are rejected like a sort of reverse osmosis. So earthen or unfired bricks are examples of 'rejects', while fired bricks have been absorbed into the semiotics of building language. Technology transfer is also dependent upon the context and culture (Figures 4.5 and 4.6). This was aptly demonstrated by the attempt to use compressed earth bricks in Sudan in 1993, using presses that used pneumatic power. These presses did not work as well as in the UK owing to the presence of small dust particles typically found in Sudan that blocked the delicate pneumatic machinery.

Figure 4.5 'Ceramic architecture' derived from traditional Iranian kiln construction (architect Nader Khalili). These structures are made of unfired bricks with high clay content, the whole construction fired both externally and internally to create a joined-up, glazed structure that provides earthquake resistance (see also page 120).

Photo: Author.

Figure 4.6 Case of technology transfer that proved not so easy? A jali wall in North London, home of architect Ken Rorrison. Masons in the UK found this common construction of India difficult to understand. Rorrison then used a scale model to demonstrate and it was built.

Photo: Author.

Embodied energy

> No building contractor came within ten miles of it. It contains no concrete, no steel, no materials at all except what were produced on the spot. It took a week to erect …
> (Hassan Fathy, talking about an earth brick building he designed at Gourna, Egypt)[10]

The embodied energy of materials is the hidden energy expended in the extraction, manufacture or refining, transportation, use and finally disposal of the materials. All these processes have costs – for the environment, financial and even social. Some of these costs are subsidized heavily. For instance, some years ago, in trying to work out costs for an unfired brick versus a fired brick, I came across the anomaly that it was cheaper to use the fired brick. That is because the firing process is heavily subsidized through reduced energy costs. The disposal costs of material can be heavy. In the case of asbestos, a material very popular in the 1960s and 1970s for roofing but now found to be carcinogenic, disposal by experts can be an expensive and time-consuming process. Transport of building materials rather than using locally available building material adds to the cost and the embodied energy.

There are many who feel that as long as building materials can be recycled or reused, it is okay to produce as much waste as you like. There are now new terms for secondary use capability – 'down-cycling' and 'up-cycling' – the prefix up and down referring to downgrading or the enhancement of the waste respectively. Michael Braungart and William McDonough invented these terms. Their book, the international bestseller, *Cradle to Cradle*, has even a chapter called 'Waste equals food', although elsewhere it says that 'the creative use of down-cycled materials for new produce can be misguided, despite good intentions'.[11]

Reducing vs. reusing vs. recycling

Reduction of use of materials during design and construction is the most effective means of reducing the waste produced. Reduction can take the form of more efficient construction, such as slimmer metal or glulam beams instead of large timber beams – parts of the building that can be prefabricated or constructed in the factory. Many traditional building types, such as tents, tipis, yurts and huts, with the knowledge of centuries of use, are built using a structurally efficient form and materials and this can be an inspiration for modern architecture too, as Michael Hopkins and many other architects have discovered. Reduction can happen in the design and planning stage with careful thought given to waste reduction. This is also cost-effective. Materials and parts can be reused with some success. Bricks, especially those taken from a wall using lime mortar, can be reused as they would be intact. Steel girders and posts can be reused. Concrete can be ground up and used for foundations with some success. The very last thing to consider should be recycling, as this can be the most energy-intensive way of using most waste.

Metals though are particularly good for recycling, using anything from 70 to 90 per cent less energy for recycling than for processing from raw ore. These percentages are separate from and do not take into account the environmental and landscape destruction wrought from the mining of metals. In October 2010, the Indian company TATA Steel Colors became the first UK steel business to be certified to the BES 6001 Responsible Sourcing standard for construction and has been awarded a 'very good' rating. It would appear that, slowly, construction companies are recognizing the need to prove that their buildings are built with sustainability in mind, and that includes responsible sourcing of materials. The BRE standard BES 6001 enables construction product manufacturers to ensure and then prove that their products have been made with constituent materials that have been responsibly sourced. The standard describes a framework for the organizational governance, supply chain management and environmental and social aspects that must be addressed in order to ensure the responsible sourcing of construction products. Independent, third-party assessment and certification against the requirements of BES 6001 then give the organization the ability to prove that an effective system for ensuring responsible sourcing exists and adds credibility for any claims made.[12]

WRAP (Waste & Resources Action Programme) works in England, Scotland, Wales and Northern Ireland to help businesses and individuals to promote and understand the benefits of reducing waste, developing sustainable products and using resources in an efficient way. According to WRAP, there are 120 million tonnes of construction, demolition and excavation waste every year – around one-third of all waste in the UK. In England alone almost 13 million tonnes of this waste ends up in landfill without any form of recovery or reuse.[13] Recognizing the environmental and economic impacts of these levels of wastage, the joint government–industry Strategy for Sustainable Construction established a target (in England) of a 50 per cent reduction in construction, demolition and excavation waste to landfill by 2012. The target of halving waste to landfill by 2012 also supports the Scottish Government's Zero Waste Plan and construction waste reduction policies in Wales and Northern Ireland. In 2010, such actions reportedly reduced construction waste by 28 per cent.

The most graphic way the building industry and consumption produce waste is evident from my annual visits with students to a building materials recycling plant for several years now. This is Powerday, one of the very few plants addressing building waste, based in North-west London (Figure 4.7). The 9-acre site is divided into several areas serving different materials to avoid contamination. Timber, metals, plastic and also household waste totalling up to 1.6 million tonnes per year are sorted out for distribution to other industries that can either use or recycle this waste. High-value metals such as copper command good prices while household waste, mainly paper and plastic, left after other recyclables have been removed, are shredded into 20–30 mm pieces suitable for use as fuel. Powerday operate two 'undercover' recycling and recovery plants and an external reprocessing area at the materials recycling facility at the West London site as well as three other sites around London (Figure 4.8). How Powerday operate their plants using the latest machinery and computer technology to sort out waste is very different from the way waste is sorted in Dharavi, Mumbai. Here, the percentage of waste recycled, including building waste, is similar to that achieved at Powerday, but most of the work is done by human hands, in dangerous health and safety conditions (Figure 4.9).

There is an ongoing problem with not just the carbon trading going on between rich and poor nations but also with the trading of waste. A lot of the waste produced in the rich countries is sent to poorer nations where even basic health and safety conditions are not followed. There is a not-in-my-backyard (NIMBY) attitude along with the rather dubious reassurance that such waste trading provides income to the poor. From computers to ships, waste that might be contaminated or even radioactive is sent for dismantling, sorting and recycling, and finally the richer countries even buy back the recycled product. For example, in Mumbai, the goods made from recycled plastic are mainly exported – there is a Mumbai plastic bottle that can bought in London

Figure 4.7 An information board from WRAP and Powerday recycling plant showing how aggregate meant for recycling can be identified for sorting and reusing, Northwest London.

Photo: Author.

on a well-known website selling eco-products. But the price paid by these waste sorters and collectors is ill health, a fluctuating income and further contamination of their land. For richer countries to reduce their waste instead of dumping it elsewhere should then become a huge social imperative.

Some poorer countries are recognizing and dealing with this problem within their own countries. In Venezuela, the oil, steel, gold and aluminium industries create toxic waste for the landscape and the environment. Wastewater is often disposed of untreated, and untreated waste usually ends in open pits. One of Venezuela's most modern waste recycling sites is

Figure 4.8 Disused wooden pallets being turned into chips, Powerday building materials recycling centre, West London.

Photo: Author.

Figure 4.9 Plastic recycling in Dharavi, Mumbai – these tiny pieces will be sorted by hand by type, hardness, colour and size and reused for bottles and other plastic goods. Around 200 types of plastics are recycled.

Photo: Author.

located in the small city of Guacara, South-west of the country. Initially the recycling centre was simply a collection of open pits where the poor came every day to sort, collect the waste and sell it to local traders. These traders, who were often part of the local mafia and involved in drug trafficking, paid a low price for waste collected. According to Eduardo Sanchez, president of the recycling centre: 'These people had no workers' security; they used to work with their bare hands. A lot of them got ill, because of the poisonous contents among the waste.'[14] Now, about 600,000 people benefit from the improved facilities, which cost $15 million, built with Canadian expertise. In total, some sixty people are working at the station, most of them organized in autonomous cooperatives. Sanchez says that the new recycling station has had three positive impacts: environmental, health and social. In his words: 'We have proven here that it is possible to work as brothers, without corruption. We are able to create a new social structure, including the inhabitants of the *barrios* in our work.'[15]

Buildings and energy

A Western European uses 17 tonnes of materials for construction and housing alone with a corresponding amount of energy to produce, transport, and process it.[16] In 2008, global material consumption was 52 tonnes per person annually – a Western lifestyle requires 30 per cent of natural materials' consumption per capita annually and this is rising. It has been calculated that keeping in mind the population growth in the poorer countries, if their consumption rate approaches that of an average European, then seven times the resources will be needed to cater for that scenario.[17] However, the irony is that by 2008, about 75 per cent of the buildings needed by 2020 had already been constructed. More than 70 per cent of the buildings in Western Europe were constructed in the last twenty years.[18] This year, as I write this, 2011 has seen a steady decline in built projects and, considering these earlier issues, it is not surprising. So, this makes a very strong argument for reuse of not just building parts but entire buildings, particularly in richer countries, as their buildings are more energy-intensive.

The other way in which buildings influence the environment is through the energy they consume while in operation. The global contribution of carbon emissions from all types of buildings has steadily increased, reaching figures between 20 per cent and 40 per cent in richer countries, exceeding the other major sectors: industry and transport. Growth in population, increasing demand for building services and comfort levels, together with the rise in time spent inside buildings, assure the upward trend in energy demand will continue in the future. The rising trend in many Western countries for single-family dwellings also contributes to this rise. According to calculations by Architecture 2030, the American building sector uses up 76 per cent of all electricity generated by US power plants to operate buildings. Among building services, the growth in HVAC systems energy use is particularly significant (50 per cent of building consumption and 20 per cent of total consumption in the USA). Over 40 per cent of the UK's energy consumption is building-related.[19] This in turn produces about half the UK's carbon dioxide emissions and many other environmentally damaging pollutants that contribute to global warming. For this reason, energy efficiency in buildings makes for not only a social obligation but also a strong economic case too.

Buildings can kill

In 2009, the survivors of an earthquake in China gathered to pay respect to the 68,000 people killed a year before but also to criticize corrupt authorities for building sub-standard schools that collapsed, killing thousands of children.[20] Earthquakes fall under 'events not under human control' but the poignant reminder that materials and technology do, comes from tragedies like this. There are many more tragedies as a result of construction that happen every year, mostly in poor countries. In Istanbul, for example, according to Istanbul Technical University, 70 per cent of its buildings constructed within the last thirty years were built illegally or improperly and if there is another earthquake of the scale of the 1999 one, this could contribute to the death of 100,000 people in the city.[21]

By far the most incidents caused by poor building happen in slums and informal settlements. They may also happen in the poorer parts of the countries' cities. Nigeria came up several times during Internet searches on building collapse and not without reason.[22] That the phrase 'incessant incidents of building collapse' has been used in a technical report for Nigerian building collapse is very worrying indeed. India has had many cases of building collapse owing to poor construction. There were eighteen incidents of building collapse in Ahmedabad, India, in 2010 alone. In these incidents, seven people died and fifty-six others were injured. The situation was not much different in 2009 when seventeen such incidents were reported in Ahmedabad. Most of the collapses happened in *pol* areas, which are the older, denser and traditionally designed parts of the city. In all the cases, police were informed but allegedly no action was taken.[23] Even more chilling was the single comment that claimed that no action is taken against builders in India because they are the 'single biggest contributor to political parties'.[24]

The most common issues relating to poor building construction in less literate and poorer countries appear to be:

1 Drawings and instructions

Drawings produced for building are either structurally unsound or have been altered to fit time or budget after they were approved structurally. In some cases, drawings showing poor designs and technical aspects were approved either through lack of time in checking or through corrupt practices. Apart from the cases from Nigeria, recently in India, the rush to complete buildings for the Commonwealth Games in 2010 led to many mistakes and collapses. There are also common cases where building commences without approved building drawings, either in the hope that drawings will be approved in time or in the optimism that the building itself will not be noticed. There are times when construction commences without any drawings at all (Figure 4.10).

2 Lack of supervision

Even where a structural design is not deficient, absence of proper supervision on the site by qualified personnel or lack of statutory inspection can lead to building failure, according to the Nigerian case studies. Although this used to happen in the past before the formalization of architecture and building, a qualified person was usually on site all the time to supervise construction and any changes required.

Figure 4.10 Collapsed concrete building, Delhi.

Photo: Author.

Cost- and time-cutting measures mean that a material such as reinforced concrete, which needs to be checked rigorously during technical specifications and construction, can be used when not cured completely or lacks proper reinforcement.

In some cases, Town Planning Authority inspectors may not carry out visits to inspect or monitor progress of work. Sometimes, the inspector or the supervisor cannot read the drawings or technical instructions properly, and this leads also to faulty construction. This may happen owing to illiteracy or the language used being something other than the inspector's own, i.e. English, or simply a lack of knowledge (Figure 4.11).

3 Alterations and extensions

Sometimes, buildings in older parts of the city and in the slums are altered without proper drawings, technical assistance or even suitable materials (Figure 4.12). This kind of subversive building work usually happens because the original building perhaps did not have planning permission in the first place and therefore there is a need to avoid attention being drawn to the new building. Sometimes the existing building needs special technical efforts such as conservation techniques and materials that the owner cannot afford and the result is that both the old and new buildings are affected negatively through the use of 'short cuts' in time and materials. There are documented cases in India where archeologically protected documented monuments have been repaired using substandard or incompatible materials, leading to their collapse.

Occasionally, the laws and ideas regarding certain building materials act in a perverse way, such that the very fabric of the construction is threatened. For example, the concept of fireproofing earth buildings by using cement render simply for insurance reasons actually causes their collapse as has happened in a number of cases in Devon, UK.

4 Use of substandard materials and poor workmanship

Substandard materials, especially reinforcement rods, steel sections and cement can contribute immensely to the failure of buildings. The use of low-quality materials is one of the major causes of structural failure. Inefficient and fraudulent labour input can also contribute to the failure of buildings. When a contractor cannot read drawings or where he refuses to listen to the instruction of the consultants, anything can happen. Oyewande (1992), quoted in the Nigerian report, posited that faults on construction sites account for 40 per cent of collapse of structures.[25] The Nigerian paper discusses how the use of acidic and salty water, sourced from oceans and seas in port cities such as Lagos and Port Harcourt, can affect the strength of concrete (drinking quality water is advised for such construction).

Figure 4.11 A badly constructed stone building 'corrected' by concrete, in the village of Jaba, East Jerusalem, Palestine.

Photo: Author.

Figure 4.12 Older buildings in high-value areas are quickly taken down and high-rise structures are built, without proper drawings, supervision or structural advice – New Delhi.

Photo: Author.

5 Location

Many of these squatter buildings are located in geographically less desirable areas, such as steep slopes, in seismic zones or next to drains or rivers. In such cases, even if the building were to be constructed carefully, during landslides or floods, buildings can collapse. It has been argued that loss of lives and buildings in the 2004 tsunami could have been much lower if there had been fewer built-up areas near the sea. The volcanic eruption and tsunami caused by Mount Krakatoa in 1883, for example, had much lower casualties.

Scarce resources and scarcer technology

It is commonly thought or assumed that poorer parts of the world do not have the materials available for construction and that is why more buildings collapse there. However, the real reasons for the collapses are lack of time or supervision, or incorrect use. While building the British High Commission in Dar Es Salem, UK architects Manser Practice commented that it was easier to find glass, cement and other modern materials in Africa than in the UK. I am always surprised to see how easy it is to find modern building materials anywhere. Visiting a DIY centre in Caracas in November 2010 (Figure 4.13), I was not only amazed to see the size of the warehouse but also the wide variety of materials being sold there. A quick survey of the people shopping there revealed that they were mostly from the poor parts of the city, the *barrio*, probably doing repairs to their houses. I saw that many of the building materials came with no instructions at all, so perhaps it was left

Figure 4.13 DIY centre in Caracas, Venezuela.

Photo: Author.

to the people to interpret their use. DIY is not a new thing – people have been building and repairing their own homes for centuries. In the past, the homeowner could do small repairs and construction, while larger buildings could be put up with a little help from the community. The timber barns of the Amish and the Shaker communities are well-known examples of communal building activity.

'Sweat equity' is a term used to describe the contribution made to a project by people who contribute their time and effort. It can be contrasted with financial equity which is the money contributed towards the project. The term can also be used to describe the value added to a property by owners who make improvements, such as those made by people living in slums (Figure 4.14). In squatter settlements where, having obtained the land for a high price, people spend their savings doing up their homes – the idea being to move out after selling. In a successful model used by Habitat for Humanity, families who would otherwise be unable to purchase their own home because of their income level contribute up to 500 hours of sweat equity to the construction of their own home, the homes of other Habitat families or by volunteering to assist the organization in other ways. Once moved into their new home, the family makes

Figure 4.14 Barrio Julian Blanco, Caracas – people wait to collect money and find time to build their homes. Here one can see homes in various stages of construction, with materials ranging from temporary to permanent.

Photo: Author.

monthly, interest-free mortgage payments into a revolving fund, called 'Fund for Humanity' which provides capital to build homes for other partner families (see case study by a student in Chapter 9 about this).

However, the concept of sweat equity means different things to different people in a cultural sense. While the Habitat for Humanity scheme has been a success in the USA, in India things have worked out differently. Here, residents were given the infrastructure support such as a toilet and centralized sewage systems – 'Starter homes' was a concept very popular in the late 1980s and 1990s. It was accepted that if people were given infrastructural support, they could create homes using sweat equity. However, in many well-known projects, the infrastructural support was missing or incomplete, or adequate support was not given to the people wanting to build their homes and the required result did not happen. Gita Verma documents two such award winning projects in her book, *Slumming India*.[26] In the book, *Toilets of the World*, a starter home in central India is shown in which the toilet has become the household store while the family build a shack for living near it and use the fields for toilets.[27]

Old materials, aspiration and the wider environment

> We should remind ourselves that it is not 'Advancement' or 'Development' or 'Progress' to indulge in modern building materials and techniques at tremendous expenses and to no good effect when there is no justification or reason for their use, instead of older, simpler, inexpensive methods.
>
> (Laurie Baker)[28]

Most buildings of the past were made of a limited palate of materials and even so the materials were relatively easy to build with and their technology had been tried and tested for centuries. Such materials include earth, timber, thatch, tiles, bricks and stone. It is indeed an irony that as the use of earth, timber, thatch and stone has declined, the use of such materials has become a 'specialist' area. The cost of repairing and building using such materials has also gone up – the cost of repairing a thatched roof is almost astronomical in the UK. Use of such 'traditional' materials requires more rigorous testing and statutory approval as in the building of the Globe Theatre in London which has a straw roof.

The Green Building Bible classifies building materials according to five aspects: renewable, extracted, extracted and processed, extracted and 'highly processed' and recycled.[29] It also talks about natural and synthetic building materials although, like most medicines, all building materials are made of natural materials, except that some are more processed than others. It is useful to remember that in the debate about old and new materials, many building materials are simply a more processed form of an existing material.

For example, concrete, bricks and glass have been used for centuries – only now they are made in big factories and have become sophisticated materials capable of doing many other things. Glass, to use an example, can now be energy saving and also provide privacy. In the debate about embodied energy of materials, again it is useful to remember that much of the energy could be in the extraction or transportation; stone is a good example of this. I have included in my discussion later the most commonly used materials I have seen used by people living in areas of rapid change and scarce resources – bricks and earth, stone, timber, concrete and glass (Figure 4.15).

Another useful aspect to consider in the reuse of materials is their potential for recyclability and the energy required for recycling. Poorly-made or dismantled bricks from existing structures may not be usable. Metals, on the other hand, although requiring more energy to manufacture into structural elements, can be recycled almost endlessly. Recycled aluminium, for example, requires 95 per cent less energy than processing aluminium ore. For green buildings, it is good to be flexible rather than pedantic about what is green and what is not. In a well-known office building, the architects were very keen to use recycled bricks from the existing office that was demolished. However, they did not notice that the recycled bricks were of a different dimension to

Figure 4.15 Home made of recycled bricks, Agra, India – however good this looks, the owners told me they wanted a 'proper' house, namely, a pukka house with new bricks.

Photo: Author.

the modern ones. They had planned to use them in a modern cavity wall construction in the new building and so the entire stock of carefully dismantled bricks had to be thrown away. In order to keep to the green agenda, bricks from a hospital about 100 miles away were brought in to construct the cavity wall. This was rather pointless.

Earth as a building material

Among the so-called 'traditional building materials', no other traditional material has been regarded with so much suspicion as earth. Use of timber and stone have increased while knowledge of earth building has declined, although earth is found practically everywhere. Writing in 1992 in *The Independent*, I described how in the summer of 1992, Desiree Ntolo, a 34-year-old mother of six, completed a 7ft-high, 54ft-long hut from 20 tons of Essex mud in the garden of her house on the Becontree Estate in Dagenham. She said she wanted to remind herself of her childhood home in Cameroon and to have somewhere to escape from her children to practise her religion.

I wrote then,

> Neither her neighbours nor the local council have been amused, and there is little doubt that Mrs. Ntolo's loose interpretation of a traditional West African home has reinforced the poor reputation of earth as a building material. She has been told by Redbridge Council that her hut must go because it does not fit into the local vernacular.[30]

It is estimated that more than one-third of the world's population lives in earthen buildings, including the South-west of England, where Laurence Keefe, secretary of the Devon Earth Building Association, estimates that there are at least 20,000 houses constructed either fully or partly in cob (earth), along with an equal number of barns, outbuildings and boundary walls in Devon alone. Windswept and rain-beaten cob houses have survived for centuries, with walls sheltered by waterproof plinths and deeply overhanging roofs (usually thatched).

Using its compressive strength, earth has traditionally been used in the form of sun-dried bricks and blocks and balls, cob and beaten earth walls, and as an infill in other structures such as wattle and daub. Earthen construction has now spawned more avatars in the form of blocks, which are now machine made and rammed earth structures. From the huge L'Isle D'Abeau housing experiment in Southern France (Figures 4.16 and 4.17) to Grimshaw's earth centre in Doncaster, UK, earthen construction is seen as an exciting venture but it is yet to take off on a wider scale. The late Iranian architect, Nader Khalili, who brought ceramic architecture to California, found it useful in preventing complete structural collapse during seismic movements. Ceramic architecture involves making structures of clay blocks and firing the

Figure 4.16 The biggest housing experiment in earthen construction, L'Isle D'Abeau, Southern France.

Photo: Author.

Figure 4.17 Artist studios and housing – architects: Francoise Jourda and Gilles Perraudin, L'Isle D'Abeau, Southern France.

Photo: Author.

whole structure together so that it fuses like a giant teacup. He also experimented with earth-filled sand bags housing while Mike Reynolds in Taos, New Mexico, has pioneered earth-filled tyres for housing (called 'earthships'). Khalili even proposed that structures could be built on the moon by gathering moon dust and firing them using solar power (I was shown a small sample when I visited his offices in 1995). The L'Isle D'Abeau housing is now more than twenty years old but, apart from some housing and hotels for the middle class, there is no noticeable worldwide uptake on earthen construction from people living in poor areas (Figure 4.18).[31]

Timber sophistication

Timber technology, on the other hand, has improved steadily. Timber is a renewable resource and also very important for the environment. Trees capture carbon dioxide, support other forms of life and help in soil and land stabilization. However, again, demand is for certain kinds of timber, especially slow growing hardwoods from rainforests. These varieties are visually exciting and very durable and thus demand has made them virtually 'extinct' – mahogany being a good example. (Just on the subject of terminology, it is important to remember that softwoods are not really soft and that balsa wood is a hardwood.) However, recycled timber which often has hardwoods, is a good option for designers with a conscience (Figure 4.19).

Figure 4.18 A poignant reminder – cement-rendered earth brick house in Gaza, Palestine. People prefer to be homeless than to have the ignominy of living in earthen housing; some cover earth bricks with cement render to disguise it as shown here.

Photo: Yara Sharif.

Figure 4.19 Recycled timber sorted out for selling to the public, a social enterprise project working with young offenders, Didcot, Oxfordshire, UK.

Photo: Author.

The Timber Research and Development Association (TRADA), based in the UK, is an internationally recognized centre of excellence on the specification and use of timber and wood products. TRADA's origins go back over seventy years and it aims to provide designers 'with the highest quality information on timber and wood products to enable them to maximise the benefits that timber can provide'. Timber is now being used in various large-span and complex structures in modern buildings, which other materials cannot lend themselves to; for example, the impressively curved ceiling for the Welsh National Assembly (by Rogers Stirk Harbour) and the gridshell structure of the Savill Garden building, Windsor Great Park (by Glen Howells Architects) (Figure 4.20). Unlike many other materials, timber can come with a Forest Stewardship Certificate (FSC), certifying its origin and eco-credentials. However, FSC does not yet take into account embodied energy such as transport over long distances. For example, despite having a favourable climate for softwood, in 2006, 80 per cent of British timber products made of softwood were being imported from Scandinavian countries.[32] A visit to the Ecobuild 2011 exhibition clearly showed that this trend had not changed.

Stone and energy

The Stone Federation in the UK and similar organizations elsewhere work tirelessly to promote the use of stone in building. Although a 'traditional'

Figure 4.20 The Savill Garden building, Windsor Great Park (by Glen Howells Architects).

Photo: Author.

material, it has been over-quarried with serious consequences for the environment and human health. The Stone Federation is a representative of the stone industries of the UK and as such it sets some guidelines for stone quarrying and environmental issues. The website of the organization states:

> Stone Federation members recognize that their operations impact upon the environment and therefore endeavour to ensure that the potential harmful effects of their actions are minimized wherever practicable. Stone Federation members are committed to considering and conserving the environment during the course of their activities.[33]

It encourages its members to comply with its policies, which include:

- Identifying and complying with all relevant legal requirements.
- Striving to attain a satisfactory balance between economic, social and environmental responsibilities.
- Reducing energy usage in all areas of the business where possible.
- Minimizing the amount of waste produced by reducing, reusing and recycling, and ensuring careful and responsible disposal of any waste we produce according to legislation requirements.

- Endeavoring to source materials from sustainable resources wherever practicable.
- Ensuring awareness amongst all employees of the importance of environmental issues, and providing training appropriate to their responsibilities.
- Ensuring their activities are safe for employees, associates, delegates and others who come into contact with their work.
- Monitoring purchasing practices and internal operations including energy and transport to ensure best use of natural resources and minimum environmental impact.
- Developing relationships with suppliers, customers, contractors and relevant third parties to discuss and promote improvements in environmental performance.
- Seeking to incorporate environmental considerations into future decision-making at all levels.
- Making this policy publicly available to any interested parties.[34]

However, this is a very loose set of guidelines incorporating health and safety, general environmental issues and information dissemination. How this is interpreted and followed is very much dependent upon individual companies and countries. The ten principles for FSC wood are much more rigorous and extensive and include, among other things, the rights of indigenous peoples and the economic well-being of forest workers. In Palestine, I visited the village of Jaba (Figure 4.21) near East Jerusalem, which is just metres away from two big stone quarries. Using dynamite to blast away the rocks, the quarries are exporting the sought-after Jerusalem stone to the world. Cases of asthma and other lung diseases are on the rise in the village while agricultural land is being chipped away in the operation. Stone is a big export for both Palestine and Israel and we were told that both nations were complicit in the environmental and health degradation of the villagers. Charges of corruption involving the way stone is being imported also add to the problem of over-quarrying and other subsequent problems. A news report in 2009 said that Palestinian stone workers and Israeli traders are joining forces to aid the passage of products from Palestinian workshops in the West Bank into Israel.[35] Such issues make the use of stone frought with ethics and environmental degradation, even though it is a durable, reusable and recyclable material.

Bricks and tradition: a case study

Bricks are one of the oldest building materials in the world. Beautiful and daring structures are found all over the world (Figure 4.22), whether made from fired or unfired bricks. However, as the demand for bricks has gone up, agricultural lands are being swallowed up with added problems of pollution, illness

Figure 4.21 Stone quarries, East Jerusalem, just metres away from homes of the Bedouin people.

Photo: Author.

among workers and toxic waste. In India, brick kilns are to be found outside every village – I remember looking out of the train window as a child, travelling from Delhi to Kolkata and realized that, whenever I saw the tall chimney, we were approaching a village. I carried out a study of brick-making technology in my village, Bamundiha, which had a population of about 500 people (2001 figures). Bamundiha is located in West Bengal, India. The British introduced the Hoffmann and Bull's Trench kilns to India in the late nineteenth century. They are still found all over the Indian subcontinent and have remained essentially the same in technology and capacity. They are in the form of an elongated trench measuring up to 10 metres in length and 2.5–5 metres in width. Green or unfired bricks are stacked in the bottom with an insulating roof layer made of rejected burnt bricks, ash and earth. A metal tube chimney is moved around and along the kiln as firing proceeds from one end to the other. The fuel used is coal mixed with cinder. In the more efficient kilns, over 70 per cent of the bricks may be usable while the rest can be crushed to make *surkhi*, a cement-like pozzolanic material.[36]

Despite their efficiency, these kilns have a much a larger impact in terms of air pollution, total fuel consumption, space requirement and employment (Figure 4.23). As the firing trenches spread horizontally they take up precious agricultural land and leave behind a scarred landscape with toxic waste. There always seem to be landowners needing quick money (and usually a brick house) who are ready to sell or lease their land to brick kiln operators. When I visited the village in 1993, I noticed for the first time black soot on

Figure 4.22 At 72.5 metres, the world's tallest brick tower faced with sandstone, the fourteenth century Qutub Minar, Delhi.

Photo: James Jordan.

Figure 4.23 Brick kilns take up agricultural land and also cause pollution. This is a brick kiln just outside the city of Tétouan, Northern Morocco.

Photo: Author.

my bare feet – the fall-out from the kilns. As coal prices go up, operators use lower-grade coal, wood and even rubber, thereby lowering both the quality and quantity of their product and, at the same time, increasing environmental degradation. In the absence of coal, wood is burnt but the amount needed is quite large. In India and Nepal, the wood needed for firing the kilns aggravated the deforestation process in the Gangetic plains, leading to floods and soil erosion. Further, lung-related illnesses have been reported in the workers, owing to poor ventilation and use of substandard fuel.[37]

Approximately 5 per cent of the village population are potters who work on terracotta products and the repair of cob houses. The brick kilns are destroying part of their income. However, the main effect has been on agricultural labourers who mainly comprise the lower and economically deprived castes, who are losing their livelihood from farming on the leased land. They have not found alternative work in the kilns because, as one of the kiln operators commented: 'I like to employ migrant "Biharis" [people from the neighbouring state of Bihar whose border is 100 kilometres from Bamundiha] as they are more sturdy and work hard for less money.' Hassan Fathy noted in the Egypt of the 1960s: 'the industrialization of crafts can produce so much unemployment that any increased production is quite outweighed by the resulting social misery.'[38]

Sometimes there is almost 40 per cent wastage from the kilns as the soil is not ideal for brick making. Soil is not tested prior to use, as this facility is not available in the area. The kiln operators compensate for these losses by paying their labourers less. Most of the kilns such as those operating in Bamundiha are not licensed or monitored and so their efficiency and pollution levels go unchecked. Meanwhile, masons who are not familiar with bricklaying are erecting new buildings. The result is waste and dangerous structures; several new houses are reported to have collapsed soon after they were finished. Traditional building skills are being abandoned fast, although the new brick building skills are still not in place. As a solution to the problem of land pollution and efficiency, the Indian NGO, Development Alternatives, has developed vertical shaft brick kilns. They take up less space and cause less pollution and wastage (5–7 per cent). However, what is needed is a way of monitoring and controlling the existing trench kilns, closing down those that cause the most pollution and wastage and licensing kilns only after the appropriate soil testing and fuel resourcing have been conducted. The village council or district authorities could address the problems connected with local employment. Recycling and reuse of bricks could be encouraged in all types of construction in India.

Concrete and glass

Concrete and glass are two other materials used in modern building construction and also in squatter settlements, especially in Latin American countries. While concrete has originated in various forms all over the world, particularly in ancient Italy and Greece, today concrete is to be found everywhere as it is regarded as a durable and fire-safe material. Concrete structures also provide good resistance to high winds, hurricanes and tornadoes owing to its lateral stiffness which results in minimal horizontal movement and can also provide superior resistance to seismic events. As a result of all these benefits, insurance for concrete homes is often 15–25 per cent lower than for comparable wood frame homes. Economical and efficient use of concrete such as 'micro-concrete' has been used for making roof tiles (Figure 4.24).

It is one of the most widely used construction materials in the world with annual consumption estimated between 21 and 31 billion tonnes. Concrete absorbs carbon dioxide throughout its lifetime through carbonation, helping reduce its carbon footprint; however, how much is actually absorbed in what period of time is open to debate. Concrete consists of between 7 per cent and 15 per cent cement, its only energy-intensive ingredient. A new environmentally friendly blend of cement known as Portland-limestone cement (PLC) has been developed and is used in concrete. It contains 15 per cent limestone, rather than the 5 per cent in regular Portland cement and produces 10 per cent less carbon dioxide emissions. In Europe, PLC-based concrete has replaced about 40 per cent of general use concrete. A nearly

Figure 4.24 Roofing tiles made of micro-concrete, one of the most successful products developed by Development Alternatives (India) in collaboration with SKAT, Switzerland. Over 40 million of these have been installed and successfully imported worldwide, including to Latin America, Africa and Asia.

Photo: Author.

inert material, concrete is suitable as a medium for recycling waste and industrial by-products using materials such as fly ash, slag and silica fume. Much of the recycled concrete is used in road building although, from time to time, architects have used it for foundations.

Glass has again been used in various forms for centuries. Glass was (and still is) one of the most energy-intensive building materials. Therefore it is not surprising that a glass tax was introduced in the eighteenth century in the UK (along with a 'brick tax'), so that only the most important buildings such as religious and royal buildings had glazed windows. However, glass is very popular in modern architecture and it is a rare building that does not use large areas of glazing these days. Common types of glazing that are used in architectural applications include clear and tinted; float, tempered and laminated glass; as well as a variety of coated glasses. Combinations of all glasses can be used singly, doubly or even three combined, or as glazing units (Figure 4.25).

Such specialized glazing is used commonly in Western countries, and it has become a material of prestige and thus highly desired in poorer countries, where often such units or the technology to fit them are not available. Many an architect trying to use the Western architectural language of glazing in tropical environments with high dust and pollution have come up with

Figure 4.25 Low E-tinted glazing in housing project, Caracas. Architect: Lab.Pro.Fab, Caracas. This project is for the rich. The poor use single glazing and in much less quantities.

Photo: Author.

buildings that are energy and labour intensive. Indeed, looking at some cities in hot climates such as Hong Kong, Singapore, Mumbai and Dubai, it is difficult to see why so much glazing has been used, resulting in the overuse of air-conditioning systems even in residential buildings. Even in the 1950s, Corbusier was careful to use less glass and more shading in buildings he designed for Chandigarh, the capital of Punjab.

Appropriate materials and technology

As discussed in detail, materials selected by people for building may not be appropriate climatically or environmentally – these may be cultural choices over which single architects or buildings have little influence. The role of the development activist could then be to disseminate information about materials and their appropriateness to the climate, technology and cost. Many books about green buildings talk about natural materials as if these were the only choices for people. Many scenarios described in these books apply only to rich Western societies and ignore the billions that live in insalubrious buildings, thereby offering no solutions for them. For many, being green is about being middle class and rich. As we have seen in the discussion about the most commonly used modern building materials, all of these have 'natural' origins, being made from minerals and metals found commonly. The major differences between materials are only about the energy and technology required for processing, transportation, use and disposal. In the *barrios* of Venezuela, even with a very limited palate of materials such as concrete frames, hollow brickwork and timber, they managed to express a great variety of architectural structural forms and aesthetics. My sketches from December 2009 are shown in Figure 4.26.

Appropriateness therefore can be seen from three simple guidelines of culture, climate and context, and consumer points of view:

1   *Culture*

   Is this material culturally acceptable?

   Is the technology to work with it available easily and locally?

2   *Climate and context*

   Is this material suitable to use in the local climate?

   Will this material be durable in the context of the site (this includes possible environmental and natural disasters)?

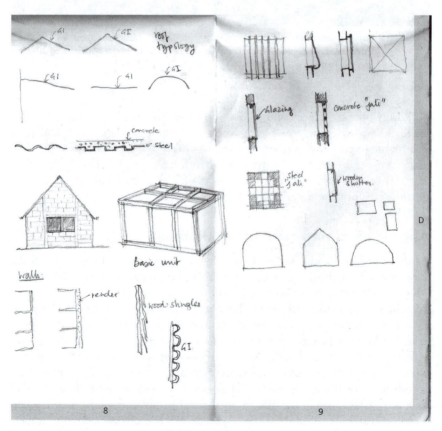

Figure 4.26 From my sketchbook of Barrio Julian Blanco, 2009, Caracas.

3   *Consumer*
   Is this material affordable?
   Will the financial cost vs. environmental cost be compatible?
   Once demolished/dismantled, how will the material be reused or recycled
      and is there a cost or incentive to the client for this?

I have used all sorts of waste materials – straw, earth, demolition waste, bottles and cans in my work in the last twenty years. However, I continue to see that the poor and the homeless do not believe in these materials as much as I do (or did) (Figures 4.27). I believe that with putting a little more thought into the materials and designs that we really do use, we can create efficient, eco-friendly and culturally suitable buildings. Reduction of building waste and energy use and reuse of buildings will become the most important issues for development activists and designers in the future, especially with climate change. Advances in building technology and materials have to work within the cultural context – this will be a very significant step forward. As Paul Oliver cautions us: 'A Luddite mentality which protects the status quo and is in conflict with innovation out of fear of the displacement it may cause, is far from uncommon.'[39] However, he also says that one of the reasons for resistance to change could be isolation (social and contextual), which 'insulates [the people] from outside influence and reinforces their dependency on the security of what they know, and have inherited.'[40] And, what they know and aspire to are concrete and brick buildings, not buildings made of tyres, plastic bags or bottles and not even earth in its latest technically advanced manifestation. I believe that the development activist has an important role to play in this crucial matter.

As the world population rises, so will the numbers of the homeless. These homeless people have to be housed in environmentally and culturally acceptable homes, otherwise these structures will become redundant in one way or the other and contribute to global warming. According to Carole Ryan, oil reserves, which are the basis of organic chemical products and deleterious to health, will determine our choice of building materials and as they run out, we will have to find new ways of using traditional technology.[41] Again, there is no incentive for good energy efficient design to be rewarded, although designers are doing it anyway owing to a social and environmental conscience (Figure 4.28). Instead of statutory pressure, which can be negative and counterproductive, designers should be rewarded if their design and construction reduces carbon emissions. Laurie Baker, Geoffrey Bawa and Hassan Fathy were masters in creating beautiful and sustainable buildings, by taking in and transforming, not destroying, local architecture and knowledge. Thus, we can learn from them and also learn from the context – there is no need to reinvent the wheel or to thrust technology or materials that cannot be used or accepted by the clients.

Figure 4.27 The author building with earth bricks, Toulouse, France, 1988.

Photo: Author.

Figure 4.28 House extension and refurbishment designed by the author (Ecologic Architects), West London, using recyclable and recycled building materials.

Photo: James Jordan.

Discussion points

- 'The problems of why societies have determined the forms of building that they use seem far more challenging, ultimately more important, than the question of how' (Paul Oliver).[42] What do you think?
- Do you think that 'alternate materials' will one day become desirable to all as more and more middle class use them?
- Regarding the appropriateness of materials, how far do you agree that sociosemiotics have a large role to play in their choice and acceptance in a particular society?
- Every material manufacturer appears to claim that their product is 'green'. How can the development activist learn to see beyond the 'greenwash' and convey this to their clients who may not have access to specialist knowledge or understand the technical aspects?

Chapter 5

Learning from tradition
Sustainable cities

There is a perversity in the learning process: We look backward at history and tradition to go forward; we can also look downward to go upward. And withholding judgement may be used as a tool to make later judgement more sensitive. This is a way of learning from everything.[1]

Sustainable 'development' and cities

What is sustainable development? Can 'development', as a byword for progress, ever be sustainable? Does sustainable development mean discarding tradition and embracing 'industrialization'? As a child, I used to look forward to having tea in an unpainted and unglazed terracotta cup, the *kulhar*, in the morning on Indian Railways on the 36-hour journeys we took to get to our village in West Bengal from Delhi in the summer. After use, the *kulhar* could be thrown out of the window as biodegradable waste. Besides being hygienic and sterile in the tropical climate, it was also a considerable source of employment for the village potters. Also the tea tasted wonderful, apparently as the tea soaks into the wall of the *kulhar*, enhancing the taste (some posh restaurants in Delhi still serve *kulhar* tea if patrons ask). After the Indian Railways Minister visited the UK in the late 1980s, polystyrene cups were brought in as a 'sign of progress'. People continued in their habit of throwing these new cups out of the window, now causing littering along the tracks and in the fields. These cups being light, travelled further in the wind than the terracotta cups. Some enterprising villagers started collecting these cups, washing them and reselling them to back to the Indian Railways or reusing them. So the next time I travelled on the train, I noticed a new instruction: 'Crush after use'. At a press conference in London in 1992, I asked the then Indian Railways minister about this and received the usual evasive answer that only politicians can give (unbelievably he even argued that crushed polystyrene cups could be collected and used in domestic insulation or as fuel). In 2004, there was an attempt at reviving *kulhar* tea by Indian Railways. However, environmental critics argued that the production of 1.8 billion *kulhars* annually used on Indian Railways would be polluting, owing to the use of kilns, and so this practice was not revived (Figure 5.1). However, I am happy to report that during my recent travels on Indian trains, I have been given china cups for having tea. Although this does not have the taste of *kulhar* tea, at least they are reusable.

The story of *kulhars* illustrates for me the interconnections and the contradictions inherent in our attempt at building sustainable cities and development. The Bruntland Commission first coined the phrase 'sustainable development'. It has become the most often-quoted definition of sustainable development, being described as development that 'meets the needs of the present without compromising the ability of future generations to meet their own needs.' The very fact that by 1992, three years after the Bruntland report, there were 92 definitions of 'sustainable development' shows that it is a very difficult thing to describe accurately. Sustainability along with other words such as 'diversity' is such a 'buzz word' that it is being used indiscriminately. Writing in the *New Statesman* of 20 May 2011, Will Self says of his frustrations with the use of the word 'sustainable':

Figure 5.1 Traditional kiln, producing soot and pollution, Dharavi, Mumbai.

Photo: Author.

When we look forward to 2012 and consider what sort of strategies may be sustainable, given emergent trends, we need to bear in mind that sustainable can mean any – or all – of the following: maintainable, supportable, viable, self-supporting, justifiable, defensible, expedient, deniable, larger (as in the expression 'sustainable profits'), smaller (as in the expression 'sustainable rates of emissions') and the same (as in 'sustainable growth'). So long as we remain absolutely clear about this, I feel certain that a way of bullshitting that we've all come to revere will remain, in the medium term, sustainable.

As I write this, British MPs are debating the phrase 'sustainable development' in parliament. So let's look at the city to understand urban sustainability.

The city and its components

Apart from people who live or work in the city, urban systems can have four basic components:

1   Connections: roads, water supply, electricity supply, sewerage systems.
2   The hard city: the built environment of the urban systems that are connected by the roads and supply systems. In this broad category, I have included homes, factories and everything that is built.
3   The soft city: the institutional, political, social and cultural arrangements of the people, their health and education.
4   Ecosystem: the natural environment of the city, including the wider area that serves the city, which also forms part of its 'ecological footprint'.

A holistic picture of urban sustainability then examines how these aspects interact and influence each other. In particular, the connections and the ecosystems have a direct connection to the well-being of the residents and overall sustainability. Clean water supply and proper waste management, for example, have the most dramatic effect on the health of the people. In 1824, with the removal of a single water pump located in Holborn that was being polluted by waste, cholera was eradicated in London (see Chapter 8 for more on this). The soft city, on the other hand, is decisive in the distribution of resources and their management. The buildings and their occupants are usually the consumers of supply systems and major waste producers. The ecosystem, on the other hand, often comes at the bottom of the ladder – once the other three aspects are somewhat satisfactory, there is an interest in overall ecological issues. It is a rare city, such as Curitiba, Brazil, where 'sustainability and people' are the driving factors in 'the development' of the city, as we will see later.

As cities grow ever larger – in 1950 there were four megacities, in 1980, twenty-eight, in 2002, thirty-nine, and it is estimated that in 2015 we will have fifty-nine of these[2] – the problems of distribution of water, electricity and sanitary facilities also grow bigger. Many of the hearts of these cities were planned for a certain level of growth (New Delhi) or they were part of a traditional city (London). For example, between 10 and 20 per cent of electricity is generally lost in transmission[3] and in many parts of the world, electricity is 'non-revenue', that is, stolen – as much as 42 per cent in Delhi.[4] Many sources of alternate power production such as tidal, solar and wind are to be found far from the city where it is needed – so again transmission losses can occur when using such sources. Sixty per cent of Delhi's water is non-revenue.[5] Sanitation is another issue. New Delhi was one of the few cities designed in the 1930s that had a separate rainwater and waste-water system – the rainwater discharged directly into canals or the river. Now, these two are combined and one-third of Delhi does not have access to proper sanitation (Figure 5.2).[6] It is not much fun being a megacity, it appears, especially in a poor country.[7] Life

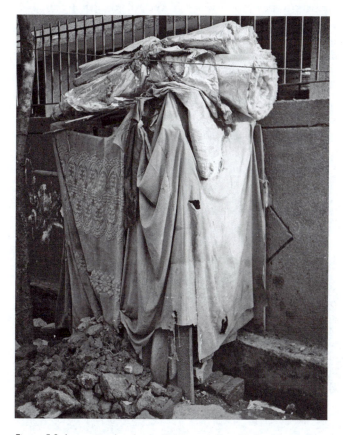

Figure 5.2 Improvised toilet in Kalyanpuri, East Delhi. Many urban poor 'improvise' their own infrastructure, given lack of other help.

Photo: Author.

is even harder for those living within and outside the megacity in squatter settlements or slums.

There are two significant factors that influence urban sustainability – the population served by a particular place and the resources available to meet that demand. We would expect that as the population grows, resources would have to grow too. However, this is not possible because we live on a planet with limited land on which resources can be grown or extracted. So we have to be careful in how we manage the use of our resources – to put it very simply. The growing population presents another problem – the waste produced also grows. At present, the planet is being overrun by waste – on land, air and water (Figure 5.3). Some countries produce more than others. For example, the USA, with about 5 per cent of the world's population,[8] produces 30 per cent of the world's waste.[9] It is interesting to note that Iceland is the third largest producer of per capita waste in the world, although it has very few people, ranking 179 in population statistics. In most industrialized nations, one household bin full of waste (most of which may be non biodegradable) has the hidden 'embodied energy' of seventy full bins that went to produce that waste[10] – a sign of a highly inefficient production system.

Economy and development, that is, progress, have limits placed by their environment and available resources. The popular understanding is that the key indicator of economic progress and sustainability is a state where people are buying more goods 'to keep the economy going'. Thus, modern goods do not only come with a 'a planned obsolescence' but also a 'perceived

Figure 5.3 Plastic bottle in an otherwise clean stream in a national nature reserve, Brasov, Romania. We found several along the trek.

Photo: Author.

obsolescence', so one is always trying to get the next best thing. Shopping has become the symbol of national economic health. After the tragedy of 9/11, the then US President, George Bush, asked people to 'shop' to show the world that Americans were okay and to keep the economy going.[11] A Legal and General report (2010) claims:

> China is now overtaking Japan as the world's second largest economy. Buoyed by *massive government spending*, the country's domestic economy continued to fizz due to *soaring consumer activity* ... Recent data released provided further confirmation that China is firmly in the *driving seat of the global economic recovery.*[12] (Emphasis my own.)

I used this extract to show that the use of words and phrases such as soaring, massive, driving seat and global recovery confirms the idea that consuming keeps the economy going (Figure 5.4).

Figure 5.4 Goods from China being unloaded at a West London warehouse. Goods from China are now not only flooding the rich Western countries but also the emerging economies such as India.

Photo: Author.

Though people are asked to shop to keep the economy going as if it were a cyclical process, the production of goods continues to be thought of as a linear process. However, production is also a cyclical process. So it follows that waste produced at the outset will come back to haunt the producer at the end. Good practice would be to make the process different so as to have no waste, or biodegradable waste only, but the best practice would be to reduce the want for things. However, as people become used to better lifestyles, they do not want to downgrade and have less. In Greece with its continuing national debt crisis, two people were killed in the protests again the austerity measures in 2010. For these people, they would rather sacrifice their lives than sacrifice their lifestyles. These issues are still going on in Europe as I write, with the economies of Ireland, Portugal, Spain and Italy 'going down the precipice', taking the rest of Europe with them.[13]

Rapid urbanization is taking away land on which food can be grown while small farms are being consolidated into 'mega farms'. There is also migration and change in the way food is grown. Also, land suitable for agriculture is diminishing, owing to desertification, depletion of minerals, pollution and other uses of land such as mining, roads, industries, etc. Food quality of the poor in poorer cities as reviewed by the World Health Organization (WHO) is another big concern.[14] In the city, diets contain fewer nutrients. A recent review of differences in urban and rural dietary intake indicates that, on average, energy intake of urban residents is around 200 kcal less than that of rural residents. There is a need to produce food closer to where people live (Figure 5.5). Add to that the allegation that bad-quality or high-fat food discarded by richer nations is being dumped on poorer countries so that, perversely, one in three obese people are from the poorer countries.[15] However, the relationship between good health and lack of diseases to that of access to sanitation, water and food is a natural one. Vaccination is only a preventive measure and does not always work. As a personal example, I have had all the vaccinations and also all the diseases ranging from smallpox to whooping cough, perhaps owing to where and how I lived as a child in Delhi. (My children are not vaccinated and I know that I can take this 'risk' because we live in London.)

Crops and animals are farmed on a large scale in one large holding. Instead of farmlands interspersed with small towns, the world looks like 'either or landscape': a conglomeration of big cities with big farmlands. In India, there have been attempts to use new types of seeds, chemical fertilizers and pesticides to make food crops grow quickly, called the 'Green Revolution' in the 1970s. However, the much touted success of the 'Green Revolution' in India did not succeed in reducing the mortality of children as a result of malnutrition and it showed that productivity and profitability did not increase appreciably, compared to non-chemical agricultural practices.[16] Now a second 'Green Revolution', based on genetically modified seeds, is being publicized as the way to appease world hunger. The book *Hungry City: How food shapes*

Figure 5.5 Local produce being brought in carts for selling door to door, West Delhi. Despite the advent of supermarkets, this practice still survives which is helpful for those unable to go far such as the elderly. However, many supermarkets are cutting out small sellers like these as the middle-classes prefer these to Western style markets.

Photo: Author.

our lives by Carolyn Steel documents how cities have become mega-sprawls that not only take food from the surrounding lands but also from abroad.[17] Demand for 'out of season' food fuels this airborne traffic of food to the industrialized nations. In London during winter, green beans are flown from Kenya and strawberries come from Peru. Even organic produce from abroad adds to the carbon emissions – an organic kiwi fruit flown from New Zealand produces five times its own weight in greenhouses gases.[18]

As the urban economy shifts to 'blue collar' work, the low-value work falls to the rural migrant or the squatter. The already abandoned farmlands become even more desolate as migration to cities takes place (in the USA, only 16 per cent of the population live in rural areas, with cities in recession such as

Detroit turning into ghost towns). About 2,000 people are moving into cities every day throughout the world, looking for work or better circumstances. Thus migration adds to the city's density. Consequently, urban density becomes another issue that makes sustainable projects unworkable. Typically, poorer countries have the world's densest cities. Mumbai with 29,650 persons per square kilometre is much denser than London, which has 5,100 persons per square kilometre. However, more waste is recycled and reused in Mumbai or Kolkata than London. I watched a garbage area in Kolkata, where most of the edible or food waste was eaten by the cows and crows working alongside their human counterparts – the rag pickers who took the plastic, glass and paper. As Bharati Mukherjee and Clark Blaise say, 'True garbage is what no living creature has further use for. And by that definition, Calcutta [Kolkata] is a lot cleaner than Montreal.'[19]

There are also cultural aspects that shape the way people view their city's sustainability and solutions to the problems. Some are based on national pride, some on modern myths that are ingrained as part of the society – many can be quite dangerous. In a TV programme, I heard a Chinese urban designer say that climate change would not affect the Chinese because of the protective dragons that secure the land. An architect in Caracas told me that there could be no pollution despite the large number of cars in the city because 'the wind simply takes it away'. Even many educated Indians believe that the river Ganges is so holy that one can throw anything in it and the water will not be polluted.[20] Eating meat regularly is apparently a perceived sign of progress, according to Jason Burke, writing in *The Guardian* about China[21] (what would he say about the vegetarian diets that the rich eat in countries such as India?). Indians were told by their health minister that they were not susceptible to the AIDS virus because they were Indians (similar views were also expressed in South Africa); these myths that are a mixture of pride and ignorance but presented in a half scientific manner by professionals, journalists and politicians, may be quite convincing to the uneducated and the superstitious (for more see Ben Goldacre's book *Bad Science*, London: Harper Perennial, 2008).

The two historical cities: London and Edo (Tokyo)

Cities before the Industrial Revolution were sustainable – only because they were small, the population was small and waste was either minimal or biodegradable. After the Industrial Revolution and imperialistic conquests of other nations, European nations were awash with things and plenty of things for the first time. And for the first time in history it became possible to really have more than one needed, even to waste and discard unwanted things without thought or consequence. I saw the Lost Gardens of Heligan in Cornwall which has a huge heap of Victorian glass bottles. The people who lived in that era did not know what to do with the discarded bottles and so the hill of bottles grew and remains today as a reminder of waste without thought. In Barrio Julian Blanco, Caracas, I saw another hill composed of plastic bottles and other trash. When I asked if people were aware that these could be sorted out and sold, there was not much response. Compare this to Dharavi slums, Mumbai, where 85 per cent of waste is recycled, particularly plastic. Of course, Venezuela is a petroleum rich country where plastic production is easy and so recycling may not be an issue. However, in the *barrio*, this waste hill was a source of smell and disease.

As the population moved from the country to the cities in search of the jobs that the Industrial Revolution offered, the population rose dramatically in cities such as London. London was once the largest city on the planet but life in it was hardly easy. The River Thames became the 'Great Stink' in 1858 with no form of life in it, polluted with sewage and other waste.[22] Until the late sixteenth century, London citizens used water from shallow wells and springs, the Thames and its tributaries. Water used by tradesmen such as brewers, cooks and fishmongers was taxed, wealthy Londoners living near to a conduit pipe were permitted to connect a direct supply pipe to their homes. So, the unauthorized tapping of conduits was also common.

In 1815, household sewage was permitted to be disposed of into the Thames. The popularity of flush toilets replacing the chamber pots meant that more sewage was flowing into the Thames via the cesspits and overflow drains. In addition, waste from the industries and abattoirs was also being dumped in the river. This effectively meant that the people who did not have access to water from the springs or wells were drinking water from the river contaminated with sewage and waste. Water-borne diseases such as cholera and bacterial infections were very common along with diseases carried by vermin. The air was full of smog. The romantic paintings of London-born painter J.M.W. Turner possibly disguised the pollution, smog and dirt and made London seem a great place to be. However, as the novels of Dickens show, London was far from being salubrious. It was much later that London was cleaned up, and at great cost in every way. Today, London is emerging as an exemplar in promoting sustainability – there are not many cities in the world where the prime minister and the mayor of the city cycle or take public transport. The so-called Boris bikes in London have been very popular and many buses are running on dual fuel made of vegetable oil. Power-saving devices are being used on modern trains. City Hall, designed by Norman Foster, and other buildings and institutions in the city, work to minimize their power requirements.[23] The association between environment and economy is being finally realized.

The Japanese city of Edo (present day Tokyo) offers an example of sustainability from the past. During the Edo period, from the early seventeenth to the mid-nineteenth centuries, Japan faced environmental problems similar to London: large population, fuel scarcity, limited arable land, deforestation, a damaged water basin. The primary design response to material and energy scarcity of that era was to apply 'multiform solutions' or solutions that achieved several aims at once. The development of the rice paddy irrigation systems, which were almost entirely gravity-fed, acted as cascading aerobic filters. They could also function as solar-heated warm-water tanks for processing hemp and other plant-based textile fibres. The rice paddies were also wetland habitats for many species, thus preserving biodiversity and sustainable agricultural systems. Forest management was recognized early on as an essential resource.

Solar energy, gravity and human labour were the mainstays of technology.[24] The city water system was also gravity-fed. Transportation and agriculture were progressively refined to largely eliminate the need for animals. So the scarce arable land, in elegantly cut terraces to make the best use of natural resources, was mostly used for food production for people, not for animals. The meat-free diet reinforced this efficiency of land use. Unlike their Western counterparts, Edo streets were free of animal manure and therefore healthier. In Edo, animal dung was used as fertilizer in the fields after aerobic treatment. In contrast, Roman waste was thrown into the river while water was brought into the city from afar by the construction of expensive aqueducts – a rather pointless and expensive venture, although these are admired now for their structural daring. So unlike Rome and London, the river water in Edo was kept clean for human and animal consumption and waterways were vital for transportation and as a food source (such as fish). The ecosystem of the river also kept itself naturally clean – and is well documented in the Edo period drawings, which became an art form in themselves.

Metals, which were scarce in Japan, were used minimally. For example, the use of iron was minimized through either the absence of nails in buildings using purely timber construction systems or the careful reuse of any nails. Even after the Second World War, the spirit of recycling was kept up with guns and metal ammunitions being turned into household products (as also in Europe after the war). In most cases, these requirements were never spelt out as a cost–benefit analysis or embodied energy calculations, but were inherent in the design. Any proposed solutions were considered adequate only if they addressed a number of secondary problems in addition to the primary purpose, namely, the multiform solutions. Even in Japan today, a great many of the underlying values – anti-waste, frugality, reuse, conserving energy – survive, as seen in the technology and car-manufacturing industry. However, the complex interconnected system that was the basis of the urban sustainability disappeared with the advent of the industrial revolution in Japan in the late twentieth century following the Second World War.

It is believed by scholars that the success of Edo lay in its diversion from war efforts to city sustainability. Edo was the most populated city of its time, but owing to investment in the city's sanitation, water supply and transportation systems, there was a lack of promotion of weapons, so 'people had forgotten how to use guns'.[25] New cities are emerging today, each trying to be more sustainable than the other. The idea of a city as a 'workshop' for new ideas on design and sustainability is not new. As said earlier, Scandinavian countries have taken a lead in promoting sustainable buildings (Figures 5.6 and 5.7). Many design and multidisciplinary practices are working on new sustainable cities. Dongtan, China and Destiny, Florida, are now being master-planned by Arup in London, an international firm of designers, planners, engineers and technical special-ists.[26] They are meant to be showcases of new ecological sustainability. Destiny will have an electric light-railway system, solar water taxis, biomass, solar farm, recycling, geothermal heat pumps and even green jobs. Nothing has been left out but will the Americans buy it? According to Arup, sure they will, once the price of oil rockets up. Even in the oil-rich Gulf states where electricity demand is growing by three times the world average, Saudi Arabia is taking the lead through the design of Masdar, the $22 billion carbon-free metropolis being built in Abu Dhabi. It is expected to have the world's largest solar power plant, enough to provide electricity for some 55,000 residents. Berlin and Barcelona were among the first cities in the world to sign up to the 'solar ordinance'. As Peter Droege says, 'too much of this wider, fossil-fuel drenched urban reality is not conducive to sustaining such great civic aspirations.' In contrast, Droege reports that 'future-minded cities are increasingly focusing on limiting their dependence on large centralized coal, oil, and nuclear power supply systems', and instead focusing on renewable energy.[27]

Figure 5.6 'Grey water', i.e. water from kitchen and bathrooms (excluding toilet) being cleaned, co-housing scheme, Stockholm.

Photo: Author.

Figure 5.7 House with recycled steel walls, 'Thermologica', Egebserggård Housing Exhibition, 1996 (architects Dissing & Weitling, Copenhagen, Denmark).

Photo: Author.

Curitiba: the maverick city

Curitiba[28] is an unusual example as it has had a mayor, Jaime Lerner, who is also an architect and urban designer concerned with sustainability.[29] He has been mayor three times (1971–5, 1979–84 and 1989–92). In 1994 and 1998, Lerner was also elected governor of the state of Paraná, in which Curitiba lies. Lerner used unorthodox solutions for Curitiba's geographic, social and economic problems. For example, instead of building levées to protect Curitiba from floodplains like wealthier cities such as New Orleans and Sacramento in the USA have chosen to do, he made them into wetland parks. In the early 1970s, when the rest of Brazil was being heavily industrialized, Curitiba allowed only non-polluting industries in an industrial quarter with green spaces. At that time, it was derided as a 'golf course'. The city now has one of the highest per-capita park areas in the world. Instead of using lawnmowers for the parks, Lerner's innovative response was 'municipal sheep' that kept the parks' vegetation under control and whose wool funded children's programmes. During his first term, Lerner implemented the Bus Rapid Transit system. Lerner began a programme that traded bags of groceries and bus passes for rubbish bags and paid fishermen for any garbage they retrieved from the bay.

Although his term as mayor was not without controversy, it says something for Lerner that Curitiba does not have such high crime rates as other more populous Latin American cities such as Caracas or Rio de Janiero. The city's thirty-year economic growth rate is 7.1 per cent, higher than the national average of 4.2 per cent, and per capita income is 66 per cent higher than the Brazilian average. Between 1975 and 1995, Curitiba grew 75 per cent more than the state of Paraná in which it lies, and 48 per cent more than Brazil as a whole. In 2010 the city was awarded with the Globe Sustainable City Award, which recognizes excellence in sustainable urban development around the world.[30]

Learning from Jaisalmer, India

So what happens if a city does not have a maverick mayor like Jaime Lerner? I have chosen Jaisalmer in Western India as an example of a city that was sustainable in the past and then had some successes and failures adjusting to the modern reality of urban pressures and management of resources (Figure 5.8). In 2009, I took my MA students for a closer look at what sustainable means to a 'heritage' city. I have chosen two issues very significant to Jaisalmer – water and electricity supply. Both are crucial to the city and its habitants; clean water being of prime importance in health and sanitation. Jaisalmer is a desert city, located in the sands of the Great Indian Thar desert. Another reason for choosing Jaisalmer was because at the time it was a self-sustaining city, in contrast to London which was at the height of the Industrial Revolution and highly polluted, as described earlier. Thus it offers an interesting paradox on the nature of development and progress.

Jaisalmer was positioned strategically as a station along the traditional trade route traversed by the camel caravans of Indian and Asian merchants (see Chapter 2). The main source of income for the city was the levies imposed on the caravans that passed en route. However, Jaisalmer's importance faded when Mumbai emerged as the main port of India during British rule and sea routes replaced traditional land routes. It also suffered from major famines in 1897 and 1900. The Independence and Partition of India in 1947 led to the closure of the trade routes on the Indo–Pakistan border. Ironically, military skirmishes between India and Pakistan now give Jaisalmer a strategic importance and function as an army supplies depot, which has made it a 'modern

Figure 5.8 City of Jaisalmer, Western India – the wind turbines in the distance can be seen from every part of the city.

Photo: Author.

fort city'. With the decline in trade, the population decreased to 18,000 people in the city in the late nineteenth century. However today, Jaisalmer has a population of more than 60,000 (according to the 2001 census). Males constitute 57 per cent of the population and females 43 per cent. Jaisalmer has an average literacy rate of 64 per cent, higher than the national average of 59.5 per cent. The principal export is in wool, ghee (clarified butter), camels, cattle and sheep. The main imports are grain, sugar, cloth, small electrical items and other goods.

Ecological issues for Jaisalmer

Jaisalmer has an average elevation of 229 metres above sea level. It covers an area of 5.1 square kilometres. The maximum summer temperature is around 42 °C while the minimum is 25 °C. The maximum winter temperature is usually around 24 °C and the minimum is 8 °C. The climate is hot and dry and there is a large variation in the diurnal temperatures. The region has the lowest average annual rainfall in India – just 250 millimetres. Despite the area being in the low rainfall desert region, it has a very high population density and a substantial cattle density in comparison to the other desert regions of the world. The density of the city is 11,429 persons per square kilometre (the fort area will most probably have a higher density but figures were difficult to obtain). The density for the rest of the district is only seventeen persons per square kilometre (in comparison, London has 5,100 persons per square kilometre).

Water is scarce, and generally brackish; the average depth of the wells is said to be about 75 metres. There are no perennial streams, and only one small river, Kakni, which, after flowing a distance of only 28 métres spreads out on flat ground to become a lake – the Bhuj-Jhil. Forests constitute an important component of the physical environment of the state influencing the microclimate. Many communities, especially tribal or migratory, are directly dependent upon the forests for both food and as a means of employment. The majority of the population outside the city lead a wandering life, grazing their flocks and herds of camels, horned cattle, sheep and goats. In the desert, some sand hills rise to a height of 46 metres with extensive grasslands around them. These are unique ecosystems with species of animals (wild as well as domesticated) that have adapted over the ages to the harsh conditions of the region. Overgrazing, encroachment and infestation with exotic species have led to adverse changes in composition, ecology and productivity of the grasslands. In the Biodiversity Conservation Prioritisation Project (BCPP) of the WWF conducted in 1998–9, eight grassland ecosystems were identified as of special importance in terms of priority and three of these ecosystems lie in Jaisalmer district.

Streets and general planning

The listing of Jaisalmer as a protected heritage city has limited its growth and spread. There are strict rules about house building, styles and density. The city has provided inspiration for designers and architects throughout the ages – in building both traditional and modern styles. In the sixteenth century, Emperor Akbar, a Muslim, used Rajasthan *haveli* styles for building his capital, Fatehpur Sikhri (Figure 5.9) while Edwin Lutyens, the British architect, referred to it in building the Viceregal lodge and the city of New Delhi. The architect Charles Correa has explored the language of courtyard buildings, use of sandstone and details in his buildings. Many government offices continue to be built in this style – perhaps to denote power and resistance – both of which have been part of Rajasthani history. The fort area lies some distance from the main city and is very densely populated with winding and narrow streets.

In both the city and fort, the streets are outdoor spaces, used at all times, especially by the men to gather and talk (Figure 5.10). In the absence of a *chowk* with a tree or temple, so common in other parts of India, the street itself becomes a public space to gather. The close spacing of buildings with their dense fabric ensures that buildings shade each other. The narrowness and alignment of the streets against the prevailing wind ensures that sandstorms do not affect the streets and homes. Most houses and the *havelis* are traditional courtyard plans, which, combined with the height of the houses, gives a depth that ensures a cool, shaded and protected space. Each *haveli* has a dog leg entrance, that is, the courtyard is never visible from the street. This provides privacy and

Figure 5.9 Fatehpur Sikhri, near Agra (a UNESCO World Heritage site).

Photo: James Jordan.

Figure 5.10 Streets in Jaisalmer.

Photo: Author.

security while also preventing sand and dirt coming in. Under the conservation programme, three out of the five main stately homes, the *Haweli* palaces, have been restored. Streets were paved in 2004. Upgrading of the sanitation and drainage system is under implementation by the Government of India.

As the architects Revathi and Vasant Kamath say:

> The architecture and the urban form of Jaisalmer are not the product of a self-conscious process of design, nor are they of theological origin; they are the physical expression of forces that affect the daily lives of the people, representative of their self-image, wealth and aspirations. Assimilation of the forces of social patterning, historical consciousness, political and cultural influences, religious habits and ritual, symbolic associations, topography, geography, climate, the restricted availability of materials, behavioural patterns, functions and most of all the institutionalized craftsmanship have led to the richness, variety and vitally human qualities of the built environment.[31]

Materials and details

Yellow sandstone, which is the local building material, has been used extensively in the fort area and outside it. The thick masonry walls with small and very few openings on the outside, especially the South-facing sides, are good for retaining heat within. So the interiors are cool during the day while at night the heat is reflected out as the diurnal temperature difference is big. This diurnal range is lowered as a result of the courtyard planning of the house. The use of delicately carved screens in the exterior and interior facades maintain an air flow while providing shading and privacy, and preventing heat gain and sand from coming in during storms (Figure 5.11). The 'double curve' shape of the roof is carved from stone imitating the form of a cloth awning. This shape helps in 'throwing' off sand during sandstorms (and water in case of rains).

To reduce glare and provide shade, sandstone overhangs – *chajjas* – extend out of walls. This feature is common throughout Northern India. In the interior streets, the intricate and delicate filigree stonework not only reduces heat gain, glare and dust, but also allows ventilation without compromising privacy. In a land where women were used as wages of war, privacy and security for women were essential for Rajasthani society and architecture. As this feature had a social reason, not just an environmental one, so this tradition continues today in the modern *havelis* coming up in Jaisalmer and elsewhere.

Sustainable infrastructure

Rainwater harvesting was undertaken on a city scale from as early as the fourteenth century. In most traditional cities, rainwater harvesting was very common.[32] Gadsisar Lake (Figure 5.12), which was excavated in 1367 by Rawal

Figure 5.11 The screened windows give a deep shade to the house and reduce glare, Jaisalmer.

Photo: Author.

Figure 5.12 Gadsisar Lake, Jaisalmer.

Photo: Author.

Gadsi Singh, is a rainwater lake surrounded by small temples and shrines. It was used for the water supply to the fort and the city but now with the advent of piped water, is used for recreational purposes only. On a smaller scale, we observed the storage of rainwater in covered stone troughs – underneath external sitting areas (in the threshold area). The troughs had removable stone seats that could be lifted when it rained to hold the water (Figure 5.13). Now many of these features are connected with the mains supply and we saw plastic pipes inserted crudely into the intricate stonework (Figure 5.14). Also near the entrance would be sandstone troughs where peelings and other food waste would be dropped. The cows on the street would eat these (Figure 5.15). Thus each household produced very little waste. Fortunately, as cows are considered sacred, this tradition continues to provide a sustainable means of disposing of food waste.

In most traditional cultures people's sense of place and identity is strongly linked with the landscapes, flora and fauna that surround them.[33] For example, the Khejri tree is as much a sacred symbol of worship to people in Western Rajasthan as the Pipal tree in the rest of India. Herds of chinkara and black buck deer can be seen around villages for whom they are sacred animals (like

Figure 5.13 Traditional rainwater collection trough being constructed, Jaisalmer.

Photo: Author.

Figure 5.14 Clogged up drain in the fort area, Jaisalmer.

Photo: Author.

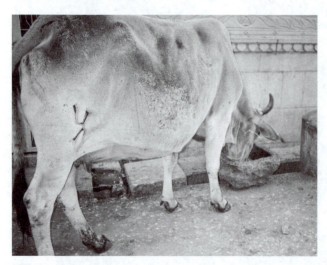

Figure 5.15 Cows eat the vegetable waste thrown into the troughs in front of each house.

Photo: Author.

cows). Sacred groves called by various names – *orans*, *deovans*, *banees*, *jors* and *birs* – have their origin in the traditional life of people living closely with the nature around them.

Despite this ingrained biodiversity in the culture and religion of the people, there are environmental problems:

- overgrazing in forest areas, commons and other wastelands with natural vegetation is the most important pressure on the forests and biodiversity resources of the state;
- increasing human population and consequent demand for forest produce;
- encroachment for marginal agriculture and for settlements;
- mining, construction of roads, expansion of urban areas and establishment of industrial centres near or inside forests;
- demand for both industrial fuelwood and animal products.

Thus, there are now laws and institutional mechanisms for the management of biodiversity. Biodiversity as an explicit concern became a legal requirement only in 2003. With India having signed the UN Convention on Biological Diversity (CBD), the Government of India through the Ministry of Environment and Forests prepared a National Biodiversity Strategy and Action Plan. The State of Rajasthan also prepared its own Biodiversity Strategy and Action Plan.

Modern water management: the Indira Gandhi canal

The Indira Gandhi (IG) Canal is one of the biggest canal projects in India, named after its most enthusiastic proponent, Mrs Indira Gandhi, former prime minister of India. It starts from below the confluence of the Sutlej and Beas rivers in Punjab state in Northern India, filling with waters released from a dam there. Its construction started on 31 March 1958 and is still going on. It was built with the aim of converting part of the Thar desert to agriculturally productive land, checking desertification of fertile areas, sand-dune stabilization in the areas around Jaisalmer district, and creating shelter and green belt for preservation of wildlife. The canal cuts through seven districts of Rajasthan, including Jaisalmer. After the construction of the Indira Gandhi Canal, irrigation facilities were available over an area of 6,770 square kilometres in Jaisalmer district, along with 3,670 square kilometres already provided. Potable water was introduced to the fort in the 1970s. The 128 Infantry Battalion, Territorial Army (Ecological) Rajputana Rifles played the dual role of protecting the country at this strategic location while also being involved in 'greening the desert' operations – an idea promoted by Mrs Gandhi. The unit planted over 11,000 saplings in an area of 7,330 hectares, and grass slips for pasture development over 3,540 hectares on the West bank of IG Main Canal and other areas near Jaisalmer.

Along with deforestation caused by excessive population and livestock, excessive irrigation and intensification of agriculture over the years have caused new environmental problems. Water-logging caused by excessive irrigation, seepage from canals and poor drainage have produced a rise in the water table, leading to increased salinity in the agricultural land. These problems have been exacerbated by the cultivation of water-intensive cash crops such as mustard, cotton and wheat. The rise in water tables, increased use of piped water with leaks, illegal tapping of water supply pipes and occasional heavy rains are affecting the yellow sandstone masonry work of the fort – the main tourist attraction of the city.[34] In one case, owing to the increasingly saline waters unfit even for cattle, the people in a village in Bharatpur, Rajasthan, have come up with their own ingenious solution, by constructing their own feeder canal linked to the river Yamuna (which also flows through Delhi).[35]

The enthusiastic planting programmes of the forest department, the army and *panchayats* (village councils) have led to either domination of monoculture of certain plants or the uncontrolled spread of exotic species. Exotic species such as *Acacial tortilis*, *Prosopis juliflora* (Mesquite) and Eucalyptus trees have accounted for 30 per cent of all trees planted under various afforestation and reforestation programmes; 20 per cent of the trees planted belong to a single species – *Acacial nilotica*. This puts the ecology under more stress in an already fragile area. Mesquite (*Prosopis juliflora*) has already spread far and wide in the state and, once established, is extremely difficult to eradicate. Owing to the law on biodiversity, preference is now being given to local species of trees and shrubs.

The success of small-scale interventions in water management

The Indian Centre for Science and Environment (CSE) through its small grant programme assisted the Thar Integrated Social Development Society (TISDS) in reviving *Paar* – a traditional rainwater harvesting system in Jaisalmer district. TISDS, a Jaisalmer-based NGO, had been actively involved in addressing the regional ecological issues since 1994.[36] It started when a group of fifteen higher secondary school students got together in Jaisalmer in 1986 to address the environmental issues related to forestry, sacred groves (*oran*), traditional rainwater harvesting systems and land management. In April 1994 they registered the group as TISDS.

For some years, owing to the poor rainfall during the monsoon season in Western Rajasthan, villagers had been forced to move to other villages. In April 2003, Jethu Singh Bhatti, the Chairman of TISDS, started an experiment of using the traditional *Paar* system in a village of Jaisalmer district. This was predominantly a tribal village where 90 per cent of the habitants were below the poverty line. The village with seventy households was totally dependent on agriculture and livestock, with people farming on leased lands. Bhatti approached the *Panchayat* in 2003 and convinced them to lease out common land for five years to TISDS. The *Paar* system he proposed consisted of:

- *Naadi* (village ponds): rainwater falling in the catchment area (*agar*) is collected in the village ponds and tanks.
- *Kui/beri* (traditional wells): the naturally percolated rainwater through sand is accessed through the *kuis* or *beris*. *Kuis* or *beris* are normally 5–12 metres deep. The structure is constructed using traditional stone masonry.

The cost for this project was INR221,600 (£3,270). Work began by developing the *agar* to catch rainwater. Later, *kuis* were constructed in the *agar* to access the water. There were certain immediate benefits as a result of the *Paar* system. The village now has a perennial source of water. Previously the villagers, especially women and girls had to walk up to 7 kilometres to fetch water. The *Paar* not only provided employment for the villagers but it also disseminated the traditional technology to the younger generation, making them self-sufficient and confident. People from adjoining villages have already started to approach TISDS to replicate similar work in their villages.

Experience of Tarun Bharat Sangh and water management

Tarun Bharat Sangh (TBS) is a voluntary organization registered in Jaipur in 1975 and started by a group of university professors and students.[37] However, as they say themselves, their journey only became a practical one when, on 2 October, Mahatma Gandhi's birthday, they 'started a mission to move the people out of their feeling of helplessness in the face of the ravages of nature and an indifferent administration'.[38]

Four youths, including Rajendra Singh (present chairman), inspired by the Gandhian model of rural development, went to live in a village of Alwar district of Rajasthan. They started a school for children but three of them left owing to the unenthusiastic reception by the villagers. However, Rajendra Singh was undeterred but puzzled by the villagers' reticence to come forward to what he thought was a good thing. He fully understood the dilemma when a village elder told him, 'You have not understood what is needed here. We want *WATER* first!' So he started the construction of a traditional *Johad*, a small check dam. He says:

> Once the first small *Johad* was ready, the villagers saw water and the ecology changed in the next monsoon. *For Tarun Bharat Sangh, it became an approach of rural development through restoring the ecology for better food production, vegetation rejuvenation and river restoration.*[39] (Emphasis my own.)

Between 1984 and 2008, around 10,000 rainwater harvesting structures were constructed through the support of national and international donors. The rainwater harvesting also revived five rivers, which had been reduced to seasonal rivers, benefiting some 250 villages. Thus the harvesting of just 3 per cent of the rainfall has enabled the economic and ecological turnaround of the region. As TBS says:

> The issue of water is not about scarcity but about its careful use and about its equitable and distributed access. In the above context, traditional community based water management systems pave way for identification of appropriate adaptation and mitigation strategies to address the implication of climate change on economy and ecology.[40]

The story of Jaisalmer and the wind farm

Normally, wind farms are associated with sustainability. The cover of Peter Droege's book *The Renewable City* has an image of wind turbines with a background of Rajasthani architecture, perhaps suggesting that wind power has been successful there.[41] This is not always the case. In Jaisalmer, Rajasthan, the politics, location and the benefits of wind farms appear to have helped only the big players. *Geography and You*[42] conducted questionnaire surveys in summer 2006 and winter 2008 to study the effect of a wind farm built by Suzlon and Enercon near Jaisalmer.[43] Suzlon Energy is a global wind power company formed and based in India. Enercon, based in Germany, is the third-largest wind turbine manufacturer in the world.[44]

Non-agricultural land belonging to the government was leased out for the establishment of the wind farm. Natural gas was found in the region in 1988 but local electricity supply has always been erratic, so the use of wind power to generate electricity appeared to have been a good idea initially. The Global Wind Energy Council (GWEC) estimates that the world can expect a rise in wind power capacity by 160 per cent over the next five years. 'Even in the face of a global recession and financial crisis, wind energy continues to be the technology of choice in many countries around the world,' GWEC Secretary General Steve Sawyer said in May 2010.[45] The GWEC expects that the United States and China will continue to be the main drivers of wind capacity growth. The industry group expects Asia to overtake Europe as the leading region in terms of installed wind capacity by the end of 2014, when Europe's installed capacity is expected to have risen to 136.5 gigawatts, compared to Asia's 148.8 gigawatts.[46] The three objectives of the study conducted by *Geography and You* were:

1   To locate positive impacts.
2   To record negative outcomes.
3   To suggest possible remedies for problem situations.

Residents of seven nearby villages with eighty-one households were involved in the study. Thirty-nine households from Jaisalmer city were also consulted. The research appears to have been done through interviews and questionnaires.[47]

Noise and effect on the landscape

Apart from the continuous drone and flickering shadows of the moving blades, the villagers did not seem to mind other issues such as bird hits and the effect on the landscape. The noise levels of the wind farms were measured to be high, well above the threshold of 50 decibels. In fact some of the wind turbines were placed within 400 metres of the villages where the sound levels were nearer 100 decibels, equivalent to an aeroplane flying close by. The noise levels were further accentuated over the barren sand hills with no vegetation. Some respondents in the area feared that during heavy sandstorms the blades would fall off their hinges.

Although familiar with wind farms from their own countries, the foreign visitors who were interviewed for this project felt that wind turbines should be located at least 5–10 kilometres from heritage sites such as Jaisalmer. They apparently felt that the haphazardly placed wind turbines were an 'ungainly sight'.

Socio-economic impact

The most significant issue for the villagers, however, was they felt completely left out of the process of design and implementation of the project. The contracted labour as well as the personnel were and are still being sourced from outside the region, although from time to time part-time jobs are available at the wind farm. Charges of nepotism were also levelled against the companies – the villagers felt that the better connected such as those from the families of the *Panchayat* members, and *sarpanch* (head of the village council) were given jobs and even electricity supply. According to the villagers, the job that is most frequently advertised is that of a watchman or guard. Technical jobs are few and often offered to people from outside the region.

The wind farm has had little effect on the electricity needs of the local residents. The electricity generated in the wind farms is fed directly into the grid and the locals do not benefit from the arrangement. The villages around Jaisalmer are electrified but, as for most of India, many households have either no electricity or receive electricity for only a few hours a day. Ironically, the respondents feel a sense of pride that the wind farms near them are now 'turning the wheels of large industries' miles away. The households in the city of Jaisalmer also experience electricity shortages. Use of generator sets run on diesel is common in these households – another source of noise and air pollution.

The issue of water management and supply remains a major concern for the villagers – they feel unhappy that this primary need was not given any concern by the big companies. The road networks to and within the wind farm, built recently by Suzlon and Enercon, are in excellent condition. This may be as they require little maintenance because the local residents rarely use them. The existence of the wind farm for the last seven years has hardly had any impact on the availability and access to these basic facilities by the people that live under their shadow. As perhaps a happy footnote for these people, the wind farm has been up for sale since October 2009.[48]

Recommendations from the survey

While the project outlay of wind companies is lower than that of conventional systems such as hydel or thermal power plants, it is possible that, consequently, the environmental and social commitments of wind farms are lower. However, the research recommended that the wind energy companies should:

- be involved in the socio-economic development of the region. This should include not only local employment, education and provision of medical facilities but also rainwater harvesting and alternate power supply such as solar power;
- allow local usage of electricity by using mini transformers on site;
- compete with each other on the basis of their environmental, social and economic commitment to the local area, so that the best company may win the contract;
- be sensitive to the local landscape, especially the nature of heritage sites. A recommended distance of 5–10 kilometres from the outskirts of the city should be permitted for wind farm location (the wind turbines are clearly seen from the fort area as we saw in 2009).

Lessons from tradition

From studying Jaisalmer, we realize that cities today are struggling to support not only people, but also the larger environment. Management of resources such as electricity and water in a high density city with strict planning conditions is a very difficult process but one that provides lessons for other cities. It is difficult to fathom why and how decisions were made – for example, the decision to install wind turbines instead of using solar power installations, and to construct a canal that has taken the best part of fifty years and is still not complete, are not sustainable solutions. It is estimated that the desert regions of the world (many of which are in poor countries) receive the same amount of energy in six hours as the world consumes in an entire year, so why is it that Freiburg in West Germany is called the solar capital of the world? Solar-power generation systems are being used in the Northern Sahara led by a company called Desertec.[49] While countries such as Morocco, Tunisia and Algeria stand to benefit from this programme, Desertec also hopes to supply 15–20 per cent of Europe's energy needs by 2050 (Figure 5.16). Solar power collection would have had less impact on the landscape and certainly less noise and disruption for the villagers of Jaisalmer, so why was it not considered? Also, as Desertec says, solar plants have been in operation for the last twenty years in the Mojave Desert, USA, and have not been affected by sandstorms and storms – things that can affect wind turbines.

The issue of appropriate technology transfer is another issue highlighted by Jaisalmer. Even though a system may have worked in one country, even though it might be a 'green' system, it does not always work in other places. Systems have to be chosen carefully, especially those that are expensive and impact on the whole city. For example, Delhi has tried to emulate Curitiba's Bus Rapid Transit (BRT) system without much success. Delhi's unmanageable BRT system has led to fatalities almost daily, not to mention the general traffic confusion (Figures 5.17 and 5.18).[50] The Metro system in Delhi, based on a Korean and Japanese system, has been criticized for its high running costs.

It is not always the following of Western ideas that is responsible for throwing away traditional approaches in non-Western countries. We cannot go back to a kind of Luddite tendency advocated by some and, as it is clear,

Figure 5.16 2,400 solar panels on the roof of the papal audience hall in Vatican City. The solar roof installed in 2008, reportedly worth nearly $1.5 million, should need only minimal maintenance for the next 25 years. In 2007, the Vatican announced its intention to become the world's first carbon-neutral state.

Photo: Author.

Figure 5.17 Cycle lane in the BRT system, Delhi, clogged up by parked cars.

Photo: Anuj Shrivastava.

Figure 5.18 Truck leans over the edge at the beginning of the BRT system roundabout, New Delhi.

Photo: Chater Paul Jordan.

the poor want to have the same conveniences and circumstances as the rich. Sometimes it is expediency and thoughtlessness that makes us not look at what has worked to see if it can be used again. An example is the Indian 'cooler'. In Northern India with its hot and dry climate, a grass mat, *khus khus*, was kept dipped in water while an obliging servant pulled a large fan above his master and mistress, serving up a cooling breeze. In time, when servants disappeared, the 'cooler' appeared. Here in a large box, the same *khus khus* was used on three sides, one side was attached to the window of the room. Water was fed on a bottom tray and, instead of a servant, a small electric fan supplied the same cooling breeze. A newer portable version of this cooler has now appeared in Delhi (Figure 5.19). Apart from the problem of mosquitoes breeding in the water tray, the main issue is that the fan uses mains electricity. Delhi is a city with frequent power outages and sometimes people use generators to run the coolers, causing noise and pollution. It would have been better to have used solar power, which is found in plenty there, for running this fan. In Freiburg, Germany, solar power is being used for running air-conditioning units, so running a small fan on solar power in Delhi would not have been a problem. However, this required lateral thinking on the part of the designers. The lesson here is that we can take the traditional and adapt it for modern use in an age of rapid change and scarce resources (Figure 5.20).

Now that over five million people have died as a result of wars over the use of natural resources in the 1990s,[51] the management of power and water supply is a crucial global concern. The war over water takes place between

Figure 5.19 Portable *khus khus* water cooler, Delhi.

Photo: Author.

Figure 5.20 Terracotta 'fridges' on sale in Dharavi, Mumbai. These are derivations of the unglazed terracotta water storage vessels in which the water tastes delicious.

Photo: Author.

states and regions in a country and even between countries. Many regions in Northern India, for example, are unhappy about the huge proportion of water diverted towards the capital, New Delhi, while they go waterless. The IG canal, as we have seen, has had limited success in 'greening the desert', while diverting water from other regions. The implementation of India's interlinking thirty rivers programme, especially the River Ganges, could affect Bangladesh's water shortage. Its government called the Indian scheme a 'weapon of mass destruction' as the livelihoods of more than 100 million people are at risk there. There are conflicts between countries in North Africa about the use of the water from the River Nile by Egypt and Sudan, based on past colonial treaties of 1929 and 1959. However, the most destructive water-based dispute has been in the Middle East, where 5 per cent of the world's population lives on just 1 per cent of the region's water. Israel, Syria, Jordan, Lebanon and Palestine are engaged in 'water wars'. Construction of large dams has also attracted negative publicity about the human and cultural costs – for example, the Three Gorges dam in China and the Narmada dam in India.

So what are the lessons here for the development activist? While some projects are small buildings, architects and designers naturally get involved with the city, whether the projects are themselves small or large. Similar to the human body, the arteries of the city are water, the electricity is like the neurological network while sewage disposal could be compared to the waste system in the body – all have to function well to provide a healthy place to live (Figure 5.21). It is certainly true that many micro-level traditional approaches cannot be applied to the city and dense squatter settlements. Reed beds need smaller communities to function properly[52] and the *Paar* or *Johad* system will not be able to cope with the demands of even a small city such as Jaisalmer. Many NGOs such as Oxfam, for example, prefer to deal with private companies for water and electricity supply to cities, using conventional systems.

Ways to deal with the larger demands can be found through using the concept favoured by E. F. Schumacher – that of smallness in scale but more intensive use. In the Philippines, GTZ (German technical cooperation) has forged partnership with the University of the Philippines Environmental Engineering Unit and the UFZ Centre for Environmental Research Leipzig-Halle of Germany, to implement a reed-bed system in the city of Bayawan, Negros Oriental Province. This project is currently being implemented through a participatory approach, where the main stakeholders are involved in planning, design and construction, as well as in the operational phase. The

Figure 5.21 A jumble of wires, leaking pipes and drains, illegal construction in shopping street, Delhi. Such dangerous and insalubrious conditions add to the problems created by urban density and make it almost impossible to resolve or transform the situation.

Photo: Author.

plant serves as a pilot measure to demonstrate the applicability and efficiency of engineered reed beds as a low-cost alternative technology for waste-water treatment in a high-density area. This is for a 1,000-strong community. In Delhi, the Sulabh Shauchalaya, the composting toilet, is being used as a paying toilet facility in South Delhi, as mentioned before (Figures 5.22 and 5.23).

Squatter settlements with their chaotic arrangement of houses and structures present not just a problem with volume but also with the arrangement and construction of, particularly, the infrastructural systems. Here, small-scale interventions such as the *Paar* system supplemented with a conventional supply may work if a clean surface, soil and rainwater can be assured. Electricity supply using solar power or solar-power heating works when there is no overshadowing and a good all-year supply of light can be found (sunlight is not essential all the time). Natural treatment systems – specifically, constructed wetlands – provide a good and robust solution for the rising waste-water problem in the Philippines. Compared to common treatment facilities, wetlands are lower in cost investment, less costly to maintain and are ideal for densely populated rural or suburban areas.

By 2015, about twenty-six cities in the world are expected to have a population of ten million people or more. To feed a city of this size today, at least 6,000 tonnes of food must be imported each day (to compare, 20,000 tons

Figure 5.22 Shulabh Shauchalaya complex, Delhi. It consists of public paying toilets fronting the road, biogas plants that power the office and a museum which displays the uses of human waste and types of composting toilets. Many Metro stations in Delhi have Shulabh toilets.

Photo: Author.

Figure 5.23 A lamp is lit using biogas (mainly a mixture of methane and carbon dioxide) produced from the Shulabh composting toilets, Delhi.

Photo: Author.

of food are transported to New York City daily, and half of it, in the form of organic waste and sewage, is hauled away). The rest converts to carbon dioxide and greenhouse gases. In 1988, about 25 per cent of the world's poorest were living in urban areas. Today, 56 per cent of such people live in urban areas. The world's urban poor spend much of their income on low-quality food, in many cases more than half of their income. Apart from food, much of their income is taken up by rental payments, sometimes with people signing leases they do not understand. Food then comes on a lower rung of needs. However, even in dense cities, this need not be the only way forward.

In Cuba, there are small organic city gardens numbering almost 7,000.[53] The government, encouraged by the success of the small gardens, converted most of Cuba's large-scale, mono-cropping, export-oriented farming system to an alternative food production system using low-input, sustainable techniques. The Cuban government now states that 50 per cent of the vegetables produced on the island come from urban gardens. By the end of 2000, food availability in Cuba had reached daily levels of calories and protein considered sufficient by the Food and Agriculture Organization (FAO). It is claimed that, in Havana (average population density 2,970 persons per square kilometre (2009 census)), 90 per cent of the city's fresh produce now comes from the 200 local organic urban farms and gardens. By 2003, consumption of diesel fuel was down by more than 50 per cent on 1989 levels, and chemical fertilizers and synthetic insecticide usage were less than 10 per cent of past levels. Bio-pesticides, soil treatments and beneficial insect breeding are being used to protect crops. Scientists and farmers are feeling so successful about their gardens that they claim that, even should the blockade fall, they will not shift their methods back to industrial monoculture. Inspired by Cuba's success, Venezuela is following its lead (Figure 5.24). In the UK, people have had a long tradition of allotment gardening and find ingenious ways to farm in small urban spaces (Figures 5.25 and 5.26).

Even in such a big country as China, which has a one child per family policy, there is a feeding problem because only 12 per cent of the land is arable, less than half of India's (17 per cent according to some scholars).[54] Most of the agricultural land, it appears, is being used for city building and roads. So intensive agriculture is being used in China. Farmers have commonly used 'night soil', a very good fertilizer, for this purpose. However, this is often untreated, a practice which is not recommended by the WHO. However, now, treated urine and faeces are being used to grow corn, rice and bamboo. Urine-diverting toilets separate liquids from solid human waste. In Guangxi province, urine diversion is popular, and also because it has reduced the unsavoury practice of carrying 'night soil'. Rooftop gardening uses urine to grow vegetables, such as tomatoes, cabbages, beans and pumpkins. Treated dried faeces are used in the fields. As urine diversion has become more acceptable, more than 20,000 urine-diverting toilets have been built in the province since 2003, which includes both densely populated rural and urban areas. In addition to China, human waste is being used in Vietnam, the Philippines and India. In some of the island communities, such as Fiji, toilet gardens in homes and schools have been installed. These systems combine the use of urine and faeces as well as grey water in urban gardens. Human waste systems are used

Figure 5.24 Organic gardens, central Caracas. Produce is sold at very low prices to encourage people to eat well.

Photo: Author.

Figure 5.25 Plan A: Selma Gunes, originally from Istanbul, Turkey, planted this kitchen garden in West London from where she gets half of her food in the summer.

Photo: Author.

Figure 5.26 Plan B? A tiny herb garden planted in the street, West London, around a lamp post.

Photo: Author.

in dense parts of Bangladesh for pisciculture. Thus, waste from the city has become a generator of economic growth and food sufficiency in many parts of the world (see case study of organic gardens in Caracas in Chapter 6).

I believe that these examples of Jaisalmer, Curitiba, London and other places have lessons that can be summarized as follows:

- *Start small, think big*

  The success of small projects such as rainwater harvesting using traditional techniques enhanced with modern technology but always keeping in mind the bigger picture, shows that both details and holistic approach count (Figure 5.27). For instance, small-scale, localized power production such as combined heat and power (CHP) not only reduces dependency on centralized systems but can also help reduce waste as it is under the control of a smaller organization. The other way with this idea is to work with larger systems already in place – especially natural ones. So, if the

Fig 5.27 Sheltered housing for the elderly which uses passive heating and rainwater recycling, Copenhagen.

Photo: Author.

climate is windy, use wind power; if you live on slopes, use gravity-fed systems, and so on.

- *Environment, health and wealth*
  The three-way connection between the environment, health and the economic growth of the city is an important part of the process of participatory and integrated design. One part of this triangular relationship influences the others. The sustainable design of rainwater harvesting led the way to better health and employment in the region. Good health from having good sanitation, access to clean water and nutritious food cannot be substituted by vaccinations alone.

- *Involvement of people*
  Participatory design process works better than a top-down approach. The wind farm appears to have failed locally owing to the lack of any participatory process, even though on paper it was an 'environmentally friendly' project. In the Tarun Bharat Sangh project, it was the village elder who pointed out that water supply was a problem, not education. People instinctively know what is required – the development activist has to listen.

- *Re-look at history, learn from the past*
  Traditional knowledge systems, combined with modern technology work best in the new context, as cities grow bigger and denser. It is not an 'all bells and whistles' approach, as the wind farm project shows, but neither is it a return to the past or about rejecting technology. Conventional values should be re-examined and unconventional solutions proposed too, such as the example of Curitiba. Precise and efficient application of technology – whether from the past or present – can be used to solve urban problems.

- *Closing the loop in design and production*
  The closer urban systems come to closing the loop between production and disposal, the cleaner the local environment will become. Using a production system that only creates minimal waste and that is even biodegradable will mean that waste disposal systems can be simplified, and people's health improved. 'Multiform use' would be a good system to use in a world of scarce resources.

- *Lowering vulnerability by diversifying*
  According to Peter Droege, vulnerable communities can be managed by preparing for future risks, urban and regional autonomy by diversifying energy systems, food sources, water supply, places of production and employment.[55] Social and environmental capital are other things that should be protected. Vulnerable populations – the poor, ill, elderly, disabled, infants and the homeless – are more vulnerable to climate change exposure; therefore, the availability of urban infrastructure to cope with such problems is a direct measure of the urban vulnerability of the area.

Discussion points

- Can cities ever be truly 'sustainable' as they grow larger?
- What does the word 'sustainable' mean to you?
- In light of increasing pressure on resources, can traditional technologies have a place in today's cities? Can these work on ever-larger scales? Or do we rethink the way our cities are designed?
- Will passive technologies fare better than active technologies in our attempts to provide more energy or 'save' energy?

Chapter 6

Participatory design for scarce resources and rapid change

'[Poverty] is also characterised by lack of participation in decision-making and in civil, social and cultural life'.[1]

Participation as a methodology

Participatory design can be defined as an approach that attempts to engage everyone in the process to ensure that the designed product or service meets his or her needs. The participatory approach ensures that everyone in the community including women and children can be empowered to transform their environment (Figures 6.1 and 6.2). This approach can be used in software design, urban design, architecture, landscape architecture, product design, sustainability, planning or even medicine as a way of producing designs or products that are more responsive and appropriate to their users' cultural and practical needs. Participation encourages a collaborative process that can be more complex and slow but enriches the end product, which then has more significance to the users. Through participation, the participants can also influence decision making for future projects and strengthen democratic processes. As Sherry Arnstein has argued, citizen participation is ultimately citizen power.[2]

In his essay, 'The architecture of complexity', Lucien Kroll, one of the earliest proponents of participatory design, says in this provocative statement:

> Diversity encourages creativity, while repetition anaesthetizes it. Often architecture is too homogenous, sometimes because of a self-centred desire to see buildings apart from their context, sometimes because of an exaggerated aesthetic commitment, which tends to a precious 'architects' architecture'. But whatever the cause, such homogeneity makes it difficult for the users to add anything of their own, and we lose that rich source of popular creativity, which can transform a space into a place and give it life. If we were able to obtain the space and the means to allow the inhabitants to organize their own buildings, they would by their own efforts generate both the diversity and the close relations to the fabric which is lacking.[3]

Figure 6.1 Women's community action group, Kalyanpuri, East Delhi. This group has been responsible for reinstating toilets in the slum and for women's rights, using the Right to Information (RTI) Act 2005 of India.

Photo: Tatum Lau, University of the Witwatersrand, Johannesburg.

Figure 6.2 Community gardens project, Islington, Ecologic Chartered Architects. Here the community and children came forward to build structures using used cans and bottles.

Photo: Author.

Although participatory design began in the 1970s and participation has existed in design and construction throughout history, it is not yet accepted as a 'mainstream' design methodology. Participatory design is not taught formally at most schools of architecture. A student who attended the participatory design workshop organized at London Metropolitan University in 2010 (Figure 6.3) commented: 'I think it [the workshop] was very effective, I've been involved in community engagement sessions through work but *I've never seen it taught at university*' (emphasis my own). Another student, though having had some experience in participatory design, also echoed this view:

> I learnt the importance of gaining the views of as many stakeholders and not being too influenced by the first one you speak to. I also gained more confidence to do participation in the future, even having done it before.

However, now with more public say in how resources are used, and corporate responsibilities, ethical concerns, scarce resources and environmental issues coming to the forefront, participatory design is seen as the way forward (Figure 6.4).

Games people play

Participatory design activities invariably have to have an element of fun and irreverence, frankness and surprise along with interaction. They range from

Figure 6.3 Participatory design workshop, October 2010, London Metropolitan University. Organised by the author with the Projects Office, London Metropolitan University.

Photo: Steve Blunt.

Figure 6.4 Gaza design workshop, participatory design day organised by the author with the Projects Office and Women's Library, London Metropolitan University, July 2011. This day also included a workshop on Sendai, Japan, see p. 218.

Photo: Steve Blunt.

interviews, debates and discussions to more 'serious' activities such as 'Planning for Real®' where models are used to encourage people to think about solutions and 'planning games' derived from monopoly board games, derivations of flash cards to trigger ideas, drawings, post-it notes, posters, etc. (Figure 6.5). In 2005, the Royal Institute of British Architects through their think-tank, Building Futures, commissioned a new planning game called 'Building Futures'. This was designed by Virtualization Oriented Architecture® (VOA) architects and Spring Graphic Design and aimed at neighbourhood-level planning consultation, although it also came to be used for other things such as transport planning and urban design. While such games offer the people a chance to understand planning issues, I am not convinced that it makes them into planners. It certainly informs and educates but does it make one participate in real terms? One of my postgraduate-level students who used the 'Building Futures' game writes: 'My own frustrations with a game which is so well used, yet *inadequately explained and difficult to grasp* inspired me to research into this essay' (emphasis my own).

Participation with storytelling and plays is also a powerful tool. Augusto Boal started the forum style of theatre, where the affected people play the roles and the audience participates through acting out possible solutions; this is not only participative but also therapeutic for those deeply traumatized by their experience. I have participated in a play put on by Cardboard Citizens,

Figure 6.5 Pop-up Fayre, participatory exercise with the community at Mile End, London.

Photo: Tina Jadav, Diploma Unit 12, London Metropolitan University, 2010.

an organization campaigning for the homeless in London, founded by Adrian Jackson in 1991. It is the UK's only professional theatre company made of the homeless and the displaced, performing in hostels, schools and prisons. For its production in the summer of 2011, it took on the story of the people of the island of Diego Garcia, whose entire population was made homeless on an eviction order by the British government in the 1960s.

There are problems with engagement – the development activist might want to engage in more participation and engagement with the 'client' but the client might not be inclined to do so. As Hasan Fathy observes: 'The Gournis could scarcely discuss the building with us. They were not able put into words even their material requirements in housing; so they were quite incapable of talking about style or the beauty of the house.'[4] Illiteracy or cultural issues may prevent participation of all people in the community, especially women. In my work with participatory and community design, I have often used a range of activities depending upon the situation and people involved.

In a project based in Birmingham, UK, we found that Muslim women did not like 'door knocking' interviews. During meetings, we found that more men and usually the same men were turning up and dominating the discussion. So, instead, we approached the women after they had dropped off their children at the local school and also put up a fun stall with models of the area at the local community fair where families could come with their ideas and questions. I have found that young men and teenagers tend not to want to engage in the usual participatory dialogue. Sometimes, walking around with children or teenagers in an area or building and simply asking them to point out things that matter to them have also worked well in teasing out design issues.

Holding a children's drawing competition or drawing workshops are other ideas I have used to involve families and women. In a memorable participative design exercise with 2–4 year olds, I used drawing and stories to generate ideas for a wildlife garden – most of the ideas were surprisingly practical as well as being creative and innovative (Figure 6.6). In the community garden project described later, held in Venezuela, I used meetings, interviews and a children's drawing workshop to generate ideas (Figure 6.7). I have come to believe more in the real world, rather than in games and tools. In my experience, games and tools used in many participatory exercises can be rather off-putting to those who are illiterate. Simple conversations about their work, life and aspirations work much better as participatory tools.

Participation on a community level

According to Friends of the Earth (FoE), allowing people to participate meaningfully (and politically) in official actions that affect their environment is extremely effective. Through the setting of 'Factory Watch' by FoE, which informed people about polluting factories in the UK, people felt empowered. In April 2005, through the 'Big Ask', fronted by rock band Radiohead's Thom

Figure 6.6 Participatory design workshop for 2–4 year olds, West London, 2006 (courtesy of Ecologic Chartered Architects).

Photo: Author.

Figure 6.7 Community group meeting, San Agustin, Caracas, looking at and commenting on a drawing for a proposed community garden.

Photo: Author.

Yorke, people campaigned effectively to get the climate change bill through in 2006. Of course, NGOs and charities are encouraged to take participative action. However, in the absence of any overseeing mechanism combined with lack of international laws governing their actions, it can be difficult to observe how effective NGOs are in facilitating true empowerment.[5]

Significant actions can be carried out individually by a 'stakeholder' or through a citizen's group – and there are several kinds of citizen's groups around the world. One of the oldest types is the Gram Panchayat of India.[6] Gram Panchayats are literally the self-governing village councils headed by a *Sarpanch* (who could be a man or a woman). In 2002, there were more than 265,000 Panchayats. The elected members of the Gram Panchayat elect from among themselves a *Sarpanch* and a deputy *Sarpanch* for a term of five years. The Panchayat meets twice a year, June and December, to decide on the following matters:

- Development work such as street lights, construction and repair work of the roads in the villages and provision of facilities for sanitation, drinking water, etc.
- Village markets, fairs, festivals and celebrations.
- Registrar of births, deaths and marriages.
- Education and schools.
- Implementing schemes relating to agriculture and animal husbandry.

The main source of income of the Gram Panchayat is the property tax levied on the buildings and the open spaces within the village. In 1996, the Dr S.B. Sen committee suggested the following broad principles of local governance:

- Subsidiarity – actions taken by the smallest, lowest or least centralized competent authority.
- Democratic decentralization of power.
- Delineation and delegation of functions.
- Convergence and agreement.
  Convergent participation is a collaborative process in which raters negotiate an evaluation on several dimensions of quality.[7] After an initial individual evaluation phase, raters meet to compare and discuss their assessments. A moderator selects and prioritizes the items (quality dimensions) so that those showing the greatest disagreement are discussed first. The evaluators may alter their individual ratings and comments as the meeting proceeds.
- Citizen-centred actions.

However, even Panchayats can be sometimes hopelessly mired in nepotism and corruption as shown in the case study of wind farms in Jaisalmer (Chapter 5).

Some citizens' groups may be set up by the government (sometimes Gram Panchayats are also set up by the government). Since 1998 in Venezuela, the 'Consejo comunale' (community councils) have been set up by the government with similar goals as the Panchayats. However, there is critical disagreement about whether these councils achieve similar levels of participation and empowerment. In my experience, the two organizations were not necessarily equal in their access to the community, especially in decision making and technical help (see case study of Caracas community gardens later in the chapter).

An alternate model for Venezuela is the Centro Ciudades de la Gente (Centre for People in the City), evolved from a research group to a community action group. This group, Redsca (Red Solidaria de comunales autonomas; note 'red' means network in Spanish, not political allegiance), set up in 2005 by Professor Teolinda Bolivar, architect and planner, consists of professionals such as engineers and architects as well as local community leaders. The group, working in Caracas' biggest squatter settlement, Petare, meets once a week to discuss community issues and development work (Figure 6.8). In terms of Nabeel Hamdi's model of the development activist providing technical support, this appears to be a more enlightened way of working participatively. According to Hamdi, participative design is not about abrogating responsibility, but instead, 'taking responsibility with authority'.[8]

Figure 6.8 A meeting of Centro Ciudades de la Gente, in Barrio Julian Blanco, Caracas, 2009.

Photo: Author.

True participative action

Many people fear participative design, believing that it is another way of 'designing by committee', therefore time consuming and sometimes inconclusive and weak. In order to appease people, however, consultation or even provision of information classified as consultation is pseudo participation or 'tokenism', according to Sherry Arnstein.[9] True participation is about equal participation and trust – the stakeholders need to feel in control of their environment and how they design and build it. Community architecture is participative design, according to Peter Blundell-Jones.[10] And Jeremy Till is even more conclusive – he defines the architect as the 'possessor of knowledge' and therefore able to facilitate the process of design.[11] In the book, *On Being Human*, Guy Bourgeault gives us three models of medical professionals working with patients that can be adapted for development activists: the paternalist – a person to whom we surrender our authority; the expert – where the client is treated in isolated intervention; and finally, the Partnership model – where the 'expert' and the 'client' work together.[12] In participatory design for vulnerable clients, the ideal combination would be 25 per cent of the expert model and 75 per cent of the partnership model.

Sometimes, participation can be skilfully (and unscrupulously) used to move people towards a set goal – Robert Chambers, from the Institute of Development Studies, Brighton, calls it 'Facipulation' from a combination of the words facilitation plus manipulation. I remember listening to a well-known British architect who told me that he always drinks with the 'locals' in the pub and then it becomes easier to persuade them to use his designs. I have seen such methods used by others in their overseas work where under the guise of 'cultural interaction', designs or concepts are thrust upon an unsuspecting community. At other times, participation in the form of consultation is merely a cloak for a decision that has been taken at government level when, despite people's objections, projects get the go-ahead. In May 2011, for example, the UK government granted planning permission for 25,000 tonnes of soil and rubble from old nuclear power stations to be stored in King's Cliffe near Peterborough. This happened despite strong opposition, where 98 per cent of the local people voted in a referendum against this scheme. Local planning permission from Northamptonshire County Council had also been denied for the project.[13]

From my experience, I believe that participation is about the following issues that are interconnected:

- *Responsibility*: each stakeholder takes responsibility for his or her actions in the process.
- *Authority*: someone has to take a facilitative action to make sure everyone is engaged; this is usually the architect, designer, engineer or the community representative – otherwise called the development activist.

- *Sustainability*: the solution proposed has to be sustainable in the long term – environmentally, socially and culturally.
- *Accountability*: along with responsibility and sustainability (long-term vision) comes accountability. That stakeholders are accountable for the project makes them aware of long-term implications, unlike buildings designed by someone who does not live there or has no engagement with the community.
- *Locality*: we must not forget that communities and people are based in a place that has specific characteristics. The context again gives rise to a sense of responsibility, accountability and sustainability.

Further, participatory work must involve dialogue and ethics. Dialogue is a necessary element of participation. All people must be given the chance to speak, although all suggestions cannot be used. The reasons for accepting or rejecting a suggestion in the participatory process must be explained at some point, otherwise people feel disheartened and disengaged from the process of participation. In my experience, conducting meaningful dialogue with a purpose and responsibility is a skill that the development activist must have. In some communities, owing to religious and social reasons, it can be difficult to engage all members of the community. These include women, children and the community elders and, in some countries, the socially excluded classes such as tribal people or aborigines or the lower castes (as in India).

As mentioned earlier, trust between parties is an essential part of this dialogue. The facilitator must always be on the lookout for people who are not engaging and try their best to draw them in. Often the body language of someone betrays a lack of trust or engagement in the process. It is the work of the development activist to draw such people in. Often I have observed that the person leading the discussion becomes so engrossed with the more vocal members of the group that sometimes they do not notice what is going on with other members. A skilled facilitator draws back and lets the dialogue happen naturally, with the mildest of prompting (Figure 6.9).

Dialogue is important not only throughout the process but also at the end. Some issues come out at the end and especially, as the facilitator may not always be resident in the community, it is important that there is a closure and that feelings are discussed. In the work with a community in San Agustin, Caracas, Venezuela, a skilled facilitator as well as a team of psychologists were used for a sensitive project. Sitting at one of the discussions later on, I observed how the members of the community group were able to talk about issues that made them angry, and the air was cleared. Robert Chambers talks about 'democracy of the ground' where participants, through the simple action of sitting together on the ground, are placed physically on an equal footing, thereby no one can dominate the other (Figure 6.10).

Figure 6.9 A skilled facilitator is required at meetings, San Agustín Community group meeting, November 2010. Can you spot if anyone is feeling uncomfortable here?

Photo: Author.

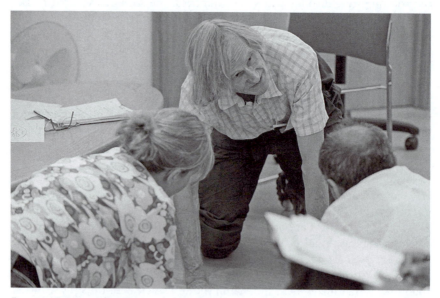

Figure 6.10 Robert Chambers demonstrates 'democracy of the ground' at the participatory design day, July 2011, London Metropolitan University. Organised by the author with the Projects Office and Women's Library, London Metropolitan University.

Photo: Steve Blunt.

Ethics and participation

Dealing with people who have no perceived power can make a development activist feel powerful (more on the subject of ethics is discussed in Chapter 7). However, the point of participation is the empowerment of the people to carry forward the project without needing an 'expert' all the time. An ethical and equal exchange can take place when both sides feel empowered. Being honest, explaining the purpose of the participative process to everyone and letting them know the results of the process – all are part of participation. A paper from the International Institute for Environment and Development offers simple and direct advice on ethics and participation:

Ethics
In relation to interactions with communities, we strive to:
- achieve mutual respect, including a commitment to long-term partnerships;
- be honest with ourselves about our own objectives; and
- be open, honest and transparent about our objectives with all community sections.

Equity
We recognize that:
- Different groups, as defined locally by age, gender, well being, ethnicity, religion, caste, language, etc. have different perspectives.
- There should be commitment by outside organizations to understand different needs and multiple perspectives within communities.
- Responding to the needs of the vulnerable involves respect for all groups. This may mean challenging asymmetrical relationships via conflict resolution methods.
- Timing and pace should be governed by local context of separate sections of the community.
- Information is generated by local people and so ask their permission to document, remove and use information. When possible, ensure that original diagrams and copies of reports remain in the community.[14]

The five Ps of participatory design

1 People: What do people want?

People are the most important part of the process and what they want is the key issue for participative action. Participative action is not top down and not about coming in with solutions and ideas – these are to be generated within the community. As Nabeel Hamdi says, 'Do not bring issues that do not engage the people'.[15] We saw in Chapter 5 how the school in Rajasthan, India, could not function because it was not what the people wanted – they wanted water, not education. In her book *Slumming India*, Gita Verma describes a couple of award-winning projects in India that were at best incomplete and at worst, faulty because they did not engage with real issues.[16]

When working with illiterate people, talking is often the way to consult. However, official reports and scientific references do not give much credence to oral testimonies, anecdotal evidence or dialogue. Nigel Cross says:

> The problem facing those who give weight to indigenous knowledge is that they come face to face with the weight, indeed might, of the multilateral and bilateral aid business with its armies of highly qualified agronomists and economists with its satellites, laboratories and computers. Oral testimony is regarded as anecdotal, even endearing.[17]

From foreign funding bodies to NGOs, organizations that do not use participative action based on equality and respect may be in danger of imposing projects that do not engage the people.

2 Place: the local environment – context, climate and culture

The place or the context of the project brings unique characteristics to the final design. The microclimate, the natural environment, culture and site shape the people and the project – again an outsider would not understand the subtle nuances unless they are actively engaged and present. Design by fax and computer do not work here. The work of the armchair architect and the development activist differ in the sense that active participation not only with the people but also with their environment is required.

There are organizations and architects who design the project in their offices and bring it to the site and local contractors carry out the building work. In many pro bono projects and some educational institutions where 'development practice' is taught, this becomes a practical and financial necessity. The people are grateful for the work done for them, so they do not want to question for fear of sounding ungrateful and, even worse, cutting off further funding for projects. However, to work as much as possible in the 'place' should be the aim of the development activist.

3 Project: how does the project engage and benefit the people?

The project must not only engage people in the participative design but also in the benefits associated with it. Again, the example of the wind turbines in Chapter 5 that did not benefit the local people and were constructed without consultation or participation is a good example of how even eco-friendly projects can fail. Engagement here means not only for the present but also for the future.

> The major risk in participatory planning is that any failure in the implementation of a project results in disinterest among the community which in turn shuts down any possibility of further participatory planning process with the community. The participatory planning process should try to focus on those issues, which can be solved with the available resources and gain the confidence of the community. Therefore, the key factor for successful participatory planning is to build a relationship of mutual trust and then start the planning.
>
> (Kurian Thomas, a planner involved in participatory planning in Kerala, India)[18]

4 Politics and power

Politics and power play present the most important case for why sometimes, despite public participation, projects do not succeed in getting built. As an example from personal experience, my award-winning project in West Bengal, which received great local support, remains unbuilt owing to the power play between the local and central governments, which are from different political parties. Palestine and Israel present an example where the political conflicts are affecting ordinary people and sustainable projects (Figure 6.11). During a visit to Palestine and Israel in 2011, I learned not only more about the politics of water and electricity management but also about the issue of stone quarrying which is described in detail in Chapter 4. Participation can be difficult in such extreme political situations, where different parties may refuse to talk to each other.

5 Participating actively and effectively

Often participation fails, owing ironically to equal importance being given to all. While this may sound undemocratic, in my experience, not all participants come with equal interest and fairness in the process of participation. Giving each and every suggestion equal importance also does not work – value and priority has to be assigned to each and some ideas may have to be discarded. Not everyone is going to be happy with the consultation and participative process – some may feel hard done by. However, the best ideas have to be used, because compromise is not the solution. The development activist, whether an architect, engineer or community facilitator, has to take a leading role in drawing out the best from everyone involved in the process. This is a highly skilled process, involving dialogue, discretion and discrimination. The role of the development activist is to arrive at a solution, using the skills of every participant within a given constraint of time and finances.

Figure 6.11 Category C land – a no-man's-land, overlooked by the Israeli settlement village of Jaba, East Jerusalem, Palestine.

Photo: Author.

Participation: ending, starting and ending …

The participatory process has come a long way from its origins in the 1970s in Scandinavia. Needless to say, participation has existed in all forms of design in one way or another in the architect–client interaction. However, when it comes to designing for vulnerable communities in areas of complexity and chaos, it takes on a greater significance. There are problems too. The concept of 'pseudo participation', where the architect takes on the role of a facilitator to ingratiate themselves with the community and then apply their design regardless of the community feelings, is common. There are other motives too – such as a practice that carries out pro bono work overseas in the hope that such actions will generate fee-paying work.

There are other problems too. Another issue that crops up frequently in overseas work is that of corruption and use of money as agreed. How the money is used and whether the building is carried out in a satisfactory manner are thorny issues. Often the development activist may not be able to stay on for the whole of the designing and building process, leaving the rest to the community. There is a problem with identifying true stakeholders – at present, anyone who writes in regarding the project can be considered a stakeholder. Thus anyone with a hidden agenda or bias can enter the debate and may be able to influence the outcome. The issue of time required for the participatory process when in an emergency situation is also of great importance to the development activist. Quick action is required in such work and measures are short term, mostly without consultation. However, participation in terms of counselling and healing for a community broken by disaster is the best first step, leading to empowerment and eventually solutions.

I propose a way of working with communities that embraces the following aspects, which I call the tools of negotiation. These tools are similar to those recommended in the Harvard Business School and used in international negotiations. However, more than that, these are basic and common sense pointers that can be used by anyone. The last point is derived from the theory of 'value creation' proposed by the twentieth-century Buddhist philosopher, Tsunesaburo Makiguchi, who substituted truth with 'benefit' as a value – this has been already elaborated in Chapter 1. Although not appreciated in his lifetime, this has become very important and commonplace in marketing today. I use the word 'value' to denote the aspects of beauty, good and gain together as the goal to aim for in negotiation in the participatory process. These tools (of negotiation) are:

- mutual respect for all parties;
- focusing on common interests, not personalities;
- using objective criteria and hard facts;
- creating value for all, not just individual benefits.

In the end, the question of where the facilitation ends and true participation begins is a complex one and unique to each situation. I remember a particular conversation with someone about whether the people in the community were beneficiaries or participants at a particular stage. As designers and even facilitators, one can feel 'possessive' of the design and even the ideas generated and it can be difficult to let go. Sometimes the plight of the community is so desperate that the development activist can feel overwhelmed and emotional – this may be the case when one visits poor communities or those in disaster situations. On another note, it has often been suggested to me that participation is a 'feminine' process for women to facilitate and engage in. Having observed and taken part in participatory processes all over the world with both men and women, I disagree. This image of participation as a 'feminine way of working' is not easy to shake off, however, and there are times when men have been reluctant to come forward for meetings. However, once they have attended, they realize it is for everyone. I think this is the message we need to carry forward. I will end with Robert Chambers' guidelines for participation given at the participatory design day in July 2011:

- introduce yourself;
- unlearn;
- ask 'them';
- believe that they can do it;

- hand over the 'stick' (i.e. authority);
- embrace error;
- relax, don't rush;
- be nice to people;
- sit down, listen, watch and learn;
- use your best judgement at all times;
- challenge!!

Case studies

Freehouse project by Jeanne Van Heeswijk, Rotterdam

I met Jeanne in Rotterdam where she started and runs the Freehouse project. It is a forum for creating space, both literally and metaphorically, for encounters between local entrepreneurs, young people, local residents, artists and designers to exchange knowledge, experience and ideas. The linking of economic and cultural capital in a form of co-production reinforces the economic position of the parties involved and makes visible the cultural process of devising and implementing new products. Freehouse, or *Freihaus*, draws its inspiration from a model with medieval origins, which offered space to groups of outsiders active in alternative economies. I saw small actions of defiance and humour that allowed the community to take control of the space in their area – a good example is the use of boxes that can quickly become seats because the local law discourages seating areas on the pavement (Figure 6.12).

The Afrikaander Market, whose 300 or so stalls offer the most exotic range of produce to be found in Rotterdam, had been in decline for several years. To accentuate the culturally diverse and small-scale character that distinguishes the Afrikaander district and its market from the surrounding districts, Freehouse and Kosmopolis Rotterdam put together entrepreneurs, residents, market traders, cultural producers, social service organizations and policy makers in the roles of co-producers in the field of cultural entrepreneurship. The needs, wishes and insights of all the stakeholders and the different forms of capital (economic, social and cultural) in the district were made visible each week by means of a series of small-scale interventions in which possible innovations could be tested. Some of these innovations include:

- *Afrikaander market*
  In 2008–9 the Freehouse model was applied in Rotterdam South to give a boost to the Afrikaander district so that the people who live there could share in the economic benefits of the redevelopment; a detailed live sketch of the ideal market of the future, devoting more attention to goods and services, cultural expression, new market stalls and a renewed market organization, as well as a considerable rearrangement of the available space.

Figure 6.12 Upturned boxes used for seating in a café run by Kosovan refugees and quickly removed during visits by the police. The café had been refurbished attractively by architects, Afrikaanderwijk, South Rotterdam.

Photo: Author.

- *Branch selection*
  Themed areas were introduced to expand the range, to achieve a quality balance and to trim back on the market glut of cheap textiles and vegetables. The themed areas mean extra attention can be paid to the linking of products, related services and functions.

- *Market assortment*
  The one-sided assortment was expanded with higher quality products within the existing stalls and new stalls with biological products.

- *Presentation*
  An attractive presentation of products can lead to increased sales. During 'Tomorrow's Market' extra attention was paid to improved presentation on a stall, encouraged by using the expertise of stylists and designers.

- *Local production*

  The designer Cindy van den Bremen and women in local sewing and hand-icraft groups make clothing and accessories using fabric and haberdashery supplied by the Afrikaander market. These 'Suit Yourself' products are sold at a Freehouse stall run by the women themselves (Figure 6.13). The food designer, Debra Solomon, and local catering entrepreneurs are developing a collective local restaurant with an international menu. The ingredients for 'Lucky Mi Fortune Cooking' are bought locally and local entrepreneurs are challenged to use their skills to expand the range, from the production of ginger beer to a Turkish deep fried meat snack.

- *New market stalls*

  To enhance the presentation and retail opportunities, Dré Wapenaar and Jeroen Kooijmans/Hugo Timmermans designed new prototypes of mar-ket stalls that will influence the future organization of the market. The stalls can be opened and closed and combined to form, for example, a roofed terrace.

- *Amenities and services*

  Co-productions of amenities and/or services in combination with products were given tangible form in, for example, a demonstration of headscarf knots by a group of women entrepreneurs at a stall selling scarves. A sew-ing and repair service was added to a second-hand clothes stall.

Figure 6.13 Shop selling clothes designed and made by Turkish refugees, Afrikaanderwijk, South Rotterdam. Situated near the docks of Rotterdam, here is one of the largest concentration of immigrants in the Netherlands.

Photo: Author.

El Shanti project, Caracas, Venezuela

This was a participatory project undertaken with a local community based in Caracas, Venezuela (Figure 6.14). The various parties to the project included the San Agustin Community Group; a UK-based architecture practice, Ecologic; a UK-based charity, Charushila; and local administration and organizations based in Caracas, Venezuela. It also included cooperation with a local artist, Natalya Critchley, who organized a drawing workshop with children, specifically to find ideas for the design. *Shanti* is a Sanskrit word meaning peace and *el* is the Spanish for 'the' – the aim of the project being community unity and peace through the making of the garden. This was achieved specifically through examining and working on the following aspects:

- *Locally produced food that is healthy and fresh*
  Residents of *barrios* do not have convenient access to fresh foods. As mentioned before, the long journey to city shops and the physical strength required to haul the shopping up or down the equivalent of several storeys, necessitate the use of more 'long-lasting' food such as chemically preserved foods – dried and canned. In the long term this is not a healthy choice. People are dependent upon getting food from the city, two-thirds of which, according to some reports, is imported, some of very poor quality. Small-scale food production in *barrios* will go some way to make people self-sufficient.

Figure 6.14 The El Shanti community garden project, Barrio San Agustin, Caracas, 2010.

Photo: Natalya Critchley.

- *Organic and low-cost production*
  Using techniques learned from the organic farm in the city centre of Caracas, the garden could become a valuable community resource (Figure 6.15). The techniques of using green fertilizers and horse manure for the garden can be very effective and low cost. The community group went to see the organic gardens during the process of consultation and the consultants from the gardens came to visit the community during the works.

- *Ownership and maintenance by the community*
  There is a sense of not just physical ownership of the garden but an ongoing relationship with the garden through building it, maintaining and using it. This is very hands-on ownership. A person working with the community reports that when she asked the community to speak at a presentation about the garden, they were 'really chuffed'.

- *Use of rubble and other waste material that could otherwise be a safety and environmental hazard*
  A lot of building material was left on the site after the demolition of homes when the Metrocable (public transport consisting of a cable car

Figure 6.15 Organic gardens, central Caracas.

Photo: Author.

system) was built. This rubble adds another potential hazard in a landslip area, so using the materials was a prime consideration in the garden. We conceived the idea of wrapping the rubble in chicken wire mesh – the rubble tortilla as it came to be called – and creating planters with such units (Figure 6.16). Further, owing to the location of the garden, it is difficult to access it to remove the demolished materials, and it cannot be taken on the Metrocable. So again, the use of the material is also a necessity. Also, in a country where there is hardly any recycling, let alone the reuse of demolished materials, this was a big step forward. The use of recycled materials, the interest in the various rare medicinal plants that were found on site and the community were useful for consolidating the overall ecotourism project for the area.

- *Slope and soil stabilization*
  Use of demolished materials using a gabion construction can help in stabilizing the soil and slopes in the landslip area. Further planting will also help in this aspect.

Figure 6.16 A rubble tortilla, El Shanti project, Barrio San Agustin, Caracas, 2010.

Photo: Author.

- *Creating a space for the community to relax and play*
  There are not many areas for relaxation and play areas for children apart from the streets in the *barrios*. The garden is a flat piece of land, easily accessible by Metrocable and on foot. Using this piece of land reclaims it from various youth gangs who had begun to use it for more nefarious activities, and it is also useful for community activity for the elderly that enhances mobility and relaxation (hence raised beds).

- *Raising self-esteem and providing community unity*
  An area that the community helps to develop and take forward as collective owners can only raise the self-esteem of the community. It also provides a focus for unity in the *barrio* where there is violence and disagreements. The reclamation of wasteland for the community also helps in engendering unity and providing a focus for ownership of the land. Taking ownership of the space also helps in community empowerment.

Building the garden was not an easy project (Figure 6.17). Apart from people (especially the men) not turning up for meetings or for work, which remained an issue throughout, the weather was totally against building work. It rained heavily throughout with thunderstorms and landslides. The women were committed to the project despite the violence around them, even when

Figure 6.17 Completed planter, San Agustin community gardens, Caracas, November 2010.
Photo: Author.

they were not paid their salaries, owing to an industrial dispute. Some of the helpers had to go and work on another assignment so days were lost.

The children's drawing workshop attracted twenty-six children and produced some lovely drawings, some using stones and leaves from the site (Figure 6.18). The ideas so generated proved to be a catalyst for the garden design. The community even changed the design themselves, showing themselves to be equal partners. More work is to be carried out in consultation with the community, especially after the landslides. The last community discussion meeting was facilitated by supervisors from Odebrecht, a Brazilian building company who were also builders of the Metrocable, and the Faculty of Psychology, Central University of Venezuela (UCV). At this meeting, significant differences amongst the community emerged – such as the commitment shown by various people involved, the lack of men and youth in the participative process, and the violence in the community. The meeting, however, ended on a positive note with promises and optimistic thoughts; and, as I understand it, continues to be taken forward by the community.

Figure 6.18 Children's painting workshop, La Ceiba Metrocable station, Barrio San Agustin, Caracas, November 2010.

Photo: Author.

Discussion points

- How do we know when beneficiaries become participatory colleagues?
- Is participation necessary in designing? Is it really needed?
- How can we facilitate participatory discussion when people seem reluctant to engage?
- How can we keep participation going within the community when we are not able to be physically present?

Part III

The soft city and the development activist

Chapter 7

Culture, ethics and other travelling discomforts

'I want to dress like a Red Indian'.
(Request from an MA architecture student from Bangladesh to his Venezuelan host[1])

With this remark made with a childlike ignorance, I do not think that this student had any idea of what can of cultural worms he was opening up – racism, imperialism and political incorrectness. Not just students, I find that many architects' work or writing have a limited sense of culture and is mostly Western based.[2] To illustrate, here is one example. I was talking to colleagues and invited external critics at the end of the celebration (open) day for the course I teach. One of them asked me, 'Have you ever been to a crit? You know, when students put up their work and external critics comment on them.' Rendered speechless, I searched my mind for a reason for his question and how best to respond – had he wanted a 'crit style' presentation that afternoon? Did he think I was a student (a common experience for me)? Was he thrown by the Indian sari I was wearing at a London University? A colleague came to my rescue: 'Sumita is the course leader.' The questioner persisted: 'If you had studied architecture, then you would have known what a crit is.' My helpful colleague who was by then equally puzzled, pitched in: 'But Sumita is a practising architect.' 'Ahh,' said the external critic, 'I thought you were a sociologist, the way you were talking.'

Do architects need to think about social and cultural issues? According to Samuel Mockbee of the Rural Studio, 'Architecture, more than any art form, is a social art and must rest on the social and cultural base of its time and place.' He even insists, 'As a social art, architecture must be made where it is and out of what exists there.'[3] However, cultural and socio-economic issues are not taught specifically in architecture schools in the UK,[4] and students often finish without having any clue as to how to talk to any kind of client, let alone a client in a vulnerable situation. The cultural artefacts and decorations, symbols, heroes and rituals are the intangible aspects of a culture and remain with the community should bigger manifestations such as buildings be destroyed in a disaster. These then can be carried and transferred to another place, as commonly happens with migrating people. Symbols, heroes and rituals are what migrants and immigrants bring with them when they come to live or work in the city.

Culture is not a static thing. 'That which may be quite right and natural in one cultural environment can easily be wrong in another; what is fitting and proper in one generation becomes ridiculous in the next when people have acquired new tastes and habits,' says Steen Eiler Rasmussen.[5] Culture is always present, always changing – a living thing, the part of people and the artefacts they make and use – including the architecture and the client.

In the present academic syllabus in Britain, there is lack of study of architectural traditions and cultures, other than European ones. Students taught using Euro-centric syllabus useing iconic Western buildings as examples, will have difficulty understanding the pluralistic approach needed for working in a 'non-European' context (although many students are now travelling further and thus this knowledge gap is being closed through their own efforts). Students and architects are working abroad or alongside colleagues from diverse backgrounds.[6] Although the intake of non-white and foreign students has increased within the UK, the numbers in the profession have not increased proportionally. The RIBA study 'Why Women leave Architecture' (2003) and the Commission for Architecture and the Built Environment (CABE) research into 'Architecture and Race: the Experience of Minority Ethnic Students in Architecture' (2004) (I was in the steering committees of both), included the following conclusions: 'a lack of diversity in teaching and learning methods; in learning resources; and in role models, contributes to problems of retention and erosion amongst women and [Black and Minority Ethnic] architecture students in UK universities; and traditional studio teaching and learning cultures, and methods of design criticism, are failing to address the learning needs of the diverse range of students who now study architecture in UK universities.'

The global impact of the image of architecture, which is now largely uniform and Western, is difficult to imagine from a school of architecture but very visible when one travels abroad. Like biodiversity, diversity of architectural styles is being lost. Architects trained in modernist architecture may see decorations and symbols in vernacular traditions as something to ignore while admiring the clean lines of its simple form or functional design. Paul Oliver writes: 'For many architects, the issue of decoration on vernacular architecture remains a source of discomfort, if not criminality.'[7] Non-Western architecture, symbols and designs are treated like a strange exotic thing – embraced in fashion and music but not in buildings.

Cultural differences manifest themselves in different ways and levels of depth. Symbols can be words, gestures, pictures or objects that carry a particular meaning, which is recognized by those who share a particular culture. New symbols develop while old ones disappear. Others may copy symbols of one particular group or use similar forms with different meanings. This is why symbols can represent the different things despite having similar forms, like the 'Golden arches' and the Islamic arch. But symbols can be universal too – recognizable by all as part of popular and current culture (Figure 7.1). According to Thomas Friedman,[8] the World Wide Web is the 'symbol' of globalization, even though it is a 'non-physical' presence.

The core of a culture is informed by values. Values, often derived from religious or spiritual beliefs are the way certain aspects are perceived, such as good–evil, right–wrong, natural–unnatural. Values are often a 'given', may change in time and sometimes people from outside the community cannot directly perceive them. Sometimes, values can be inferred from observing the way people act in different circumstances. For although the issue can be the same, different societies (at different times) have different ways of dealing with core values. This affects the way spaces are used. While designers may have designated spaces for formal buildings such as schools, housing and offices, in the informal and formal areas we find space set aside for shrines, temples, memorials – these are part of the culture of that place and yet are often not given any thought or space. However, this is the value of that particular part of the culture as designated by the space in a particular spot – the 'space-value'. The development activist needs to understand the 'space-values' of a particular society and 'design' or allow for such spaces, using participation and sensitivity. The value system espoused by Tsunesaburo Makiguchi of beauty, goodness and benefit can embrace values from different cultures

Figure 7.1 Global symbol of food bows to local culture – Russell Maddicks talks about 'MacArepas', a derivation of popular Venezuelan street food by MacDonald's. According to the architect, Robert Adams, architecture has also been 'MacDonaldized' – what do you think? Bolivar Hall, London, July 2011.

Photo: Author.

and economic strata. According to Paul Oliver, 'buildings may embody in expressive ways the qualities that we relate to our value system [which may be closely bound with our religious convictions and practices].'[9]

Cultures have heroes and villains who personify values. Heroes can be from the past or present, real or fictitious, positive – such as Rama from the Indian Epic, Ramayana. On the opposite scale, are the villains, who embody what a particular culture terms as bad characteristics, namely Ravana, from the same epic. In the modern context, these heroes are very important as usually, they may have political significance and influence and references to them should be treated in a respectful and delicate manner in dealings with a particular group. Heroes can also be a collection of values they embody – the brave, the brash groundbreakers, the innovative (the good) vs. the bad who are the dinosaurs, the timid or the old fogies. As Richard Wilson puts it:

> The young, genius visionary has a radical new idea that's going to transform the world – but the old fogies just don't get it. He is Galileo, Georges Danton, Bob Dylan, Jesus Christ, Albert Einstein, Charles Darwin, and Richard Branson. They are the Pope, Louis XVI, the Pharisees, those other scientists, British Airways, and Richard Nixon … He is Captain Kirk, boldly going where no man has gone before. He is Evel Knievel, Elvis and Batman. They don't understand that they must innovate or die. They don't understand that kids just wanna rock.[10]

This can be seen in the worlds of architecture and construction too with very strong divided camps of style and innovation.

Rituals are collective social activities. They are carried out most of the times almost without thinking; for example, ways of greeting ('How are you?' is a common one even when one is not really interested in the answer), paying respect to others (touching the feet of elders in India), religious and social ceremonies, etc. These may extend into spatial expression by the requirement of space set aside for the particular ritual, such as a space for leaving shoes outside a mosque. Cultural rituals are part of the observed phenomenon and most do not have any scientific or logical explanation, such as 'detox' or fasting (Figure 7.2). Ben Goldacre, in his book *Bad Science*, says:

> Because it has no scientific meaning, detox is much better understood as a cultural product. In some respects, how much you buy into this reflects how self-dramatizing you want to be; or in less damning terms, how much you enjoy ritual in your daily life.[11]

However, for the development activist, the use of symbols, the naming of heroes and rituals in a particular culture has special significance in relation to use of space. In India, we observed particular rituals that shopkeepers

Figure 7.2 A ritual or science? Various coverings for toilets and even toilet paper, very popular in squatter settlements, Caracas.

Photo: Author.

partake in before opening their shops. The pavements outside, where some of the rituals take place, become an appropriation of space (Figure 7.3). Alpona, the Bengali decorative art for walls and floors, is both a ritual and a symbol of that culture.[12] However, most new housing designs in Bengal do not allow space for such activities. Buildings not only embody our cultural aspirations but also can be an extension of our temporal and spatial patterns through the symbols and rituals they carry.[13] Feng Shui (Chinese) and Vashtu Shashtra (from India) are rituals that specify where and how a building may be built. They have no scientific basis and yet are vital to the community's culture (Figure 7.4).

According to UNESCO, 'languages are essential to the identity of groups and individuals' and to 'their peaceful co-existence and are of utmost importance in achieving the Millennium Development goals' (MDG).[14] Ten languages die out each year according to UNESCO.[15] 2008 was designated the year of languages. Only 300 languages have one million speakers – these are considered 'healthy languages'. Just three – Mandarin, English and Spanish – are the most widely spoken of the 7,000 different languages in the world. Language has become a tool in reclaiming the past, a cultural heritage or reversing historical acts. In India, Bombay has become Mumbai, Poona is Pune and Calcutta is now Kolkata. I visited Hong Kong to document street names, parks and metro stations (some of which come from my husband's

Figure 7.3 Appropriated space from a pavement next to a community park for religious activities, New Delhi.

Photo: Author.

Figure 7.4 Vishwakarma, the Hindu god of architects, on the construction site of an eco-friendly office for Development Alternatives designed by Ashok Lall Associates, New Delhi. Builders worship the god before starting work on any building project in India and space and time must be given to this ritual.

Photo: Author.

family who are partly Armenian) and have now changed to Chinese names after the takeover by China in 1996. Street names have been changed in former Yugoslavia and other places. In other places, revival of languages such as Welsh in Wales is part of reclaiming a heritage.

Naming names as I described in Chapter 1 (third world, developing, industrialised, etc.) have a cultural impact, which goes deeper than just their literal meaning. Even words such as 'compassion' have different cultural contexts. In an article, Rabbi Jeffrey Newman, Director of the Earth Charter, UK, describes how despite two years of negotiation, this word was not acceptable in a draft principle about treating all creatures with compassion. The Inuits along with groups from sub-Arctic and Southern Africa, who depended upon hunting for survival, argued that hunting with compassion was not possible. Eventually this was resolved by moving the word compassion to another principle.[16]

'Macaulay's Children' or Macaulayism is a pejorative term used to refer to Indians who adopt Western culture and language (Figure 7.5). Lord Babbington Macaulay after whom this term originates and who introduced English as the language for Indian education in the 1830s, would have been pleased to see how well the English speakers of India are doing now.[17] Gandhi believed that Macaulay's intention was 'sincere'[18] but debates still rage about Macaulay. While many Indians believe it to be about superficial things such as clothes or accents, I believe that Macaulayism survives more substantially in the way Western ideas and culture are seen as being automatically superior. This results in 'Western architects' being given commissions in India when they hardly

Figure 7.5 The Englishman as a figure of ridicule, from a street dance performed at a popular shopping centre, Delhi.

Photo: James Jordan.

know the culture or place. Jockin Arputham, founder of the Slum Dwellers International, told me that learning about the culture of the place is essential to working there.[19] Language is a part of communication and talking is just a small part of that, while body language or non-verbal language is the major part of communication – some believe it to be as much as 70 per cent. I have travelled to thirty-five different countries but I don't speak thirty-five languages. For the development activist who is working for a short time in a place, it is best to be courteous, pleasant and at least know some basic local language, cultural traditions and gestures while working closely with a local translator. For long-term work though, it is essential to learn the language.

Cultural determinism

> Yet the evidence suggests that, regardless of our cultural background, many of us will blithely electrocute another human being if a man in a white coat tells us to, or commit gross acts of torture and humiliation if we think we can get away with it.
>
> (Richard Wilson, 2008, *Don't Get Fooled Again*)

The position that the ideas, meanings, beliefs and values people learn as members of society determine human nature is termed 'cultural determinism'. There is also a term specifically for architecture – architectural determinism. Cultural determinism proposes that cultural values can be changed externally. Architectural determinism proposes that given the right kind of houses, schools, libraries and even prison, persons can change for the better. Optimistic visions of cultural determinism place no limits on the abilities of human beings to do or be whatever they want, given the right circumstances. This view expects a person to take responsibility for their choices and behaviour.

The opposite view is that people are what they are conditioned to be; their behaviour and choices are something over which they have no control. This view holds that nature is more important than nurture. This explanation leads to behaviourism that states that the causes of human behaviour are beyond human control. Some anthropologists suggest that there is no universal way of being human. What is seen as acceptable in one culture may be not acceptable in another. I had an insight into delicacy of negotiating culture and personal issues while attending a conference about Venezuela in London. Two of the main speakers – one English and another one from Venezuela – were both late. The conference started twenty-five minutes late due to this. The Chilean organizer apologized for the 'small delay' while the English lady chairing that session apologized for the 'rather late start' and made several curt references to the delay caused by the English speaker (a well-known British MP) during that time.

Mark Tully, the BBC journalist, who has made India his home, believes that the legacy of British and Western cultural imperialism has left its mark on the Indian middle class or what he calls the 'English-speaking elite'. As someone living in India, he perceives the caste system very differently from those on fleeting visits or those reading or hearing about it from the 'elite Indians'. He says:

> It would lead to greater respect for India's culture, and indeed a better understanding of it, if it were recognized that the caste system has never been totally static, that it is adapting itself to today's changing circumstances and that it has positive as well as negative aspects. The caste system provides security and a sense of community for millions of Indians. It gives them an identity that neither Western science nor Western thought has yet provided, because it is [also] a kinship system.[20]

I have often seen foreign students go into Indian settlements and come back to the UK to design something that would 'remove caste barriers' – a system of being for a nation that has survived not only thousands of years but also the British colonial rule. While there is nothing wrong with trying to improve the housing for the poor of any nation, I think to try to use architecture to impose external values, is a different matter.

Gerard Hendrik Hofstede,[21] the influential organizational sociologist and his son, Geert, classified five dimensions of culture in their study of national work-related values:

1 *Power:Distance Index* (PDI) – This dimension measures how much the less powerful members of institutions and organizations expect and accept that power is distributed unequally.
2 *Individualism vs. collectivism* – In individualist cultures, people are expected to develop and display their individual personalities while in collectivist cultures, people are defined and act mostly as members of a long-term group.
3 *Masculinity vs. femininity* – This dimension measures the value placed on traditional male or female values.
4 *Uncertainty avoidance* – This dimension measures how much members of a society are anxious about the unknown and, as a consequence, attempt to cope with anxiety by minimizing uncertainty.
5 *Long- vs. short-term orientation (adapted from Michael Bond)* – This dimension describes a society's 'time horizon', or the importance attached to the future versus the past and present.

While visiting Latin America (Mexico and Venezuela) and India, I tried to see whether Hofstede's classification holds true and to compare 'Latin culture' to the Indian one and in particular to Bengal (a culture I come from). Most informal settlements, in my experience, tend to be feminine, where 'soft' issues prevail and collectivist and long-term goals are important. The PDI is high, so people respect political and other leaders – this I perceived in both cultures. Many of these 'disinvested' areas become a political playground during elections with political leaders trying to swing votes and opinions their way. According to Hofstede's classification[22] (the website makes for a fascinating pastime, comparing countries), Venezuela has a higher power distance rating and higher masculinity rating than other Latin American countries (Figure 7.6). It is a collectivist country. India has a high PDI and masculinity but both are rated less than Venezuela. While Venezuela has a high uncertainty avoidance index (UAI), with strict rules and regulations, India has one of the lowest UAIs of 40, compared to the world average of 65. On the lower end of this ranking, the culture may be more open to unstructured ideas and situations. This appears to agree with my own personal experiences of working in these countries. Again, the individualistic and collectivist impressions that are influenced by wealth can be carried over to poorer parts to the society, not just the countries. So people in the *barrios* were more collectivist than individualistic while the middle classes in Venezuela tend to be more individualistic. Wealth perhaps gives us more choices.

Hofstede's classification has been criticized as being too general and reductionist while not recognizing that national culture can be influenced by global culture. This theory has been also criticized because the research

Figure 7.6 Author of a guidebook on Venezuela, Russell Maddicks, expounds on its culture of power personified by Hugo Chavez, and beauty personified by its beauty queens, London, July 2011.

Photo: Author.

behind this classification was based on the middle classes of each country. While Hofstede's dimensions can give a superficial introduction to a society, they should be used lightly and critically, because generalizations do not work on individuals, whether from the middle classes or the lower classes, as we saw in that example of the conference speakers described earlier.

Reframing and re-contextualizing

Another way of understanding a place can be through reframing the situation on to a familiar context. This can be done by either contrasting or comparing and is a useful tool for those working in cultures other than their own. Usually, either a comparison or a contrast can always be found between settlements and different contexts. I was able to contrast the *bustees* of India with the *barrios* of Venezuela by examining physical layouts and social markers such as standard of living and crime levels. Another example is where a student used a garden in South London compared to a settlement in Delhi, India. Flo's garden with its shrine, journey and hideaways was easily comparable to the squatter settlement, which had its own shrine, hideaways and journeys. In another example, the students 're-branded' streets in a slum in Delhi, naming them according to their primary characteristics. The nameless main street where most of the shops were situated was renamed 'High Street' by a North American student, who was familiar with this term (Figure 7.7).

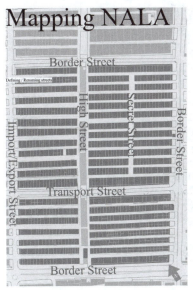

Figure 7.7 A 'high street' in a slum in New Delhi, by Heather Stuart from Canada, MA Architecture of Rapid Change and Scarce Resources, London Metropolitan University, 2008.

Reframing can happen in other ways than spatial and visual. Understanding the oral histories of people, such as comparing and contrasting the persecution of the Sansi tribe, India, to the Jewish Diaspora helped a student understand them. Many metropolitan centres have specific ethnic areas such as Chinatowns, Indian shops, Spanish or Hispanic centres which can help the development activists in understanding the culture of another country, such as the Turkish quarter in Rotterdam, the Netherlands (Figure 7.8). Before I went to Venezuela, I had the privilege of discussing the politics and society of South America with Benny from Caracas, who ran his café among the little group of South American restaurants on Holloway Road, North London.

Museums offer another way of understanding a culture. The history of the Kurds, for example, may be understood from visiting a tiny museum in Hammersmith, London, run by a former Kurdish general. There have been calls for local faiths to have museums in London so that people can understand other faiths – the Jewish Museum is often used as an example of this. Often local museums and exhibitions are useful places for finding visual and oral histories that can be discussed collectively. However, Raja

Figure 7.8 Turkish refugees in a housing estate in Rotterdam, the Netherlands.

Photo: Author.

Shehadeh cautions us about too much dependence on history, by giving the example of Palestine as seen by Israelis and others. He talks about a process that

> continues to this day of travelers and colonizers who see the land through the prism of the biblical past, overlooking present realities. Eager to occupy the land of imagination they impose their vision and manipulate it to tally with that mythical image they hold in their head, paying scant notice to its Palestinian inhabitants.[23]

Trying to view a culture from one's personal experience and understanding has to be done cautiously and lightly as it can lack objectivity as well as disguise a sentimental attachment to the observer's own perception. While reframing can be an important tool in connection and empathetic understanding of a community, on the other hand, there is a possibility that this could actually block one from working objectively by looking at the overall picture and long-term goals. Lévy-Bruhl, the anthropologist, calls this the 'participation mystique' and refers to a relationship wherein 'a person cannot distinguish themselves as separate from the object or thing they behold'.[24] This could be detrimental to the project even. The development activist has to be alert to this kind of sentimentalism. Often I have found that students and, sometimes, even I get drawn emotionally into the world of squatters and the deprived. What is needed here is a holistic approach, namely looking at the community issues and not just individual cases – that helps to balance concerns and retain objectivity.

Cultural relativism and ethnocentrism

> Modernity is seen as an exclusively European event in which self-cultivation of the human mind through exercise of reason and the study of classics had as its main purpose the creation of a homogenous, rational and beautiful society ... in this narration, colonial and imperial history has been disregarded, marginalized or simply obliterated.
> (Doris Salcedo, Columbian Artist, 'Shibboleth', Tate Modern, October 2007–April 2008, from Artist Catalogue)

There are no scientific standards for considering one group as intrinsically superior or inferior to another. Information about the nature of cultural differences between societies, their roots and their consequences should precede judgement and action. Negotiation is more likely to succeed when the parties concerned understand the reasons for the differences in viewpoints. Ethnocentrism is the belief that one's own culture is superior to that of other cultures. It is a form of reductionism that reduces the 'other way' of life to an inferior version of one's own. This is particularly important in cases of global dealings when a company or an individual is imbued with the idea that methods, materials or ideas that worked in the home country will also work abroad. Environmental and cultural differences are, therefore, ignored. In her book *Indigenous Modernities*, Jyoti Hosagrahar writes about the Delhi Improvement Trust (DIT) set up in 1936 under British rule:

> First it is assumed that environments shaped societies and people and that people who lived in similar environments shared a similar culture. Second, that architecture derived from 'scientific reason' and the principles of 'rational design' must be universally valid regardless of culture and politics.[25]

The author concludes that the presumed supremacy and universality of science that was, in fact, rooted in a particular European context justified the denigration of the walled city (Old Delhi) and its architecture as what the officials called a 'slum' and the replacement by a new kind of built form as a superior alternative.

Western formality was the ideological apparatus that sustained colonization and is one form of experimentation in the ordering of society from the European or Western viewpoint, according to Michel Laguerre. He says that it is basically a way of unifying the world through a system of logic that Western rationality can understand and manipulate.[26] He gives examples of how, in the USA, the establishment of the formal system has led to the 'production' of minority communities and contributed to the informalization of the minority institutions that now have a different political meaning from that found among the 'mainstreamers'. Laguerre explains:

> In the minority communities, informality was produced through an act of aggression and the forced subjugation of the people. In the mainstream community, formality came about as a result of victory of reason over traditions. Thus the informalisation process consisted in the imposition and upgrading of the rational Western formal system and downgrading of folk and minority ways.[27]

The price of life, it appears, is also now based on whether one is 'Western' or 'non-Western'. While researching various cities of the world and looking at statistics of crime and murder, I was startled to discover that many of these statistics were based on how many North American citizens had died in a particular city. So, for example, Baghdad is dangerous because so many American soldiers have died there, not because citizens of that city have died. Mexico city inhabitants valued their lives at $325,000 while Chinese workers thought it could be $4,000.[28] The Intergovernmental Panel on Climate Change (which won the Nobel Prize in 2007) published a report in 1995, in which they 'assessed the impact of global warming, valuing statistical lives at $150,000 in poor countries and at $1.5 million in rich ones'.[29] This caused an outcry, and they were forced to recalculate each person's life at $1 million, regardless of where they lived.

However, in reality, the price of the life of a person from a rich Western country is still held to be higher. *Wired* magazine, March 2011, ran an article by Scott Carney about where one can compare the prices of legal and illegal body parts. For a legal liver transplant, one can expect to pay £360,000 but for one from a Filipino slum dweller, one will pay less than one-third of that – £101,000. Kolkata used to produce 60,000 skeletons a year until the practice of exporting body parts was banned, but most skeletons still come from India. Bodies from graves in India are exhumed, cleaned in acid baths and sold at premium rates in Canada and Europe. People in vulnerable situations, such as a disaster or in abject poverty, will often turn to desperate means to earn money. In 2007 in Kalyanpuri in Delhi, for example, we met a mother who was going to sell her kidneys to ensure that both her sons went to college (she did not feel the same way towards her daughter's education, though). In his book, *Red Market*, Scott Carney describes an Indian refugee camp in Tamil Nadu that is known as Kidneyvakkam, or Kidneyville, because so many people there had sold their kidneys to organ brokers in efforts to raise money in the aftermath of the 2004 tsunami.[30] It is imperative that the development activist displays the same respect while working with vulnerable people, as they do with any other clients.

The invisible panapticon: the Internet

The panapticon was an architectural invention of the British philosopher, Jeremy Bentham, to watch and control inmates of social institutions, such as prisoners, inmates of asylums and workhouses. He imagined a series of rooms where one could be watched all the time. Everything would be open, transparent and, thus, be influenced. In the last 200 years, we have now acquired not buildings but technology attached to or inside our buildings that watches us all the time. Consider, for example, closed circuit television, CCTV. Using CCTV is particularly common in Britain, where there are reportedly more cameras per person than in any other country in the world.[31] In the small town of Hebron, Palestine, there were twenty-six CCTV cameras lining the main street (about 6 minutes walk) and reportedly over one thousand Israeli soldiers watching us as our small group consisting of students and staff visited in 2011. The placing of cameras and soldiers on rooftops gave a feeling of dominance and triggered fear in us. Increasing use of surveillance has triggered debates about security versus privacy. However, the computer and the smartphones along with social networking sites have brought the panapticon even closer, inside our homes. We can be tracked down easily by strangers and be visible to others thousands of miles away. Phone hacking is common. Smart cities, which depend on 'soft technologies' such as the Internet, are the next step to Bentham's panapticon. They are being designed by companies such as IBM and are to be found in Korea, China and India, along with those in Europe.[32]

Two billion people are connected digitally with five billion devices.[33] We see photographs of people we have never met, we 'like' them and become 'friends' with them (in Tokyo, people have become bored of virtual friends, you can actually hire a real person to be your friend for a few hours). Perhaps this is one step beyond Lévy-Bruhl's 'participation mystique'. There are issues of ethics in the way we use technology, who we photograph or film and how we use them. Foucault (1995) warns in *Discipline and Punishment*: 'visibility is a trap' and thus our interaction with people in vulnerable situations has to be respectful and sensitive'. In a workshop on participatory design at London Metropolitan University, we held a Skype conference with people from Sendai, the earthquake and tsunami hit Japanese city. In our enthusiasm to come up with design solutions, we almost forgot that we were dealing with people who were grieving, with a place where more than 16,000 people lost their lives (September 2011 estimates), until someone reminded us (we were glad that she did). The way we then thought about the community changed instantly and our design priorities changed too.

'The Other'

Modern ethics arose out of the philosophical questions of morality, right or wrong, and about treatment of other people (and through religion). When working with groups of people who appear to have no power or wealth or other signs of social importance, there could be a problem for the development activist in participating with equal engagement. Working with children presents great difficulty, with some either patronizing or dismissing them. Most reactions can be divided into two types – one of feelings of superiority and the other of despair. People can use a means to achieve an end for the proposer – the principle of ends and means – which may mean awards for the proposer of the project with no benefit or sometimes even negative benefit or a loss for the community. Richard Wilson's book *Don't Get Fooled Again: The sceptic's guide to life* lists the following findings from the report of James R. Schlesinger, former Defense Secretary for the USA, on the American guards' behaviour[34] at Abu Ghraib prison in Iraq (the executive summary of the Schlesinger report can be found online) – the examples are mine:

• *Deindividuation*: the anonymity, suggestibility and contagion provided in a crowd that allows individuals to participate in behaviour marked by temporary suspension of customary rules and inhibitions [examples might include two levels – group level, for example, the behaviour of English football hooligans abroad and, on an individual level, photos and information that a person might reveal to thousands of people on a social networking site].

- *Groupthink* is characterized by two main kinds of illusions – first, that of invulnerability, that is, group members believe that the group is special and morally superior and, therefore, its decisions are sound; and second, that of unanimity, where members assume all are in concurrence and pressure is brought to bear on those who might dissent.

- *Dehumanization*: individuals and groups are viewed as less than fully human [the concept of the 'noble savage' from Jean-Jacques Rousseau, although enlightened for his time, could be viewed thus now].

- *Moral exclusion*: one group views the other as fundamentally different, therefore prevailing moral rules and practices apply to one group but not the other. [An example would be the slogan 'Liberty, Equality and Fraternity' which appeared to be applicable to the people of France but not to the people in the French colonies.]

Although the development activist is not working in the stressful conditions of war and imprisonment, in working in informal settlements with vulnerable people, some of these characteristics may be unconsciously transferred in the way of our thinking. It may be very easy for a middle-class architecture student from the UK to feel superior to or in a position of power over a slum dweller barely able to find money to eat. Somehow, the normal relationship that an architect may have with their clients is abandoned the moment a development activist enters an informal settlement and sees poverty, filth and disease. Instead of seeking solutions together, the architect decides that the community needs certain things in a moment of architecturally deterministic thinking. Peter Singer in his classic book *Practical Ethics* provides a way of overcoming this problem and also racism, sexism, disability or intellectual slavery by using the principle of 'Equal consideration of interests', that is, looking at the interests rather than at individuals, thus ensuring true and complete participation.[35] This idea is further developed in Chapter 6 on participatory design.

Star Trek and fact mining

> The researcher who loses sight of the search for truth and acts out of selfish
> interest also loses sight of his or her own obligation to society and humanity.
> (Daisaku Ikeda in Guy Bourgealt, *On Being Human*, Middleway Press, 2003)

Ethics also consists of truth and honesty in reporting the circumstances. True research takes time and effort. In the words of John Brophy, a Pennsylvania miner, an advocate of public ownership of resources, 1921:

What is research? Research is digging facts. Digging facts is as hard a job as mining coal. It means blowing them out from underground, cutting them, picking them, shoveling them, loading them, pushing them to the surface, weighing them, and then turning them on to the public for fuel – for light and heat. Facts make a fire, which cannot be put out. To get coal requires miners. To get facts requires miners, too: fact miners.[36]

Hasty reports and 'made-up' research are results of quick visits to a country. Visiting a place with a made-up mindset contributes further – we like to find facts that prove our hypothesis. Robert Pirsig states: 'We build up whole cultural patterns based on past "facts" which are extremely selective. When a new fact comes in that does not fit the pattern we don't throw out the pattern. We throw out the fact.'[37] This excerpt from a publicly visible online post about a student architecture project is a reminder of why people make up things:

> I need to make up a story of local people in order to validate the project I am proposing … and all the stories I am coming up with are not so true but seems to be true … wish to be a writer of star trek.

Proper research takes time and money – and sometimes there is not much of either of those, especially in student projects. I heard an external critic use the term 'fudge factor' to rate the amount of 'fudging' that was done in student projects abroad. Honesty and transparency must be part of students' projects too for it is in education that the tone for the future is set. There are many links available online about lies in reports (try googling it) and one can see that this is an uncomfortable subject to discuss openly.

I have participated in many 'market research' meetings and am constantly surprised by the difference in what is discussed at meetings and what is then consequently used. A research company says candidly:

> Lies – we consider them an occupational hazard. In the course of our research at [XXX], organizations both large and small will inadvertently ask us to participate in their lies and, intentional or not, the implications are often dire. When we lie to ourselves, our users, or our team about issues at the core of a user experience project, we unwittingly accelerate the interface's demise.[38]

On a visual level, the presentation of graphs, figures and statistics can be very powerful and persuasive, as Darrell Huff proves in his book *How to Lie with Statistics*.[39] Lying, bribery and corruption that are part of many development projects and aid programmes challenge our notion of ethics while working in different cultures. Many times, I have known of foreign funders being taken to see 'beautified and sanitized' projects that have been made so only 24 hours before the arrival of the dignitary and then left to disintegrate after their departure.

Based on my idea of exploring discomforts, there could be value in using lies to design a better solution (or a better research report):

- Admit it is a lie (this is the most difficult step!).
- Discuss the lie – why did you lie? What is the 'value' of the lie, i.e. who benefits from it? (This is best done in a group discussion.)
- Use the reasons for the lie to form a solution or arrangement – What could be the solution? What could be done better? (A brainstorm session works well.)

Travelling and working in a global village

> So you are eating nothing but vegetarian curry and you can't get bacon for love or money. Visit a town like Pushkar … and you will find that religious reasons mean that meat, fish and eggs are completely banned along with any form of alcohol. This is something to take into consideration when planning your itinerary. Do you want to be stuck for three days in a town where there is not a whole lot to do and you can't even have a decent night out?
>
> (From *High Heels and a Head Torch* by Chelsea Duke (the ultimate survival tool for any glamorous girl about to set off in search of adventure))[40]

Students and architects are now working and living in a global environment (Figures 7.9 and 7.10). According to research commissioned by the Architects Council of Europe, within Europe in 2010, the highest number of architects working outside their countries were the Irish, followed by Slovenia and the UK. One can read guidebooks and websites as much aspossible, but the ultimate experience of being in a country belongs to those who travel and work with open minds and eyes. This is not a book about personal safety – it assumes that the development activist will have done their homework and read guidebooks before leaving to work elsewhere. Here I would like to discuss what it means to visit an unfamiliar culture. Many will seek familiarity not just in terms of re-contextualizing, but also by persisting in their personal beliefs about a place or seeking familiarity through their personal experiences. There are many jokes about the English wanting fish and chips in most improbable places – it is about seeking the familiar, as demonstrated by the above extract. However, one must forget the familiar, even if it looks familiar, and seek with the eyes of the inexperienced.

Before visiting Venezuela, a student who had an acquaintance in Caracas informed me (as an indication of the level of crime in the city) that this wealthy woman had to pay extortion money not to be raped. I had a vision of a Rapunzel-like figure imprisoned in a tower amid Latino villains determined to get her. However, upon checking various websites (for example, http://www.nationmaster.com/index.php), I found that the rape statistics of Caracas

Figure 7.9 Feet pedicure using Garra Rufa fish from Turkey, at an Indian Mela in West London, Summer 2010.

Photo: Author.

Figure 7.10 Two students – one from USA of Vietnamese origin and another one from Canada – cooking in my kitchen for an international food party for students, 2009.

Photo: Author.

are much lower than many cities of the USA, UK, France, Norway and even Spain (where the student hails from). This kind of cultural stereotyping of a nation and its people is more common than we like to think. The images of the punctual and tight-lipped Englishman, the lazy Latino, beer guzzling Germans, the lager louts of Australia – all have a way of diminishing the person and the country. The development activist needs to stay safe while working in different cultures by being aware that, for example, crime can happen anywhere, in any country.[41] The Foreign Office website is a good one to refer to but it explicitly warns you against visiting squatter settlements in any country. So along with that I rely on local knowledge and guidance and organizing visits with local people to slums and squatter settlements.

In asking students to 'explore their discomforts', I refer to the *positive* use of conflicts and discomforts, called 'Creative Abrasion' by Jerry Hirshberg.[42] This helps them to open up their personal beliefs and challenge established modes of thought, to understand what the mirror of society is showing them. This tool can also be very useful if used collectively, when groups of students get together and discuss their discomforts. Visiting an exhibition in London about the use of the veil in Islamic culture, we discussed with the curator of the exhibition what our individual reactions would be if asked to wear a veil and whether we could even work with a veil, given the very physical barrier that the Niquab or the Hijab presents. The idea was not to reach a consensus but to vocalize different viewpoints, literally. It was not to judge or predict but to see where we stood and whether we could set assumption aside. The year after, when one of my students visited the *barrios* of Venezuela wearing a Hijab, I saw that there was simply an acceptance of what she was by the people there, no other reaction.

I have observed people in squatter settlements getting upset if they perceive that their privacy has been violated in ways such as measuring their homes, going inside them without cultural respect (such as taking shoes off in places such as India) and talking about them in front of them while ignoring them, or ignoring the issues that they present. Some of these vulnerable people think that the measuring means that their homes will be demolished – an easy inference for squatters. One year in India, I watched as colleagues simply walked on by as they could not understand Hindi, oblivious to the distress of an old woman whose home their students had measured. I have observed students being hit with stones and threatened in settlements while on field trips with other colleagues (indeed I had to rescue two female students from a crowd in Delhi and, unfortunately, this was followed up by a local journalist) and considered this kind of extreme reaction is the last thing a development activist would want. Mutual respect and openness are things to aim for in order to work in informal settlements. In order to overcome these difficulties and also to respect the people who really are our clients is not to include measuring or going inside homes without permission during site visits. Once, after I saw students going inside people's homes during their biggest festival, Diwali, I asked a colleague: 'Would you allow people to come and measure your home without permission during Christmas?' Put quite simply, ethics is about treating another person how you would like to be treated.

Ethical consent forms in English, that are not sometimes translated (or are impossible to translate) into local languages are often used, mostly to satisfy the most basic requirements of 'visiting organizations' (usually Western) with an additional excuse that they are working with a local NGO or charity as a paper exercise. Most ethical consent forms are derived from medical origins (which, in turn, are derived from Nazi medical research) and thus can have strange questions about 'collection of body tissues and fluids' from humans and animals, even for use by architectural staff. Ethics forms should be tailored specifically, be simple to use and read, and able to be translated into local languages if they are to have any meaningful use. The same guidelines apply to Memorandums of Understanding or Agreements. Having read quite a few of them and struggled to use them onsite in informal settlements with illiterate people or via NGOs, I have found these are usually cumbersome and difficult to explain. Another issue is working with children. In the UK, participants working with children have to have a Criminal Records Bureau check and certificate,[43] and even then this is loosely followed (I have one but many people I have worked with did not appear to have one). However, even then, this is not a requirement for other countries. Thus, a good and suitable ethics form that takes into account working with adults and children from other countries becomes very necessary – we should see to it before we leave.

The function of ethics, according to Professor Padmasiri de Silva,[44] is fivefold: 1) motivational, 2) clarificatory, 3) adjudictive, 4) integrative and 5) embodying values. Motivation helps us to understand why we are doing something. Clarification looks at alternatives and why we choose a particular methodology. Adjudictive function helps use choose between values. Ethics can help to integrate the values with our work. Finally, we have to understand the plurality of values and priorities. The International Institute for Environment and Development (IIED) has produced many Memorandums of Agreement/Understanding, that take into account the different ways a visiting activist can engage with the society. While being legally binding documents, they do take the nature of participatory working in different cultures into account and thus also provide flexibility. These documents are also excellent because they present complex issues in simple language, which can be understood or even translated for everyone. There is a degree of transparency, which is very welcome in participatory working. The idea of informed consent can be simply distilled into how the person is given information about the project, that is, what kind of information is needed and how it is to be used and a simple explanation of the wider implication of this work. Participant information is the material needed for research or work, and this needs to be understood clearly by all the participants. The best tip I have received about ethics is to start researching the ethics as soon as your start the research.[45]

Case Study: Article 25's equal opportunity policy statement

Article 25 is a UK operational NGO providing technical construction expertise and management support to development projects around the world. Capacity building and community participation are central to the implementation of all of Article 25's projects in the field because they say it supports their commitment to equal opportunities not only in HQ but in the field as well. Here I have reproduced, with permission, Article 25's equal opportunity policy that shows in very simple words how to deal with cultural issues.

> In the recruitment, selection, training, appraisal, development and promotion of staff and volunteers, the only consideration must be that the individual meets, or is likely to meet, the requirements of their role (or role applied for) and the needs of the projects and work of Article 25 in which they will be involved.
>
> The requirements being met, no volunteer or employee will be discriminated against on the basis of their sex, sexual orientation, race, colour, ethnic origin, nationality (within current legislation), disability, marital status, caring or parental responsibilities, age, or beliefs on matters such as religion and politics.
>
> We also encourage our staff and volunteers to be additionally mindful of the cultural issues and sensitivities required when working on projects overseas, sometimes with vulnerable groups. This means that staff and volunteers applying to and working with Article 25 should ensure that they are commensurately sensitive to the potentially diverse viewpoints of those they work with through Article 25, who may be beneficiaries or partners, and who may differ in viewpoint – even in relation to the equal opportunities policies espoused herein.
>
> Article 25 is committed to provide a working environment in which the rights and dignity of all its members are respected, and which is free from discrimination, prejudice, intimidation and all forms of harassment.
>
> Article 25 is committed to ensuring that this policy is implemented and monitored at an organizational and individual level. This means in practice: factors such as sex, sexual orientation, marital status, ethnic origin, race, religion, colour, nationality, political beliefs, disability and age should not be taken into account for the purposes of recruitment, appointment, training, appraisal, promotion, discipline, application to and acceptance on to a project.
>
> Selection for a role or project within Article 25 is made solely on merit.

Tips for development activists

Based on my observations and work, I propose the following:

Innocence

We should become keen observers and listeners and, even, according to Edward de Bono, 'listen with our eyes',[46] that is, watch out for the unsaid. We could learn to leave our preconceptions behind and embrace what we see. We can become objective evaluators of oral and visual evidence in this way. In some ways, foreign students working in different cultures already possess this innocence. However, even if you know the culture, there are always new things to be seen, so a 'cultivated innocence' or even a 'cultivated ignorance' is required. The American poet, Wallace Stevens, said that 'poetry must resist the intelligence almost successfully'.[47] I believe that this must be so for the work of the development activist.

Sharing perceptions

According to Carmona *et al.*, perception is not just a biological process, it is culturally and socially learned. Individuals differ on how they filter information – thus, each person experiences the same space differently. Male/female experiences are keenly different for people working in informal settlements in different countries. So, shared mental maps are useful in developing an idea of the space. Sharing perceptions, feelings and evaluations can also be a useful tool for a group working in such areas.

Create value

Following the idea of Makiguchi's value creation mentioned earlier, it is possible to create value from whatever circumstances one finds oneself – whether societal or personal benefit including public reputation and satisfaction. According to the report 'The Architectural Profession in Europe 2010' commissioned by the Architects Council of Europe and researched by Mirza and Nacey, Sweden and Denmark were top scorers in both reputation and satisfaction, although the largest architectural market was Germany and the largest number of architects came from Italy. Creative solutions and personal pride in work do not come from quantity (size and numbers of projects) but from quality. The humble projects in which the development activist may find herself or himself in, can create value in all areas, including personal satisfaction, and build reputation.

Tips for development activists (from UNFPA)[48]

The following are excerpted from a UNFPA publication *Working from Within:*

24 tips for culturally sensitive programming

1 Invest time in knowing the culture in which you are operating.
2 Hear what the community has to say.
3 Demonstrate respect.
4 Show patience.
5 Gain the support of local power structures.
6 Be inclusive.
7 Provide solid evidence.
8 Rely on the objectivity of science.
9 Avoid value judgements.
10 Use language sensitively.
11 Work through local allies.
12 Assume the role of facilitator.
13 Honour commitments.
14 Know your adversaries.
15 Find common ground.
16 Accentuate the positive.
17 Use advocacy to effect change.
18 Create opportunities for women.
19 Build community capacity.
20 Reach out through popular culture.
21 Let people do what they do best.
22 Nurture partnerships.
23 Celebrate achievements.
24 Never give up.

Discussion points

1 Are forms for ethical consent and memorandums of agreement necessary? What can we do to make such issues more accessible to local people?
2 How can we reconcile our different cultural backgrounds to those of the people we visit? Do we need to let go of our values and embrace theirs or can there be a half-way point?
3 Should we speak up if we observe corrupt practices or unethical behaviour from the people we are working with? Is it better not to rock the boat in such circumstances?
4 Given sometimes the lack of time in which projects have to be finished, how can we make sure that our work is correctly researched and written?

Chapter 8

Observing and recording the soft and hard cities

Tools and (cautionary) tales

> The city as we imagine it, the soft city of illusion, myth, aspiration, nightmare is a real, maybe more real, than the hard city one can locate in maps and statistics, in monographs on urban sociology, demography and architecture.
>
> (*The Soft City* – Jonathan Raban, 1974[1])

Informal settlements such as *bustees*, *barrios* and slums are soft cities – with no plans, no addresses, made of found materials, on land that is not owned by the occupiers (and sometimes by no one). Taking Raban's definition, I have called the informal city also the soft city. Some call this the 'everyday architecture' or the 'architecture of the everyday'. I think this last definition misses out on the multitude of characteristics that are very significant while the phrase 'everyday' has implications of the ordinary and these places are far from being ordinary. These soft cities, of course, are not places for experiencing Vitruvius' three qualities of architecture – firmness, commodity and delight. These places, although made of hard materials and situated in hard landscapes, have complexities and pluralities that defy conventional exploration and classification. In contrast formal cities are places with hard data – formal plans, infrastructure, land registry title deeds and safe from future demolition and moves.

Recording soft cities or settlements needs unconventional and multiple approaches to be taken. Hard data such as statistics rarely tell a full story and can be twisted to present a different image or idea.[2] The history of a city is never an exact science, neither is the evaluation of an ever-changing informal city. If even one contextual element changes, it gives rise to other complexities. Formally recognized markers such as street names, house numbers, a planned rational layout, a transport system and other such methods for orienting oneself, do not exist in such placces. In a Channel 4 TV programme *Slumming it*,[3] the British presenter, Kevin McCloud, visiting Dharavi, panics trying to find a shop – there are no street names, no names for shops or offices. We have become used to formal markers whereas in the squatter settlements children from an early age recognize informal, social and cultural markers and make their way in the settlement (Figures 8.1 and 8.2).

Figure 8.1 Lack of street names in early colonial settlement, La Pastora, Caracas – only crossroads and junctions are named using directions.

Photo: Author.

Figure 8.2 Project to name streets in the *barrio* of Julian Blanco by Central University of Venezuela, Caracas.

Photo: Author.

Squatter settlements are built quickly, in order to take advantage of the scarce materials and spaces available. The slow deliberation of plans, orientation and views are luxuries that are not available to the builder. The modern architect and the informal builder have different aims – the former encourages the single, the stable and the iconic while the squatter will want pluralistic, the informal and the everyday in design. Habraken says, 'In this new situation, unspoken ways of ordinary environments must be articulated. We cannot revive the naïve past. We dare not promise an unrealizable future. But to make peace with our task of designing the ordinary we must seek more intimate knowledge of it ... Anew, we observe what always has been with us – not to discover, much less to invent, but to recognize.'[4] In the following sections, I describe and evaluate different techniques and tools that have been used in observing and recording the soft city.

Experiencing spaces in the squatter settlements

> The life of our city is rich in poetic and marvelous subjects. We are enveloped and steeped as though in an atmosphere of the marvelous; but we do not notice it.
> (Charles Baudelaire in Robert Williams, *Art Theory: An historical introduction*, Wiley-Blackwell, 2004, p. 127)

Slums and traditional settlements are chaotic, kinaesthetic places – full of movement and tightness without the sight of planned and neatly delineated areas – even a *'terrain vague'*.[5] The emergence and stitching of complex spaces and buildings through movement and appropriation is a dynamic experience.[6] Formal spaces in planned environments lack this dynamism. However, the visual chaos that is presented by the soft city can become a real barrier to understanding and recording the spaces (Figure 8.3). As Sabine Bitter and Helmut Weber comment about the *barrios* of Caracas:

> the photographs of the *barrio* are deeply embedded into a normative view of them as organic, chaotic and precarious territory which is either heroic in its insistence of the everyday and the informal, or dangerous in its darkness and otherness. Literal shifts in perspective – either sprawling aerial views or on-the-ground portraiture of people who live in the *barrios* – can be used to reinforce this polarity.[7]

This image, although describing the *barrios* of Venezuela, can apply to any slum.

Walking is the best and, sometimes, the only way to experience these 'stitched' up areas – the association, appropriation and accommodation of spaces. The view from walking is a different experience to the view from the

Figure 8.3 Julian Blanco, Petare, Caracas – note how streets and other details disappear when viewed from a height.

Photo: Author.

car, as described in the book *Learning from Las Vegas*.[8] Bosselman argues that people measure (their) walks in rhythmic spacing, related to visual and space experiences.[9] Even in formal cities, walking provides a better experience of the city and many cities hold walking tours – a 'walk workshop' organized in London in 2009 showed the walkers many different aspects of East London – regulation, ownership, place, data, nature, friendship, escape, entertainment, identity exchange, biotopes and contemplation through a range of actions that established a new condition for interaction.[10]

Once on site, the view from the ground is dramatically reduced while walking – one can no longer see wide spaces, perhaps only gaps and glimpses of what lies beyond. People moving, traffic and other sensory data quickly obliterate the physical. As development activists, we need to record the use of space, movement and other sensory data – the soft city. Walking in the soft city requires a 'soft approach' that may be quite slow as we need to move slowly through to record details not visible from above (Figure 8.4). Moreover,

Figure 8.4 Rialto market, Venice, Italy – when walking on the street, details can disappear.

Photo: Author.

the lines and boundaries in such spaces that delineate private and public areas may be invisible or apparent. These aspects, which may not be apparent on one visit, may become so on subsequent visits as described later.

Formal spaces have been classified by many according to space (organizational), temporal and perceptive elements.[11] It is interesting that formality and informality coexist and intervene – people make formal spaces informal and create formal spaces from informal spaces. According to Michel Laguerre, 'Prior to the formal use of space, there is an informal use of space. Formality invades the informal space and gives it an order. The government is always devising rules to formalize spaces.' He also notes that the reverse is true – informality invades the formal space too 'because a formal system is unable to meet the needs of every individual, they transform formal spaces into informal spaces to conduct informal activities' (Figure 8.5).[12]

Thus the key lies in finding formality and order in 'informal' spaces. I have adapted and extended key classifications of formal spaces so that they can be used also for informal spaces:

1   Space – streets, alleys, physical markers, squares and areas (adapted from Lynch, 1960).
2   Denseness – using spacing, proximity, access, volume and height.

Figure 8.5 Place des Vosges, seventeenth-century Paris – a formal space turned into an informal space by its users.

Photo: Author.

3   Closures and views, based on space rather than aesthetic judgments (adapted from Von Meiss, 1990 and Cullen, 1961).
4   Territoriality – public, private and liminal spaces (adapted from Jencks and Chaitkin, 1982).
5   Temporality – space as experienced through time and spaces (perhaps like a cinematic experience).
6   Social – including cultural, religious, political and communal spaces.
7   Sensual – including tactile, emotional, sentimental and personal experience of space. The inbetween spaces are a particularly rich mix of sensory experiences.

Data and dangers

For recording and decoding soft data such as cultural and social markers, many direct and indirect ways of expressing the spaces of squatter settlements have to be found. Direct methods include actual measuring, drawing, interviews, photography and site observation. Indirect methods are those that use Google Earth, supplied maps and plans, inference from interviews and oral histories, photographs and drawings (made by the observer or by the residents themselves).

Most data are classified as either from primary sources – collected directly from the person concerned; or from secondary sources, including books, articles, documentaries, photographs taken by another person, etc., that describe and interpret available evidence. However, both may be liable to prejudice by the collector or the originator. Testimony given several years after the event could be affected by memory, recent events and prejudice. As both sources are not infallible, all available data should be collected from a variety of different sources and evaluated so that a holistic picture emerges. Edward De Bono describes how prejudice can affect data collection.[13] He gives an example of an explorer who visits a big island country and reports that he has found a strange looking big bird and a huge rock and nothing else. So he is sent back again and asked to go to the Northern parts and record everything he finds, and carry out a similar exercise for the other directions as well. When he completes this, he finds that there are many more things than the bird and the rock. The work of the development activist is to record all events and issues without judgement or preconceptions. When collecting information for the soft city, a 'blank and extensive mind' is essential equipment.

Formal and sensory mapping

Google Earth is a useful tool for recording slums and squatter settlements and then adding details on site. Superimposing Google Earth plans on formal maps and site plans has proven to be useful for getting a sense of the settlement – size, location and placement of roads and services. However, this is the view from the top – literally and metaphorically. Most people in traditional and squatter settlements have no use for maps. Moreover, there may be copyright issues over use of Google maps, which should be checked out before use. Google maps are not always correct and there have been complaints before. In 2011, the Northwest German town of Emden complained that the map gave its harbour to the Netherlands. In November 2010, Costa Rica said Google was responsible for a border row with its neighbour Nicaragua, after a Google map placed a disputed island on the Nicaraguan side of the border. Google apologized and revised its map. While in the Medina of Tangiers, Morocco, I found that different hotels had been given the same location on the Google map.

More worryingly for development activists, Google appears to be biased towards planned and formal settlements. As announced on 26 April 2011, for instance, Google agreed to amend its map of Rio de Janeiro, after city officials said it gave too much prominence to *favelas*.[14] According to the complaint, 'their labelling on the map and the absence of wealthier districts and tourist sites gave a bad impression of the city and false impression that the urban area is nothing more than an immense cluster of *favelas*'. 'The maps turn Rio into a *favela*,' one resident apparently told the paper. 'Anyone who doesn't know the city would be frightened.' A spokesman for Google told the newspaper the company had never intended to 'defame Rio', and perhaps added in its defence that the person who drew up the maps was a 'native of the city'. However, Google told *Globo*, the Brazilian newspaper, that it would change the way the information was displayed, by changing the text sizes. Accordingly, the maps would gradually be amended to change the text sizes and to apply labels to districts. The *favelas* would still be marked, but only once the user had zoomed in. So again, it is the cautious and careful use of maps, whether from the Internet or those given to us, that we need to consider.

Other systems that appear not to have been fully explored by architects is GIS – Geographic Information System. A GIS is any system that captures, stores, analyses, manages and presents data that are linked to location. In the simplest terms, GIS is the merging of cartography and database technology. The origins of GIS lie in a cholera outbreak in London mentioned earlier in Chapter 5. In 1854, a doctor, John Snow, plotted a cholera outbreak in London using dots to represent the location of individual cases. His diagrammatic study of the distribution of cholera led to the source of the disease – a contaminated water pump within the heart of the cholera outbreak.

While software is available to carry out GIS surveys, a basic survey of the area and its facilities linking them to socio-economic issues would be a handy tool for the development activist. Learning to use GIS also involves many other skills such as critical thinking, space reasoning and organizing large data sets. GIS could be useful for looking at physical connections between buildings, such as roads, open spaces and pathways. Environmental factors such as light, sunlight, wind, temperature, rain, etc. can be quantified and qualified through space and time, as each of these is dynamic in nature and influenced by the relationship of one building to another. This is even more the case in the closely spaced informal city. These have been used quite extensively by landscape architects, urban planners and disaster management experts, and even for participatory processes, but not as much by architects.

'Nolli' or figure ground-type plans can be very useful in a squatter settlement. Giambattista Nolli (1701–56) was an Italian architect and surveyor who devised an ichnographic plan map of Rome, as opposed to a bird's-eye perspective, which was the dominant cartographic representation style. I used the Nolli type of mapping during my work in Nizamuddin and Shahjahanabad, Delhi, mentioned earlier. Combining this with a socio-economic survey of the areas and land ownership gave me a very detailed impression of the urban density and the reasons for it.

Figure–ground maps are very useful for understanding the density of an area and also to get a sense of scale. Essentially, the drawing depicts buildings as solid objects against a plain white background. Eisenman Architects, who used the figure ground in the formulation of designs for the City of Culture of Galicia Santiago de Compostela, Spain, say:

> The original center of Santiago conforms to a figure/ground urbanism in which buildings are figural, or solid, and the streets are residual, or void spaces. Through this mapping operation, the project emerges as a curving surface that is neither figure nor ground but both a figured ground and a figured figure that supersede the figure–ground urbanism of the old city.
> (See http://www.archdaily.com/141238/the-city-of-culture-eisenman-architects; accessed August 2011)

Some urban planners criticize the use of Nolli and figure–ground maps as being reductionist. I think that these maps are very useful but agree that, like any other tools, should not become the only way of observing and recording the informal city. The figure–ground is a useful starting point for the understanding of the urban form, an analysis of the relationship between building mass and open space. To this initial analysis are added the circulation patterns and other linkages, as well as important places using overlays, and the complexity of the informal city emerges and can be recorded (Figure 8.6).[15]

As the soft city is full of sensory experiences as well as emotional stories, these can also be recorded on plans. Initially, recording the sensory data is quite useful for the development activist to understand the community. This sensory data can be quite personal and thus quite revealing. Informal and even formal spaces can be feminine or masculine – I do not mean the space itself but rather, the use of the space. The Jungian analyst, Clarissa Pinkola Estes, talks about women's spaces.[16] She says that women from all cultures and ages set aside a 'sacred' space for communion and inquiry. These places were not just used for certain times of the month but were used frequently as part of the everyday architecture – such as a tree, water's edge, near the ocean, a special room, a church or a temple, etc. In all settlements I have visited, I found women's and men's spaces. These spaces are perhaps not so well demarcated in planned settlements or the formal city but can be found.

Sensory input can be very useful in understanding the space as the following example illustrates. The plan shown in Figures 8.7a and 8.7b was made by a student who was afraid of entering a squatter settlement in Delhi. Her own fears made understanding the space quite difficult for her. So she was asked to record her fears and her emotional assessment of the place on a rough map as she went there with her colleagues. The first drawing (Figure 8.7a) shows the areas where she felt fear and those where she felt 'free' and comfortable, while the second drawing (Figure 8.7b) shows the feminine and masculine places. Thus, after reading the settlement in this way, she was able to understand why women used certain areas and where men gathered. The settlement came to have meaning for her through her emotional reaction to it. Eventually, over time, she came to understand the planning of the settlement, why certain walls faced the way they did, or why the streets ran in a certain direction, etc. The emotional reaction to the settlement led the way to a physical understanding.

Figure 8.6 The final map of a settlement made using Google Earth, local maps, observational sketches and measurements on site and interviews.

Source: Viet Hoai Nguyen, MA Architecture of Rapid Change and Scarce Resources, London Metropolitan University, 2009.

Physical markers and identity

Settlements have physical markers such as social spaces in a plaza, under a tree, a junction or a special memorial. In the *barrios* of Venezuela, the plans of where one *barrio* begins and another one ends, are often loose or porous. We learned of *ranchos* physically located in one *barrio* but the residents of that say that they belong to another *barrio*. Informal soft cities, although having no boundaries – often have 'hidden' markers and lines. Like dogs that mark their territory, human beings have their 'defensible spaces' where they feel as if they can 'mark' their ownership of it.

According to Oscar Newman, planner and architect, the 'defensible space' is a residential environment whose physical characteristics – building layout and site plan – function to allow inhabitants themselves to become key agents in ensuring their security. According to Newman, designed defensible spaces have the following characteristics:[17]

• Assigning spaces to specific people on the basis of environment that they are best able to use and control. These are often dependent upon age, life-styles, socio-cultural backgrounds, incomes and family structures.

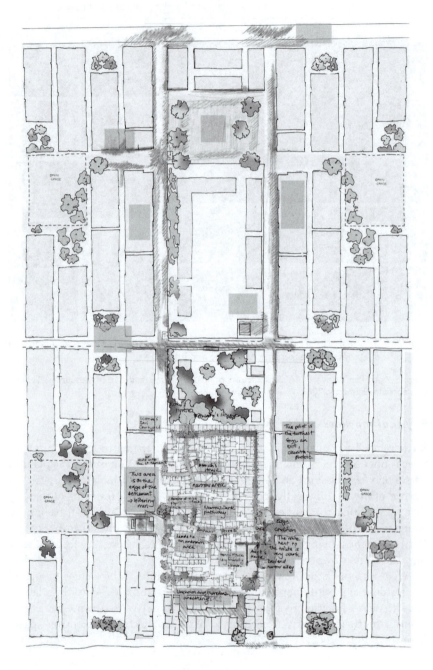

Figure 8.7a Kalyanpuri, Delhi, safe and feared spaces.

Source: Amelia Rule, Diploma Unit 6, London Metropolitan University, 2007.

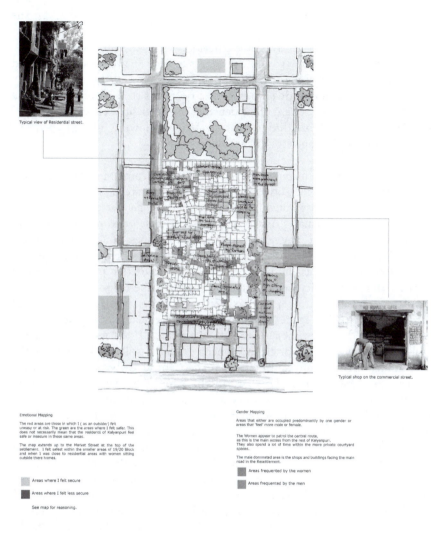

Typical view of Residential street.

Typical shop on the commercial street.

Emotional Mapping

The red areas are those in which I (as an outsider) felt uneasy or at risk. The green are the areas where I felt safer. This does not necessarily mean that the residents of Kalyanpuri feel safe or insecure in these same areas.

The map extends up to the Market Street at the top of the settlement. I felt safest within the smaller areas of 19/20 Block and when I was close to residential areas with women sitting outside there homes.

Areas where I felt secure

Areas where I felt less secure

See map for reasoning.

Gender Mapping

Areas that either are occupied predominantly by one gender or areas that 'feel' more male or female.

The Women appear to patrol the central route, as this is the main access from the rest of Kalyanpuri. They also spend a lot of time within the more private courtyard spaces.

The male dominated area is the shops and buildings facing the main road in the Resettlement.

Areas frequented by the women

Areas frequented by the men

Emotional Mapping and Gender Mapping of the Site : **Kalyanpuri**

Figure 8.7b Kalyanpuri, Delhi, feminine and masculine spaces.

Source: Amelia Rule, Diploma Unit 6, London Metropolitan University, 2007.

- A territorial definition of space in residential developments to reflect the zone of influence of specific inhabitants.
- The juxtaposition of dwelling interiors with exterior spaces and the placement of windows to allow residents to keep an eye upon exterior and interior spaces 'assigned' to them.
- The juxtaposition of dwellings with city streets so as to incorporate the streets within the sphere of influence of the residential environment.
- The avoidance of building forms and designs allowing others to perceive the vulnerability and isolation of the resident.

While designed or formal housing may make a conscious effort to make spaces defensible, in the soft city, common spaces are defined by unwritten rules, by events associated with spaces and by gender and culture (i.e. mainly through Newman's first principle). The close proximity of houses in an informal settlement may not ensure the defensiveness of a space. No man's territories exist in informal settlements. Physical closeness does not always ensure security or reduction in crime nor does it ensure that people are looked after by the community or respected by them. In the dense *barrio* of Julian Blanco, Caracas, I met an eighty-six-year-old woman, Mrs Abreu, who lives by herself and has had stones thrown at her to intimidate her into leaving her property which is on prime land (during a visit in 2011, I was pleased to see that she has now a secure brick and concrete home thanks to the work by the community organization and help from the Central University of Caracas). Figure 8.8 shows a particular space in the same *barrio* where an upturned bathtub is used by youth as a seat. Nearby is a small junction where the body of a young boy was left to be found by his mother. These spaces, used and guarded by certain youth, are avoided by others from the community.

Physical difficulties can also be a useful tool for the observer. Physical aspects such as topography, levels and slopes can naturally limit the boundaries of a 'defensible space' for someone. Observing how the elderly, children and the infirm use spaces can help in the future planning of these places and also for emergency escape. In the *barrios* of Venezuela, the number of steps to be climbed to escape for a particular resident from his or her *rancho* (shack) can be a useful element for planning for emergencies such as fire or earthquakes. Carnivals and processions, particularly the routes they take, mark the culturally important routes to the settlement. In Julian Blanco, for example, a particular route to the *barrio* was blocked during the Christmas period to let children play. This was not the most important route into the *barrio* but perhaps the most 'social' one – one that led past important physical markers for the community.

Physical markers also include the building typology, styles and materials. The visual chaos of the informal city often hides the use of a huge variety of materials – some of which may not be 'conventional' building materials. In a settlement that looks as if it has been made of a relatively small number and

Figure 8.8 Space marked by a bathtub, Julian Blanco, Caracas, Venezuela.

Photo: Author.

uniform use of found materials such as bricks, tin sheets and timber, can be found a remarkable number of other materials along with different plans and styles. The settlement of Kalyanpuri, East Delhi, at first glance looks as if it is made of bricks and corrugated iron sheets only. On closer examination, we find many other materials such as glass, bamboo and other timber, woven grass, jute sheeting, canvas and thatch, steel, terracotta tiles, salvaged materials such as parts of cars, containers, etc. Such physical markers as building materials show us the economic boundaries of the place – the richer residents have better built houses made of cement and bricks while the poor live in materials made of more 'temporary' materials such as cardboard, tin and thatch (Figure 8.9).

Photography as a tool

> If you can smell the street by looking at the photograph, it is a street photograph.
> (Bruce Gilden, Street Photography Now project, 2010)

Photography can be a powerful tool but the knowledge that derives from it can be second-hand. A photograph can be widely disseminated, especially now on the World Wide Web. Images can be quickly taken out of context to prove or show something that was not intended by the photographer (or by the subject). Steve Edwards says:

Figure 8.9 Kalyanpuri building materials, East Delhi, India – note the houses of the less well off in the foreground and the ones of the richer residents in the background.

Photo: Author.

> Much of our familiarity with our world comes through photographic visualization as a surrogate for firsthand experience of places, objects, creatures and events. Photographs have made many things seem ordinary, bringing distant places or unusual things closer to us, but, at the same time making much of our experience seem second-hand. It is startling to think of how much of our knowledge comes through a medium of photography: how many of us have actually seen a polar ice flow or a refugee camp? Yet we are able to describe both.[18]

The Internet, particularly the social networking sites, has made the world even more familiar and we are able to describe or relate quickly something we might not have ever seen or experienced.

Apart from the issue of the viewer's secondary relationship to photographs, photography can be intrusive (Figure 8.10). People who are photographed sometimes object to it: sometimes they become conscious of being photographed and may try to show certain aspects of themselves that *they* want to. Photographing children is a particularly sensitive issue at the time of widespread Internet scandals of child pornography, particularly those involving children from 'foreign countries'. The photograph in Figure 8.11 shows MA students in a park with moveable shelters that they had made from found materials. I had to explain the purpose of the project to mothers, who were curious (and perhaps a bit suspicious initially). In most circumstances, people, particularly children, enjoy being photographed, especially in the informal settlements. In the words of a student visiting a settlement in Delhi:

Figure 8.10 As with many Muslim countries, this lady in Tangiers was happy for her bakery shop to be photographed but not her face. I always ask permission before taking photographs. Many countries have areas where photographs are not allowed or restricted and it is important to be respectful and sensitive towards these rules otherwise it can be dangerous and silly. For example, one cannot take photographs near the American embassy in London. Some of my students found this out the hard way in Venezuela after the whole group was arrested, cameras taken and images deleted following a moment of bravado when two of them decided to take photographs near President Chavez's offices despite earlier warnings.

Photo: Author.

Figure 8.11 Projects in the park, Islington, London, MA Architecture of Rapid Change and Scarce Resources, London Metropolitan University, 2009.

Photo: Author.

It is an amazing thing to see how such a commonplace act of taking a picture can have such an overwhelming affect on these children. One such small device brought so much joy to so many kids. And to be warmly greeted by such cheerful children and adults was inspiring. It makes one want to pursue community base architectural work even more.[19]

However, photographs have to be taken with care and sensitivity, and aim towards showing dignity. Empowering people by giving them their own cameras and inviting them to take photographs is a technique that works well. In Julian Blanco, Caracas, I distributed disposable cameras to people to record events, places and people of importance to them. Thus, people can take photographs or take videos of their families in a more relaxed and non-intrusive way. This works well particularly with the less visible or vocal part of the community – the hidden players, as I have termed them. (Hidden players depending upon the cultural context can be women, children, youth and the elderly.)

At one site in West Delhi, by looking at the photographs of family members killed in the terrorist bombing, we realized that we were not just looking at one family, but the entire neighbourhood and community that existed before the bombing. This allowed us to construct a picture of the community that existed before the bombings and how it had been affected – some families had been thrown out to live on the streets. The children of the community had expressed their grief and worked through it by making images of their dead parents and keeping chickens as pets underneath the tree where the bomb had exploded. Somehow the simple act of empowering these 'hidden players', such as women and children, by giving them cameras can become a powerful exploratory tool for the development activist. The Participatory Video (PV) project in Rio De Janeiro, Brazil,[20] was a successful project where children carried out the filming themselves.

Sketching and drawing

Sketching and drawing on site is another technique to draw in participation from the community. Unlike photography, sketching is generally appreciated and considered non-intrusive and participatory. Farrelly points out that there are three basic types of sketches – conceptual, observational and analytical.[21] Any of these can be used to study and design in an area. However, we are particularly interested in observational sketches. These are very important because sketching can be a non-invasive and participatory experience in the soft city. Often children and other people will point out details that they would like drawn in and occasionally people join in the drawing themselves. In the words of a student sketching in Delhi:

> Through sketching, bridges to community members were created. Interest was generated; dialogue was initiated. Many community members approached me while I was sketching and mapping ... Although the initial interaction was cautious and suspicious due to the recent terrorist attack three months prior, once it was known that it was a school project, people became friendly and loquacious.[22]

The sketch in Figure 8.12 was drawn by a student; the residents of this squatter settlement wrote on it, thereby participating in the process and providing valuable clues to the community organization (see the writing in Hindi – people wrote the names of important local markers which the student could have missed). Sketching also provides a way of editing and grading aspects in importance. Photographs show the whole place – everything is recorded without discrimination. Sketching is more controlled because the sketcher can concentrate on the issues that he or she would like to highlight – this can be an advantage as well as a disadvantage. The sketch also highlights the delicate interaction of the street and the home, the threshold, the commercial use contrasting with the personal use.

Another method we have used consists of making sketches from photographs, editing or emphasizing details later – I call this the 'edited sketch'. This has been particularly useful for work in places where it can be impossible to sketch in peace. Throngs of children and people surround the sketcher, talking and asking questions, making it impossible to concentrate. In such cases, it is more useful to talk to the people and take photographs. Figure 8.13 shows sketches made by a student who used 'edited sketching' in order to concentrate on issues by reworking the photographs he took. Comparing it with photography where everything is recorded, there is a cautionary note to this type of sketch – both the sketch and the 'edited sketch' can also suffer from

Figure 8.12 Sketch of Nagla Devjit settlement, Agra, India.

Source: James Lloyd-Mostyn, Diploma Unit 6, London Metropolitan University, 2006.

Niches in adjoining wall of adjacent building

Corner of Arya Samaj Road and Gurudwara Road

Figure 8.13 'The edited sketch', Naiwallah, New Delhi.

Source: Viet Hoai Nguyen, MA Architecture of Rapid Change and Scarce Resources, London Metropolitan University, 2009.

the prejudice of the sketcher because sometimes the eye sees what it wants to see. Therefore, a sketch can be supplemented by a photograph.

Visual images and objects

> Art is important for it commemorates the seasons of the soul ... Art is not just for oneself, not just a marker of one's own understanding. It is a map for those who follow afterwards.
>
> (Clarissa Pinkola Estes)[23]

The symbolic nature of any art or visual or oral reference is of immense importance in understanding the settlement or building. The symbols as used on buildings are not only identification markers, but also denote motifs, rule systems and rituals. Through subsequent visits and observing people who use these spaces, the hidden symbolism of the space comes to light. Desmond Morris, an anthropologist states:

> [the symbol] is the basis of all games we play, all the story telling, all the theatre and cinema, all the fiction, all the fantasy, mythology and legend, and all the pictorial art. If we cannot make that leap, from the real to the seemingly real, and – just for a while – respond to them as one and the same, then art has lost one of its main functions.[24]

Another way to understand the community and culture is through visual images made or collected by the people themselves. Visual clues can be paintings, murals, votive figures, graffiti, photographs, altars and images of gods, etc. For the Aboriginal people of Australia, the same seriousness that is applied to issues of ownership of land is also applied to the making of art in the public domain. The making of the art is carried out using the 'Owners' – the people who work with others of the opposite moiety[25] – the workers are those who make the drawings in ritualistic fashion.[26] Here, the art *is* the experience. Rasmussen in experiencing art (and architecture) says: 'On the whole, art should not be explained, it should be experienced.'[27]

Project Morrinho is a social project that takes the form of a miniature city built by young people in Rio de Janeiro from brick, paint and other found materials inspired by the landscape, architecture and everyday life of the *favelas* that span the city.[28] In the summer of 2010, it arrived in London and was built with help from second generation Brazilians, some of whom had never been to Rio – thus through this artefact and act of building, these youngsters touched on the city's *favelas*. The Morrinho model has now grown to be over 350 square metres and involves not only the original eight boys but a whole cast of local youth – now more than twenty youngsters are involved in some capacity, from ages six to twenty-five. Joao Wrobel, a former student at London Metropolitan University, worked with Project Morrinho as part of Southbank Centre's 'Festival Brazil'. The Southbank project was a collaboration between six of the original Morrinho artists and youths from the Stockwell Park Estate in Lambeth, creating a landscape that fused places and stories – real and imagined – from the tower blocks of Lambeth to the backstreets of Rio de Janeiro (Figure 8.14).

Graffiti is a particular form of public expression that makes visible underlying issues – the artist is often anonymous but the message is loud and clear (Figure 8.15). In most Latin American countries for example, posters and graffiti are highly political statements. This kind of art started most famously in Mexico with the posters of Diego Rivera, José Clemente Orozco, David

Figure 8.14 Project Morrinho at Southbank, London, summer 2010.

Photo: Author.

Figure 8.15 The *barrio* boy wishes, graffiti in central Caracas, 2009.

Photo: Author.

Alfaro Siqueiros and José Guadalupe Posada, in the early part of the twentieth century, although now graffiti is used instead of posters. In the UK, the 'invisible' graffiti artist Banksy has a cult following while Blek le Rat from France, a former architect, is a visible public figure. As Banksy says: 'Graffiti is not the lowest form of art. There is no elitism or hype, it exhibits on some of the best walls a town has to offer ... A wall has always been the best place to publish your work.'[29] Where the graffiti appears is also significant; it usually appears in prominent places – junctions, just after an underpass, on buildings – where they can be seen easily either from a car or when walking.

Voices, people and histories

> Genuine dialogue results in the transformation of opposing viewpoints, changing them from wedges that drive people apart into bridges that link them together.
>
> Daisaku Ikeda[30]

Oral histories offer equally powerful imagery through words and songs. Panos is a London-based organization that promotes the participation of poor and marginalized people in national and international development debates through media and communication projects. Interviewing, note taking and listening skills are essential in this process. The problem affecting interviews and recording oral histories, however, is often of language and its interpretation. The development activist can be working in a culture and country whose language is not familiar to him or her. This can lead to what sociologist, Rebecca Abrams, describes as the language being 'injured'. According to her: 'One of the problems of translating an oral history interview ... is that meaning is injured in the process. Meaning is held not only in the words, but between the words, in the pauses and hesitations, in emphasis, inflection, intonation.'[31] As stated before, oral histories can be subject to fading memories, prejudice and the impact of recent events – thus precautions have to be taken with this.

The male/female participation in interviews is also hindered in certain religions and communities. In my work with Bangladeshi immigrants in the city of Birmingham and in Delhi, I found that in Muslim-dominated areas, female respondents were reluctant to come forward to me, even though I was another female, albeit from another culture and religion. In my work in rural areas of India, women would talk only in the presence of an elder female or a male, often the head of the household. This can also happen in non-Islamic but strongly masculine societies with high PDI (see Chapter 7) where women defer to men. In the aftermath of the tsunami in 2011, it was difficult to get Japanese women to speak about their issues, as reported by researchers from Tohoku University. Researchers for the magazine *Geography and You* also pointed out another reason for fewer female respondents. That was because questionnaires usually are based on locating the household rather than the individual (see Chapter 5 for the case study of the Jaisalmer wind farms). More often than not, it is the male who heads the household and answers the questions.[32] For interviews, it is important to seek out all participants, even using female interviewers in such communities.

Folk tales also provide a way of recording culture and social history. The professional folklorist, the ethnologist, anthropologist, theologian, archaeologist all have different aims – the development activist can use such tales to understand the community. For example, the Baniyas and other iterant tribes of India have folk songs and tales that tell us how the community moved from place to place and, more importantly, why they moved. This is important to the development activist in future resettlement plans. Migrants to the city often bring these songs and voices with them and thus they are important tools for the development activist. There are also specific times for telling stories and tales – Pueblo tribes tell stories in winter, while the cultures of Eastern Europe do it after the autumn harvest.

Folk theatre, songs and puppetry offer important clues to the community and its history. In Bengal and parts of Eastern Asia, such as Thailand, Burma and Malaysia, a person, usually a man, 'dresses up' in different costumes and make-up. He walks the streets, performing and begging. He is also a news giver and local gossip (the *bohurupiya* – person of many disguises), who wanders from place to place – a powerful personality. Storytelling is often connected with the rituals of inhabiting or even repairing buildings. In a UNESCO magazine is a description of the storyteller of the Djenne, Mali, who preaches to the people gathered to repair the earthen mosque at the end of Ramadan. In the absence of my inability to say it so beautifully, I reproduce the author's description below:

> The storyteller listened to the words, the sentences and the sounds, gathering them for a moment in his ears, his heart and his head. Then his tongue caressed them, cleansed them, drew them out, spun them, rinsed them and delivered them to the gathering, purged of all anguish and poison. For the spoken word can be a pain that kills and a dagger that scars for life ... He [the storyteller] said:
>
> > 'That walls have stopped weeping
> > That it is time to heal
> > The wounds left by winter.'
>
> (Albakaye Ousmane Kounta, *The Courier*, April 2000, published by UNESCO)

There are also modern and formalized forms of theatre for creating and documenting social urban change for the poor. The M Arch Urban Design students from Delhi School of Planning and Architecture organized street theatre to publicize the eviction of squatters before the Commonwealth Games in 2010 (see Chapter 3 for the story of the games). Radical forms of theatre have been developed by others, most notably by Augusto Boal – the Forum theatre

– a participatory form of theatre where the audience participates in forming an end or a solution to the dilemma presented (this is discussed in Chapter 6 on participatory design).

Time and patterns

Watching how a space is used at different times can be an investigative method. Different people use spaces at different times in different ways. Rituals are another way of appropriating space – through repetitive activities and visits, a person can make a place their own.[33] As architects and designers, we may assume that one space is used for one function. However, in squatter settlements where both private and public spaces are tight, spaces can be multi-functional. This can happen both inside and outside the home. I have observed a room being used as a sitting area during the day, for eating, for studying, and finally at night this room turns into a bedroom. The same space used for entertaining as well as study – the bed is used as a divan and table too. Thus, it can be incorrect to give a space a name denoting a single function in maps or plans of internal settlements.

A person's personal timeline is different too. We observed a woman in a squatter settlement going about her typical day – starting with getting up and taking her children to school and finishing with preparing the dinner and going to bed. We called her daily walk 'Sarita's journey'. The students followed her to get ideas for a project for Sarita. For years afterwards, I have followed her too and come to see how her journey has changed – new schools, paved streets and new toilets have changed her journey. In a similar manner, we observed the elderly women of a Sansi tribe who lived in the streets of Delhi – their rituals and the prayer times, the washing and feeding. The Sansi tribe were classified as 'natural born criminals' by the British in India and from this arose discrimination and prejudice against the tribe that remained long after the 'decriminalization' in 1952 (seven years after Indian independence). Most of the Sansi people we interviewed lived on the streets. By observing their pattern of living, the student proposed a museum and healthcare centre for the Sansi – a way of re-instituting their proud heritage. Public facilities in squatter settlements also show different uses at different times. While in India, a student recorded that at a particular time, a water pump was used by 300 different people while, at other times, it was used exclusively by women. The water pump thus became a communal resource – a place to meet and a social marker (lower castes in this area used a different pump).

The illustration in Figure 8.16 was made by a student who initially filmed the street and then using this was able to construct a map of the place as used by the people. So some of the areas are quite heavily used, while some are not; some are even secret watching places of people keeping an eye on their property. This was not evident straightaway from the filming but as the student gradually watching the collected films, this was revealed and then plotted on

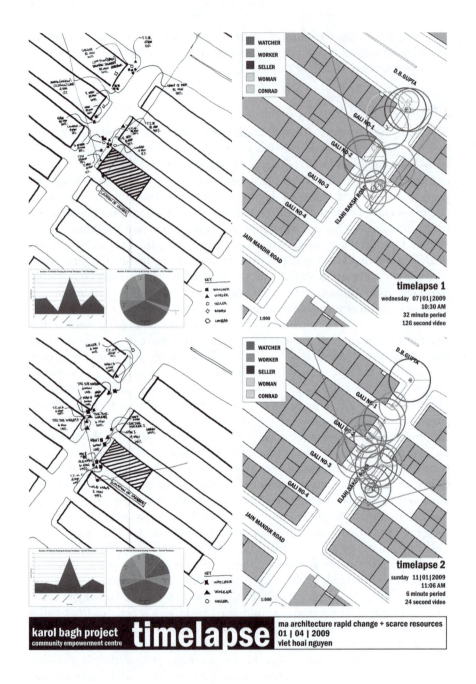

Figure 8.16 Naiwallah movement plans, Karol Bagh, New Delhi.

Source: Viet Hoai Nguyen, MA Architecture of Rapid Change and Scarce Resources, London Metropolitan University, 2009.

the street plans, perhaps similar to Snow's recording of the cholera outbreak, mentioned earlier.

Another way to get the temporal events of a settlement is by reading personal accounts of past visits and memoirs by others. Thus the description of Soweto's squatter settlements by Nelson Mandela[34] and the experience of Venezuela *barrios* in the *Motorcycle Diaries* by Che Guevara[35] give powerful images of these settlements as they existed. However, Raja Shehadeh, who has been walking the hills and areas around Palestine for the past thirty years, cautions us about accounts from past travellers. He says:

> The accounts I read do not describe a land familiar to me but rather a land of these travellers' imaginations. Palestine has been constantly reinvented, with devastating consequences to its original inhabitants. Whether it was the cartographers preparing maps or travellers describing the landscape in the extensive travel literature, what mattered was not the land and its inhabitants as they actually were but the confirmation of the viewer's or reader's religious or political beliefs.[36]

I encourage students to keep travel diaries, and do so myself, to try to record things as they are, not what they think they might be.

The participatory process of recording the soft city

> Don't be too hasty in trying to find a definition of the town; it's far too big and there's every chance of getting it wrong.
>
> (George Perec, *Species of Spaces and Other Pieces*, 1974, p. 81)

It should be clear that the soft city invites participation – one is never a bystander there. The participatory process of data collection is the best approach for a development activist – a process of collecting data together with the 'client' (Figure 8.17). Participatory design is a proven technique, so participatory data collection should be an efficient technique too. We have already seen how useful the participatory process can be in sketching, measuring, using a video camera, photographing and other ways. People living in informal settlements already have great fear of being displaced and uprooted – so although a slow process, working with the people works best.

Working in the soft city is a time-consuming process. Teolinda Bolivar has worked in the *barrios* of Caracas for the last forty years and Ashish Muni Ganju has worked in an Indian slum for the last twenty years. A true development activist has to engage in a community for some time to understand it. As Thoraya Ahmed Obaid, UNFPA executive director, says:

Figure 8.17 MA student showing her photographs to the residents, Kalyan Puri, East Delhi.

Photo: Author.

> In our development efforts in poor communities, we need to be able to
> work with people at their own level and to find common ground. We
> may not believe in what they do, we may not agree with them, but we
> need to have the compassion and the commitment to understand them
> and to support them as they translate universal principles into their own
> codes, messages and ways of doing things.
>   (See http://www.unfpa.org/culture/tips.htm; accessed September 2011)

Informal settlements are unpredictable places. Unpeeling the layers of
visual and kinaesthetic stimuli, the romanticization of the desperation of the
people, the personal discomforts and the educational barriers make a conventional approach difficult. How we approach pluralistic demands and prioritize
them in the design process are key issues for the development activist. Our
education offers us a privileged position and choices that the poor and vulnerable do not have. At present, student curriculum does not offer the kind
of perspective required to work in these areas (although poverty and lack of
housing are probably the fastest growing issues of the urban world). Essential
skills such as listening, note taking and managing meetings are needed to
work in the architecture of rapid change and scarce resources but are hardly
taught in architectural schools.

The different stimuli and conditions that the informal soft city offers can be confusing but equally creative. 'In urban environments in which opportunities for appropriating space for pluralistic purposes are all too often foreclosed by imposition of urban regulations, ask what if?' says Juliet Davis.[37] My academic approach has been to explore the 'discomforts' that a soft city offers. Architectural research can be a lonely business in which one grapples with the complexities that the design presents. Like a mirror, the discomforts we have with the projects are issues with which we have personal problems, such as the example of the female student's fears with exploring the settlement described earlier. Through confronting and exploring her discomforts instead of avoiding them, she was able to find a creative solution.

The development activist has to be flexible in his or her approach in order to work through and record the complexities present in the squatter settlements. There is no one approach, no one methodology. This often confuses architects trained in the 'modernist approach' to have one view, one methodology that is followed systematically. Then again, because of this, the evaluation of the soft city remains an exciting, open and challenging process. However, it is our human approach or reaction to a place that is most important and credible. This is not sentimentalism, but a realism grounded in practicalities of being in a place that we have no idea about. Ultimately, whatever way we choose to observe and record in the place, it is the place that is important, not us. In the words of Alain de Botton (who in turn echoes the warning of Raja Shehadeh quoted earlier):

> It is unfortunately hard to recall our quasi-permanent concern for the future, perhaps the first thing to disappear from memory is just how much of the past we spent dwelling on what was to come; how much of it that is, we spent somewhere other than where we were. There is a purity in both remembered and in the anticipated visions of a place, it is the place that is allowed to stand out.[38]

Discussion points

- 'The sole cause of man's unhappiness is that he does not know how to stay quietly in his room'.[39] In light of this, do you think it is best to leave informal settlements alone?
- What are the different ways of recording and observing the soft city that you have used? Out of these, which have been most effective and why?
- Which of the aspects of observing the soft city have you found most difficult – auditory, visual or kinaesthetic? Cultural, social or political?
- What kinds of fears and discomforts have you had in exploring the city?

Chapter 9

The development activist and new ways of working

> In this area are the professional consultants who specialize in uncertainties and value choices in their work. For them, each case is unique. In many important cases we do not know and we cannot know, what will happen, or whether our system is safe. We confront issues where facts are uncertain, values in dispute, stakes high and decisions urgent.
>
> (Ziauddin Sardar[1])

As I write this chapter, I have just received news that one of my former students is planning to buy a boat and sail around the world, carrying out development work as he stops at various places. Another writes that, feeling very inspired by one of the trips we took, he is planning to work and travel further afield. Indeed, as globalization spreads and recession hits many of the richer nations, architects are looking for work abroad. Not only are they looking for work in a conventional way in offices, some are indeed 'discovering' work that needs to be done and doing it. Some are fundraising for development projects, becoming designers, managers and builders of projects too. In an interview with *Building Design*, the architect Sarah Wigglesworth says: 'My real education came when I started thinking for myself.'[2]

Slums, informal settlements and other areas of scarce resources are complex urban forms. These complex systems are constantly adapting to their changing situation and environment. Complex systems have elements that are linked to each other – like the weft and weave of a cloth. Here our objectives cannot be to control, but to participate and facilitate. The 'post normal scientist' has much in common with the development activist working in the field of rapid change and scarce resources. The development activist like the post normal scientist stands in this complex and chaotic world, trying to make meaning of it and propose solutions.

If we can imagine a series of concentric circles denoting the ways of working in design, at the centre is the traditional 'applied science' or the work of the typical architect or engineer – the safe place in the centre. This kind of practitioner is a desk architect, perhaps with a few select clients who know what they want. These clients have money, ideas and power. In the next outer circle we come to development activists who are working in areas such as infrastructure, community projects or social housing. They have clients with whom they interact via various agents such as housing associations and local bodies. There is some consultation and participation but the whole process of design is managed in a tight sequence. But further out towards the edge of this circle is the realm of chaos and complexity – the area of rapid change and scarce resources (Figure 9.1). This is the area of 'fuzzy logic', of 'soft' information and data, of informal settlements, new types of urban morphologies such as the megacity, of sustainable development, culture, etc. Increasingly, in a world dominated by chaos, we are far removed from the security of traditional practice and the world of the 'armchair architect'. As Nabeel Hamdi says:

> All of this comes at a time when that old paradigm, based on Newtonian thinking – which is deterministic and reductive and which values certainty and predictability, trying hopelessly to pin it all down – is today displaced in favour of emergence, self-organization and holistic thinking. Holistic thinking moves us away from certainty and instead, toward an appreciation of pluralism, an acceptance of ambiguity and paradox.[3]

Figure 9.1 Flower sellers at night market, Karol Bagh, New Delhi. Working with multi-form spaces such as these requires 'pluralistic thinking'.

Photo: Author.

Here the extended peer community consists of the housewife, the slum dweller, the community groups, the stakeholders, the advocacy or human rights lawyer, etc. These people bring extended facts including their own personal experience, surveys and scientific information that otherwise might not have been in the public domain. Squatter settlements have become the playground for different players with different interests, some of which are conflicting. Modifying Malcolm Gladwell's terminology from his book *Tipping Point*, I have come up with three main players we can find in squatter settlements – the mavens, the connectors and the influencers.

The mavens (a Yiddish word) are the 'Gurus' – people with knowledge who are respected within the society. I would like to think that development activists and architects are the mavens who can facilitate the work. The connectors are people with social skills and connections within that community. In my experience, women tend to be very powerful 'connectors' in a community. Influencers are people who may or may not come from that society but have a big influence on it – such as politicians, religious leaders and even actors. As Jeff Bridges, actor, quoted in *Mail* online, 13 February 2010, says of his work with the disinvested in the USA:

> One thing I'm really proud of is the work I do with the End Hunger Network. There are many homes in the US where the mother has to tell her children they won't get dinner that night. They suffer spiritually, socially, in every way. It's hard to imagine, but the US ranks last among the top 23 industrialized nations in how it takes care of its poor and its hungry.

New ways of working

You can only predict things after they have happened.
(Eugene Ionesco, 1912–94, French playwright)

The resourceful architect of today needs to be finding work as 'conventional' sources of work such as patronage and one-job-for-life dry out. In Charles Handy's words, this is the era of the 'portfolio worker' who can show diversity of work. Many skills needed for practice in today's world of rapid change and scarce resources are not taught in the formal education of architecture. These include practical skills such as business and promotional skills, understanding of the economy as well as 'softer' skills such as using participatory design and dialogue. The resourceful architect needs to have a portfolio of both small projects and large ones – of local and global. It does not matter if these projects are real or projected (Figures 9.2 and 9.3) – the architect needs to demonstrate his or her depth and broadness of vision. For the work of the resourceful architect should not only be able to be placed in a context different from his or her 'home' country but also have an influence on the global.

Architects have always had a flexible approach to work and have been known to work in several other different areas after finishing their studies if they do not work as architects. So among those who studied architecture but have gone separate ways, we have a hair product magnate (Charles Worthington), an actor (Greg Wise), pop musicians (Pink Floyd, Pet Shop Boys), beauty queen and actress (Aishwariya Rai, Miss World 1994) and even royalty (Queen Noor of Jordan). In the April 2011 issue of *RIBA Journal*, architect and academic Richard Weston describes how he has ventured into selling scarves printed with high resolution images of crystals and leaves at Liberty store in London, all arising from his love for nature. However, some people advocate specialising in certain niche areas. Architecture, in particular, gives a good general grounding in almost all subjects so that 'there is a fear ... that this can spread [architects] too thinly across the design process', according to Ian Collins, an architect who has now started a property development company.[4] From the positive reaction to his work, Collins also advocates a more open-door policy where staff in a practice are allowed to 'explore other avenues through career breaks and sabbaticals, then welcome them back with a new outlook and experience.'[5]

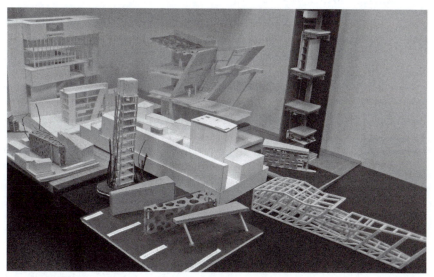

Figure 9.2 Student work from year 3, Birmingham City University, 2011, showing different 'structural design models' for a project.

Photo: Author.

Figure 9.3 Room travel project: room as the city. Students were asked to write a diary and make movies or photograph their room as an imaginery landscape.

Source: Dan Courtney, MA Architecture of Rapid Change and Scarce Resources, London Metropolitan University, 2008.

Sara Muzio: case study

Sara's case appears to be similar to many architects who have multifaceted talents and qualifications. Sara is a film director, artist and writer. Having lived, travelled and studied across Europe and Latin America, Sara specializes in cross-cultural approaches to cultural, social and economic development.

Sara has a degree in architecture and an MA in animation. Her portfolio includes films, books and large-scale public installations. Sara's architectural dissertation, 'Contested realities: new topographies of power in Caracas', focuses on the way social conflict is expressed and played out in the urban territory, and includes extensive fieldwork in Caracas, Venezuela.

As a filmmaker, Sara's films have been screened internationally at film festivals and exhibitions, including the Tenth Venice Biennale of Architecture. Sara's projects include Canning Town Caravanserai, in which 6,000 square metres of brownfield land will be transformed into a living installation by a collective of architects, artists, thinkers, makers, community groups and local residents; completing a four-part research project in Brazil; collaborating on a book with a contemporary vision of Bolivia; and continuing to teach film and animation workshops at architecture schools in the UK and abroad. For architects, as demonstrated by Sara's case, their means of expression of design and architecture lies not just within conventional practice as we understand it but also in other fields such as film-making, exhibitions and writing.

Social enterprise and pro bono work

Social enterprises are organizations or projects that apply business strategies to achieve a social purpose. This includes both a non-profit model that uses a business set-up to pursue its mission and a for-profit model whose primary purpose is social enhancement by using the profits. The primary aim is to work on projects that have social and/or environmental as well as financial incentives – often referred to as the triple bottom line. In fact, as Levitt and Dubner show in their book, *Freakonomics*, the three incentives together are very powerful – if any one of these is missing, often the enterprise does not work at all.[6] Many commercial businesses would consider themselves to have social objectives, but social enterprises are distinctive because their social and environmental aspects remain the most significant driving factor.

Many development activists and architects have branched out in the area of social enterprise, as their goals have been more altruistic anyway to begin with. This could also be an effective business model. As Nabeel Hamdi once put it, '90 per cent of architects are after 10 per cent of the jobs while 90 per cent of the world is looking for architects.'[7] The main problem with this social model is the lack of money from their 'clients'. The 90 per cent of those seeking architectural or technical assistance do not have money to pay for architects' fees. For a successful business, it must be a sustainable business. Many architects balance their social enterprise work with other work that brings in regular money.

The work of the development activist is based in the real world and tested there. However, it can be particularly disheartening when students work on academic projects that are based on incomplete or even 'made-up' research due to the pressure of academic timetables. This means that the time that was spent on the projects was merely a theoretical exercise – a waste of time if the intention of the student was to work in real development practice. Writing in the *Building Design* issue of March 2011, the architect Ben Addy from Moxon architects, sets out a case for making students examine 'real-life' issues such as business and ethics while studying. His argument: architecture is not a hobby; students cannot be expected to pick up such vital issues through 'osmosis' while working on live projects. He says that the benefits of introducing business and ethics units into courses are clear: 'It would be a fascinating and enjoyable part of their studies, providing a better understanding of their future role later on, while engendering a healthy self-respect.'[8] I get many applications from students with varied education and work experience for my course, ranging from apple-picking in Andalusia, cow milking in Norway and llama farming in Devon (all real examples), students who run bar/restaurants, to mature students with many years of work behind them. John Le Carré stated that the desk was a dangerous place from where to observe the world – I would argue that it is in the real world that students learn and that practices could be more creative in encouraging students to develop and take responsibility for projects. Many other design studios across the world are increasingly turning to the real world and socially relevant work to use in teaching (Figure 9.4).

Free work

In this category come volunteering, charity work and pro bono work. Many young people volunteer for charity work, including the areas of development and disaster. Since 1993, the United States has invested in volunteerism through a national service programme called Americorps. Each year, 75,000

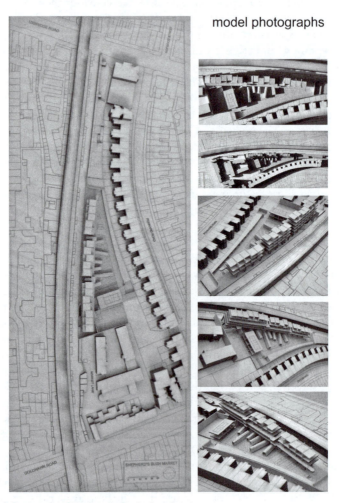

model photographs

Figure 9.4 Project for Shepherd's Bush, London.

Source: Conrad James, MA Architecture of Rapid Change and Scarce Resources, London Metropolitan University, 2008.

young people enlist in Americorps. The volunteers commit to ten months of service, fulfilling needs in under-resourced communities. This includes critical work such as tutoring children, building homes and conducting HIV tests. According to reports, Americorps has increased the organizational capacity of respected charities such as Habitat for Humanity, the American Red Cross and Teach for America.

The architecture student, not only owing to pressure of having to finish their apprenticeship, but also from an interest in further work in the area of rapid change and scarce resources, will often volunteer to work with various charities and organizations in return for a small honorarium or even just expenses (Figure 9.5). Sometimes even this is not paid. Organizations such as Architecture for Humanity, Architects Sans Frontières and Article 25 depend on such voluntary or reduced salary work. Recently, with the UK government promoting the 'Big Society' where participatory and voluntary action in communities in the form of pro bono work is being urged, many are volunteering for such work. However, many architects are seeing this as more of a 'smoke screen to cover cuts in essential services'[9] and instead would like to see more paid work for architects and promotion of architecture through schemes in the UK such as 'Open-City' and 'Architect in the house'.

The other phenomenon is that of studying and doing such work which has the additional bonus of getting one's internship or apprenticeship covered

Figure 9.5 MA students from London Metropolitan University work on a structure designed with found materials, Braziers community, Oxfordshire, 2008.

Photo: Author.

while studying and doing such worthy designs. Many architecture schools operate studios that work in such environments, so that students work on real-life projects for beneficiaries. The most well known among such studios is the Rural Studio, which is based in Newbern, Alabama, USA, as mentioned earlier. It places a great importance on the social responsibility of the architect and architectural students. According to one of its founders, Samuel Mockbee: 'If architecture is going to nudge, cajole, and inspire a community to challenge the status quo into making responsible changes, it will take the subversive leadership of academics and activists who keep reminding students of the profession's responsibilities.'[10] The Rural Studio has built more than eighty houses and civic projects in Hale, Perry and Marengo counties and received several awards since 1995. Many other initiatives operate now in the UK, South Africa, Australia, India and other countries.

Many firms allow for a small amount of free professional consultation. In the USA, John Peterson, the founder of Public Architecture, an advocacy group dedicated to making architecture more socially engaged, started the 1 per cent campaign, which has recruited nearly 400 firms to its cause. The 1 per cent campaign encourages pro bono service by architects and designers. In the UK, many firms are doing pro bono work, including John McAslan's practice, which has carried out work in Malawi and other places in Africa. However, as sometimes interviews reveal, the purpose of such work may not be completely altruistic – they get (or hope to get) other work on the back of such free work. Also, often it is easier for bigger practices to do pro bono work than for smaller or sole activists because they can absorb 'losses'. As about 60 per cent of UK architecture firms are between six and ten people strong, it may be difficult to find UK practices that take on work in areas of rapid change and scarce resources or have resources set aside for pro bono work for which the development activist could volunteer (Figure 9.6).

The biggest problem, however, comes from the lack of clear guidance over how such work is covered under professional indemnity and public liability insurances. As Paul Hyett, past president of the RIBA, asks in reference to professional identity, 'are the schools of architecture preparing graduates properly, in term of both the scope and the quality of service?'[11] Work in disaster or war zones is particularly appealing to young people and satisfying as it is easy to see the difference quickly. However, it could be quite dangerous when occasionally volunteers manage to get involved in situations beyond their control or take undue risks (Figure 9.7). The story of Linda Norgrove, the Scottish aid worker with a Master's degree in rural resources and environmental policy, who was killed in October 2010 after a botched-up rescue operation carried out by the American Army in Afghanistan is a stark reminder of how dangerous aid work can be. I had an architect friend who contracted a serious disease while working in Afghanistan. Insurance cannot prevent anyone from being killed or hurt in such conditions but certainly can help in times of need, provided of course that the insured have not recklessly

Figure 9.6 Community Empowerment Centre, Karol Bagh, New Delhi. Given adequate resourcing and support, is it possible to build student projects?

Source: Viet Hoai Nguyen, MA Architecture of Rapid Change and Scarce Resources, London Metropolitan University, 2009.

Figure 9.7 A city divided, Belgrade. It may be difficult to obtain insurance and financial backing for work in areas of rapid change and scarce resources.

Photo: Author.

placed themselves in danger.

While researching on this issue for my own small charity, I was informed that bigger charities and NGOs such as Oxfam and the Red Cross are easier to cover, as they are bigger organizations. Also, we note that these organizations do not employ architects. The RIBA discourages 'free work' and the guidance from the Architects Registration Board (ARB) is very specific and would apply while working in areas of rapid change and scarce resources. I have extracted the following from ARB's guidance on public liability insurance:

- The board is also aware that in certain instances, architects may be reliant on others to provide cover/protection on their behalf. Examples of this are those acting as consultants, through agencies, or providing casual or gratuitous advice. Architects may not need to maintain their own policy where other appropriate cover/protection is provided on their behalf, but again should seek confirmation of that cover in writing.
- Consideration needs to be given to the issues surrounding pro bono work. Work carried out for free is unlikely to be free of liability. It is not uncommon for claims to be made against architects for pro bono work and suitable protection will be required, as for other categories of work.
- Architects should ensure that any work they undertake overseas is adequately covered by their policy. They should also consult with their broker as to under which country's laws any claim might arise.

On a happy note, I did manage to obtain insurance cover for myself and any volunteers who may work for my charity. The insurers took a long time to find a quote stating that the work I proposed to do in slums and squatter settlements was something they never had to deal with. I hope that with more students and architects engaged in development practice abroad, insurance would be easier to find in the future.

Development activists: what to do

On 21 December 1931, a young man named Richard Crews sent letters to the offices of several prominent Chicago architects inquiring about the demands of daily life in the profession.[12] He received carefully written responses from at least four members of the profession: Howard White, a founding member of one of Chicago's most renowned firms, Graham, Anderson, Probst & White (successors to D.H. Burnham & Co.); Chas Morgan, an active associate of Frank Lloyd Wright; Ernest Braucher, who designed Craftsman-style residences in Chicago; and Clarence Doll. Doll, about whom not much is known, gave the most pragmatic piece of advice – that holds well even today:

> Perhaps this short narrative will surprise you, as well as many others, for an architect's work is quite varied from just drawing. He is much more of

a business man than you may imagine, and for this reason a commercial course in his education is of great importance.

Chas Morgan was the only one to offer advice of a philosophical nature: 'A real architect like a good man in any business does not waste any time whatsoever doing things of which he might be ashamed, he must above all be a sincere artist.' Reflecting on these letters, I think they are just as relevant today as they were eighty years ago. Even more than a conventional designer, the development activist must be a practical business person but yet be able to have a philosophical view.

So having introduced in the book what issues development activists must study in further detail, I can now finish with three guidelines, which I feel are the most important things that they must always do. These are not my views alone but distilled from talking to many architect and teachers. If I had to leave you, the reader, with something, then these three points are what I would like you to remember.

Talk! And listen!!

Sarah Wigglesworth's advice to someone who wants to be an architect? 'Don't worry about getting good marks, network like mad – it's the contacts that count.' The chances of finding work can be really jeopardized if the development activist does not make and keep up contacts. Filipe Balestra and Sara Göransson,[13] who are now working in India, say:

> [We] had the privilege to meet Jockin Arputham, the president of the National Slum Dwellers Federation in India, in a press conference in Stockholm. I was very inspired by his talk. After the talk was finished, I introduced myself to him and spoke about Sambarchitecture, the designing and building of a school and community centre in Rocinha – one of the largest slums in Rio de Janeiro – in a participatory design and construction process together with the community.

And it appears this worked for them.

Be honest

A fair degree of honesty is required in not only what you are doing but also in assessing your own capabilities. Do you have what is takes to be a development activist? This kind of work is not only physically demanding, it also needs the quick and rational thinking for emergencies and long-term work in areas of rapid change and scarce resources. It needs someone who is also fairly well educated in the extensive knowledge required for this kind of work – ranging from basic social skills such as talking and listening to how money is spent on projects. The extent of knowledge needs to be broad as well as deep – as sometimes it takes many years to accumulate such knowledge.

Be curious

I have talked about this quality before but need to emphasize this again, having found it in so many books written by economists, architects, designers and in fact everyone! 'Conventional wisdom' and practice can be out of place, especially in today's world of complexity and chaos. It is essential to be a sceptic but not to be a cynic. The cynic dismisses everything, thereby missing something quite valuable, while the sceptic looks at problems from different angles and will end up finding a solution. The sceptic might be slow and sure while the cynic will be quick and full of doubts.

Think outside the box

Informal settlements are complex places. Solutions can be simple but one needs to think outside the box. So think outside the box but with concern for the client and context. The uncertainties we face in real life do not have much in common with the sanitized environment of the academic world. As Alan Fletcher says, 'Everything is connected with everything else and searching for solutions often requires being alert to spot the unlikely connections.'[14]

Case studies of student work

Case study 1: the Complexities of Development in Alexandra Township, Johannesburg. Tatum Lau, MA Architecture of Rapid Change and Scarce Resources, London Metropolitan University, 2010.

In 2005, second-year students from the University of the Witwatersrand in Johannesburg documented the courtyards, homes and stories of people living in Alexandra Township (informally known as Alex). Through the process of conversation, sketching and measuring, a class of about sixty-five students was able to document information such as density, unemployment, tribal differences, crime rates and number of children per family. In the courtyard we investigated, our group came across a small shack being used as a crèche for thirty children (Figure 9.8). A woman from the neighbouring province, together with four volunteers ran the school for children aged between two and six. The 'crèche' was in reality someone's house, rented during the day and used by the owner for the rest of the time. It was made of blocks with a corrugated metal roof, perhaps the remains of a single story building from the past. The house had a small kitchen, a bedroom with no windows and an

Figure 9.8 Alexandra township 'crèche'.

Photo: Tatum Lau, University of the Witwatersrand, Johannesburg.

external space with a bucket for the children to use as a toilet. For this, they were charged R400 (£36) per month.

Parents were asked to contribute R50 (£4.50) per month towards the crèche but few parents could afford it and some children had no carers. Other than a few vegetables given by a local grocery, the crèche had no support. The volunteers told us that their situation was temporary and that they were hoping to move into a disused building nearby. They were excited about the prospect of being able to make a place their own, where they could have chalkboards and furniture and where they did not have to pack everything (even though it was not very much) away at the end of each day. It was then that as a group, we decided to assist in refurbishing their future building and supporting them in ways that we could, irrespective of what we did through the university.

Back at the studio, we put our drawings and models together to form a large detailed plan. Using conversations as data, we mapped the area and began to identify community needs, potential sites and possible interventions. Groups split up further and, in pairs, we began to design. For my partner and I, the need was obvious; thirty children from the crèche needed a safe, clean place to stay during the day as many children from the local area spent their day wandering around the streets of Alex. The challenge was to find a large enough site in a place where, whenever a piece of land became available, squatters moved in immediately.

At the same time, the Mandela's Yard Interpretation Centre was underway. The building was part of the Alexandra Renewal Project (ARP) (the name has since been changed to Alexandra Interpretation Centre) and the site for Mandela's Yard was chosen as a heritage site to mark the place where Nelson

Mandela once lived. In the parking area for the museum, a slither of land was left over, too narrow for a standard parking bay but reasonably generous in length – perfect for us. Our proposal consisted of three shipping containers of different lengths stacked above one another to create shaded areas, climbing areas and a small vegetable garden on the ground floor (Figure 9.9). The shipping container was the ideal width (2.3m) and could be locked up securely after hours. Shipping containers are structurally sound and easy to acquire, as it costs a business less to get rid of them than to return them back to their ports. At the time, the intention for the proposal was no more than a hypothetical university project.

After several weeks of returning to Alexandra, bringing with us electrical fans, stationery, books and other items donated by friends and fellow students, we began to build a relationship with the community in the courtyard. We learned that the challenges of running the crèche were not limited to the financial difficulties. Volunteers were not reliable as they themselves were faced with the harsh reality of surviving in Alex. Tribal differences and preconceptions between those who ran the crèche and others in the community meant that people could be distrusting when issues such as money arose. Alcoholism affected the employed, the jobless and the volunteers. We learned that agreements were often oral and therefore could easily be breached. We also learned that the land that was promised to the crèche had been sold to an international developer.

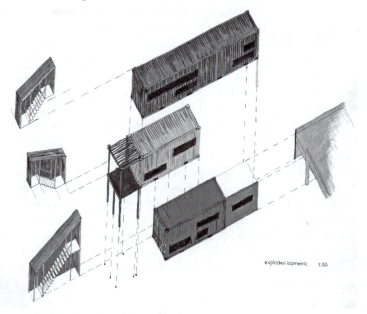

exploded isometric   1:50

Figure 9.9 Proposal using shipping containers.

Source: Tatum Lau, University of the Witwatersrand, Johannesburg.

Alexandra Township was designed to house 70,000 people but is estimated to have a population of between 350,000 and 750,000 people and is approximately 8 square kilometres in area. It is located on the banks of the Jukskei River between the affluent business district of Sandton and an industrial area, Malboro. 'Township' or 'location' is the South African term for a suburb or city of predominantly black occupation, formerly officially designated for black occupation by apartheid legislation. Alexandra is a combination of formal housing of brick and block work and informal shacks. The 1924 Urban Areas Act allowed the government to move non-whites to the peripheries of the city. Alexandra, however, was 'the only black spot in the white landscape after attempts to attract white buyers had failed'.[15] Under the Apartheid government preceding 1994, little infrastructure was implemented in black townships.

While mapping the more dilapidated parts of Alex, we found that at least half of the people from the area did not have jobs, because either they were too ill to work or because they believed that there was no work. In an essay entitled 'Crime and the Emerging Landscape', the author points out that 'areas disadvantaged under Apartheid are most vulnerable to murder, armed robbery, rape and violent assault – Soweto, Alexandra and Orange Farm'.[16]

Towards the end of 2005, we informed the architect for the Interpretation Centre, who was also our tutor at the time, about the crèche's failed plans to relocate. We found that if we could acquire three containers free of charge, the cost of the crèche for eighty children would only amount to R150,000 (£13,500). Mandela's Yard was conveniently located across the road from the existing crèche. Although our project was not part of the proposal for Mandela's Yard, which already had funding from the ARP, it seemed possible that we could slip it in as part of a late submission and since the centre had just gone onto site, it was very timely for us. Our proposal was awarded the 2006 prize by the Gauteng Institute of Architecture for 'the most convincing design proposal, which is a result of participatory research with a disadvantaged community'.

Building at Mandela's Yard began to slow down. We were informed that the future of Mandela's Yard was under discussion. We were not involved in any meetings that may have taken place with the local council and were never asked to produce more detailed information. As our proposal was never officially part of the Interpretation Centre, we thought it would be best to leave it in the hands of the architect involved. In the meantime, we began to look for independent funding and other potential sites even though we were unprepared for the possibility that a company would grant us the funding and nervous about how we could ensure it was managed correctly, as well as who would be responsible for managing the money. We knew that the donations we brought in did not always stay at the crèche. Although the crèche was a registered non-profit organization, documentation recording their activity and sponsors was limited. We were certain that putting the money directly into the crèche's account was not the right decision but we were not represented by any organization to receive money.

Throughout 2006, our group continued to work with the volunteers. It was unknown how long the crèche would have to wait for a new location but it seemed like a good idea to improve the conditions of the existing shack in the meantime, and the owner agreed that filling in a few holes and a bit of paint would dramatically improve the place or at least prevent infestation from vermin. During a term break, ten colleagues and I made plans to refurbish the house. We were able to get donations from hardware stores and friends in order to buy the necessary materials. We arrived at the crèche to find that none of the volunteers or parents had arrived as promised but at least the doors had been left open for us. We filled holes, repaired stairs, painted walls, built small benches and desks, put in a ceiling and put up shelves. The neighbours from the courtyard gave us a hand and we had lunch with them, treating their children to some sweets. A week later, we received a phone call from a community organization in Alex. The owner of the house had put up the rent as his newly refurbished house could fetch a higher price and the crèche would have to leave if they could not pay for it. We were also told that we had been discriminatory because we had bought sweets for a selected group. Fortunately, we were able to patch things up and celebrated together at the graduation Christmas ceremony in December 2006.

It was there that I met the founder of the NGO, Friends of Alexandra. Although we were not aware, he had been supporting the crèche for several months and had been looking for an architect to work with on a potential site for a new crèche. In the new year, the existing crèche had to find an additional R100 per month to pay the owner, Mandela's Yard was semi complete but put on hold owing to lack of governmental funding and the half of our original group of six that remained were left deflated. In March that year, however, on a farewell visit to Alexandra, I noticed that the foundations and columns had been laid to support future containers at the building site. Despite the fact that information had deliberately been held back from us, knowing that Friends of Alexandra had come into the picture and could find another architect was reassuring. Both of these things were signs of hope for the future.

Author's note: this account from Tatum highlights all issues involved in students working on real projects – funding, design planning, community participation and actual building. And the bittersweet experience of community engagement. Although the community got their building in the end, it may have been frustrating to work on something and not see it to fruition themselves. On a happy note, Tatum has used that experience to get more work and is working successfully with a practice in London.

Case study 2: Borderline Colonias
Bara Safarova, Diploma Free Unit, London
Metropolitan University, 2010.

In summer 2008, I spent two weeks as a volunteer, through Habitat for Humanity, building a family house in a settlement called 'Colonia Gerardo Perez' in Mexico (Figure 9.10). I worked as a labourer for Don Vicente's family in return for drinking water and lunch. The second week I was offered hospitality in their friend's house in the *colonia*, round the corner from the building site. This way I could learn not only about the process of building the house, which was to take only six weeks, but also about the parameters that give *colonias* urban form, size, material, density and social structure.

Colonias are legitimate suburbs of towns. A government representative divides land; roads, electricity, water supply and sewage are provided while private houses grow around them. Colonia Gerardo Perez was about nine years old but did not look finished. As there was 'no mortgage' there was incremental development with half-built structures. Approximately half of the *colonia* was built up, the rest consisted of provisional sheds, where people lived, while accumulating their houses in 'dry' form. When it came to building a house, it happened really quickly: with one architect – six visits, one builder – the rest of the workforce comprised the neighbours. The residents of the *colonia* would have worked on their neighbour's house. These were very often women as men had to go to work. On many occasions I was asked for professional help. I could only do as much as help mix the cement with the sand.

One phenomenon struck me, as a curious outsider and a student of architecture: despite the fact that all houses had flat roofs with water tanks, no one

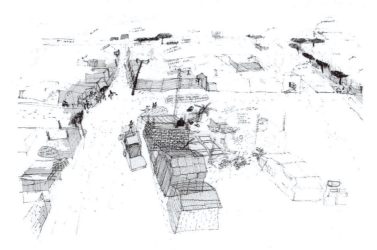

Figure 9.10 Sketch of Colonia Gerardo Perez.

Source: Bara Safarova, Diploma Free Unit, London Metropolitan University, 2010.

collected rain water, even though the *colonia* had piped water only between 11 a.m. and 1 p.m. every day. (Note: piped water in Mexico is not drinking water. Drinking water is bought in plastic bottles.) The site falls into the specific area of Cuernavaca (also known as 'Eternal Spring'), which gets heavy rain every day between 5 p.m. and 6 p.m. throughout the summer season.

In 2010 I decided to invest my time and effort of the final year thesis at London Metropolitan University and turn the paradox into a proposal. This seemed possible thanks to the structure of the Free Unit, in which students are required to bring their own projects. I was offered work on *colonias* in Texas, USA and along the Mexican border, which offers similar opportunities.

However, *colonias* in the USA are different and face bigger issues. They appear along the whole USA–Mexico border and carry the same name because they are based on the same principle – incremental development of edges of cities. The difference is that in the USA, the *colonias* are informal settlements not connected to 'host' cities. The United States Department of Housing and Urban Development (HUD) defines *colonias* as 'rural communities and neighbourhoods located within 150 miles (240 kilometres) of the US–Mexican border that lack adequate infrastructure and frequently also lack other basic services'. The Environmental Protection Agency (EPA) defines *colonias* as 'rural US settlements with substandard and poor living conditions along the US–Mexico border. These communities typically lack potable water, wastewater treatment, drainage, electricity, and paved roads.'

According to Wikipedia:

> In the 1990s, *colonias* became a common American English name for the slums that developed on both sides of the US–Mexican border. *Colonias* have existed along the border for decades, but since the passage of the North American Free Trade Agreement in 1994, the number of people living in *colonias* has increased significantly, due, in part, to the increase in low-skilled jobs created on both sides of the border through the maquiladora industry [...] From USA's point of view, *colonias* are illegal subdivisions created by rural settlers and are found near the US–Mexico border. [...] From Mexico's point of view, however, a *colonia* is a regular division inside every city, meaning suburbs or *fraccionamientos*.[17]

The *colonias* in the USA do not generate revenue; thus, cities do not provide public utilities, such as sewage, paving for roads, sidewalks, street lighting, postal services, etc.

The project suddenly lying ahead of me seemed to include rainwater collection as part of a wider strategy for rethinking the use of resources from scratch. The academic ground offered a great range of experts and a base of research and contacts. During our field trip to Texas, we visited Pliny Fisk at the Center for Maximum Potential Building Systems (CMPBS), which is an architectural studio researching use of alternative resources.

In Las Lomas Colonia, we met Blanca Juarez, the founder of Colonias Unidas, a non-profit organization helping *colonias* get funding to install basic services. At Texas A&M University which we visited, students and tutors are involved in testing local building materials and have developed IMPACT 2001, a hydraulic portable machine for making unfired blocks from widely available local soil called *caliche*. We also met representatives of Center for Housing and Urban Development (CHUD), an organization running the Colonias Program, which has opened over fifty community centres in *colonias* and is funding projects for the revival of *colonias*.

My student project was divided into two parts. One was based in Las Lomas, which is already upgraded to basic standard, yet lacks public footpaths, lighting and spaces. Using the research by CMPBS and Texas A&M, I proposed a manual for DIY making of pavements (side walks in American-English). The second part is a wider urban strategy for an alternative self-sufficient settlement built from DIY *caliche* bricks. To help them leap into reality, we went to Texas in summer 2011 to present the work to CHUD, Texas A&M and Colonias Unidas to discuss the best way forward. Both projects are currently available for contribution on Open Architecture Network.

Author's note

This work received the third prize in the Royal Society of Arts 2011 'Resourceful Architect' competition.

As these two examples of student projects show, it is not easy to get projects off to the building stage. However, it is through doing projects in the real world that we learn. Borrowing Makiguchi's idea of pragmatic education, it appears fitting to finish with his words:

> In school education should be closely connected in practice with actual life so that it can transform unconscious living into fully conscious participation in the life of society. Education integrated into the life of society will yield benefits of well-planned living, without undesirable effect of mechanical uniformity, an inherent danger in standardized education.[18]

Discussion points

1   How can we define the development activists' work?
2   What could be the essential person specification for the job description of a development activist?
3   Free work is often a necessary evil in the field of rapid change and scarce resources – how do you feel about that?
4   How can you 'future-proof' yourself as a development activist?

Appendix

Web references:

There are many references, books and websites in the suggested reading list which you can follow up. Google searches will yield many sources of information and work in other countries. Here are some to start you off, divided into two sections: one for finding work and one for information, although they may be interchangeable; that is, where you look for information may also be somewhere you can find work and vice versa.

1 Working, studying and volunteering in areas of rapid change and scarce resources (UK-based only)

http://www.actionaid.org.uk
http://www.architecture.com (useful resource to find architectural practices working in sustainable design, schools of architecture, travel and research grants)
http://architectureforhumanity.org
http://www.article-25.org
http://www.asf-uk.org/home.htm
http://www.cafod.org.uk
http://www.charushila.org.uk
http://www.christianaid.org.uk
http://www.do-it.org.uk
http://practicalaction.org (formerly Intermediate Technology)
http://www.progressio.org.uk
http://www.volunteering.org.uk
http://www.vso.org.uk

2 Looking for information

http://www.ashdenawards.org
http://www.bbc.co.uk (to be used with care)

http://www.earthhour.org

http://www.fco.gov.uk/en/travel-and-living-abroad/travel-advice-by-country
(this is a useful reference guide with current travel information to all
countries, although it specifically warns you not to go into slums and
squatter settlements. Always be careful and show respect for local traditions and cultures; listen to the advice of local people, when travelling
and working in any country. Remember that accidents and incidents can
happen anywhere.)

http://www.foe.org

http://www.greenpeace.org

http://www.guardian.co.uk (to be used with care)

http://www.iied.org

http://www.independent.co.uk (to be used with care)

http://www.indexmundi.com/g/r.aspx?t=0&v=21000&l=en

http://ngm.nationalgeographic.com

http://www.un.org/en (this website has links to other websites with useful
information such as http://www.unescap.org and http://www.unhabitat.
org.)

http://webarchive.nationalarchives.gov.uk/+/http://www.dfid.gov.uk/
Get-Involved/Developments-magazine/ (these are archived issues of
Development magazine) and also see http://www.dfid.gov.uk/Stories

http://www.worldmapper.org

http://www.wwf.org

Notes

1 Introduction: architecture of rapid change and scarce resources

1 Some of my friends questioned the need for me to do this and I agree that most fridges and some freezers are indeed very energy efficient now. Indeed, I have not heard of any teacher who goes through such drastic lifestyle changes to understand issues first hand. However, as I buy fresh food and grow some too and do not use 'convenience chilled/frozen foods', usually the huge fridge-freezer that came with the flat was empty. My experiment was simply to demonstrate that one can live without these 'necessities' – after all, I had been born and brought up in a hot tropical country without a fridge and, therefore, could not see any reason why I needed a fridge and a freezer in London. Of course, global warming might change all that!

2 Wateraid say: Both of these are from the WHO/UNICEF (2010) Joint Monitoring Programme report, available from http://www.wssinfo.org. These figures will be current until mid-2012 when the next report comes out: 4,000 children die every day from diarrhoea caused by unclean water and poor sanitation. This comes from WHO (2008) Safer Water, Better Health, available at: http://whqlibdoc.who.int/publications/2008/9789241596435_eng.pdf (p. 12 figure for diarrhoea 0–14 (being 'children' in a population context, rather than health) 1,370,000 divided by 365 equals ~3,750, rounded up to 4,000. There are newer figures (for 2004 rather than 2002) available in the tables linked below, which are slightly higher: see www.who.int/quantifying_ehimpacts/publications/saferwater/en/index.html. However, they do not disaggregate by age group. Figures we obtain directly from WHO do disaggregate by age group 0–4 (i.e. under-5s, the normal interpretation of 'children' in a health context), and using these they give a figure ~4,200, which rounds down to 4,000. These statistics are kindly supplied by Wateraid.

3 See www.un.org/esa/socdev/unyin/documents/ydiDavidGordon_poverty.pdf (accessed May 2010).

4 See www.nybooks.com/articles/archives/2011/may/12/quality-life-india-vs-china/?pagination=false (accessed April 2011).

5 Ian Ritchie, lecture at the University of Westminster, 30 January 2000.

6 See http://www.bdonline.co.uk/news/riba-gets-its-meeting-with-michael-gove/5020479.article (accessed July 2011).

7 Jessica Williams, *50 Facts that Should Change the World*, new edn, London: Icon Books, 2005.

8 See www.cellular-news.com/coltan (accessed July 2011).

9 See www.btselem.org/water/consumption_gap (accessed July 2011).

10 Williams, *50 Facts that Should Change the World*.

11 Ibid.

12 See http://en.wikipedia.org/wiki/List_of_cities_proper_by_population_density (accessed June 2011) – 2006 figures.

13   See   http://portalsostenibilidad.upc.edu/archivos/fichas/informes/huellaecol%F3gicadetoronto.
     pdf (accessed June 2011).

14   Nassim Nicholas Taleb, *The Black Swan: The impact of the highly improbable*, New York:
     Random House, 2007, p. 89.

15   Alex Wright, *Glut: Mastering Information through the Ages*, Washington: Joseph Henry
     Press, 2007.

16   Stephen Levitt and Steven Dubner, *Freakonomics: A Rogue Economist Explores the Hidden Side
     of Everything*, London: Penguin, 2007.

17   See   www.fastcompany.com/1751745/the-new-faces-of-greenwashing-and-their-mothers
     (accessed July 2011).

18   Tony Juniper, *How Many Light Bulbs Does It Take to Change a Planet? 95 ways to save the
     planet*, London: Quercus, 2007.

19   Dorothy Rowe, *The Real Meaning of Money*, London: HarperCollins, 1998.

20   See http://in.lifestyle.yahoo.com/life-work/now-snapdealcom-nagar-article-ilmx.html (accessed
     July 2011).

21   Guy de Maupassant, *The Necklace*, new edn, Hertfordshire: Wordsworth Editions, 1997,
     p. 109.

22   See http://architecture2030.org/the_problem/buildings_problem_why (accessed March 2008).

23   George Elton Mayo, *Hawthorne and the Western Electric Company: The social problems of an
     industrial civilisation*, London: Routledge, 1949.

24   Levitt and Dubner, *Freakonomics*.

25   Also, as 'You are therefore I am' – *You Are Therefore I Am* is the title of a book by Satish
     Kumar, Totnes, Devon: Green Books, 2002.

26   See www.guardian.co.uk/science/2006/feb/16/environment.uknews (accessed June 2011).

27   See www.ucsusa.org/global_warming/science_and_impacts/science/global-warming-
     faq.html (accessed May 2011). As they say, 'Because our atmosphere is one connected
     system, it is not surprising that ozone depletion and global warming are related
     in other ways.' Also see www.independent.co.uk/environment/ozone-hole-linked-to-
     southern-rain-increases-2274321.html (accessed July 2011). See also Dinyar Godrej,
     The No-Nonsense Guide to Climate Change, Oxford: New Internationalist Publications,
     2007, pp. 42–3.

28   See www.guardian.co.uk/environment/2009/dec/01/ozone-antarctica (accessed July 2011).

29   *National Geographic*, June 2010.

30   *National Geographic*, June 2010.

31   You can check your own ecological footprint here: www.myfootprint.org (accessed July 2011).

32   Juniper, *How Many Light Bulbs?*

33   *National Geographic*, September 2009.

34   You can see some evocative photographs about 'Failed States' here, called 'Postcards from Hell':
     www.foreignpolicy.com/articles/2011/06/20/postcards_from_hell_2011 (accessed June 2011).

35   Mike Davis, *Planet of Slums*, London: Verso, 2006.

36   See   http://aangirfan.blogspot.com/2011/02/third-world-british-hospitals.html   (accessed
     September 2011) and *Daily Mail*, 22 July 2003.

37   According to Nassim Nicholas Taleb's bestseller *The Black Swan: The impact of the highly
     improbable* (New York: Random House, 2007), the differences between Eastern and
     Western culture are 'superficial'. I disagree, probably because I come from India and do
     recognize the sharp ideological, cultural and social differences between India and the UK.

38   See   www.un.org/esa/socdev/unyin/documents/ydiDavidGordon_poverty.pdf   (accessed
     May 2010).

39   Kisho Kurukawa, quoted in *Theories and Manifestoes of Contemporary Architecture*, ed. Charles
     Jencks and Karl Kropf, London: Academy Editions, 1997.

40   See www.tmakiguchi.org. T. Makiguchi, *Education for Creative Living*, trans. Alfred
     Birnbaum, ed. D. M. Bethel, Iowa: Iowa State University Press, 1989.

41 Theodore Kaczynski, in an interview with the *Earth First! Journal*, Administrative Maximum Facility Prison, Florence, Colorado, USA, June 1999.

42 See http://www.ikedaquotes.org/education/education434?quotes_start=14 (accessed June 2011).

2 Big games and small money

1 See https://secure.avaaz.org/en/make_giving_powerful/?cl=891465932&v=8070 (accessed January 2011).

2 Helena Norberg-Hodge, *Ancient Futures*, London: Rider Books, 2000.

3 See www.telegraph.co.uk/sport/othersports/olympics/news/8640217/Japan-bid-for-Olympics-to-aid-tsunami-recovery.html (accessed July 2011).

4 Laura Stack, *Leave the Office Earlier: Do more in less time and feel great about it*, London: Piatkus, 2004.

5 See www.grossnationalhappiness.com (accessed September 2011).

6 John Maynard Keynes, quoted in David Boyle, *The Little Money Book*, Bristol: Fragile Earth Books, 2003, p. 65. Also see http://www.panarchy.org/keynes/national.1933.html (accessed July 2011).

7 See www.noticierolegal.com/index.php?option=com_content&view=article&id=6539%3Apersiste-alta-inflacion-en-venezuela&catid=41%3Abcv&Itemid=42 (accessed March 2011).

8 There is good explanation of this in David Boyle's *The Little Money Book*, Bristol: Fragile Earth Books, 2003.

9 In Canada, Probe International launched the debate over odious debts in 1991 with the publication of *Odious Debts: Loose Lending, Corruption, and the Third World's Environmental Legacy* (Patricia Adams, Probe International Publications, 1991). See also http://probeinternational.org/library/wp-content/uploads/2010/11/Odious-Debts.pdf (accessed May 2011).

10 Williams, *50 Facts that Should Change the World*.

11 See http://email.cogdesign.com/t/ViewEmail/r/A8D616F86BEF0B98/341DE9B1D56FC1ED2540EF23F30FEDED (accessed March 2011).

12 *Evening Standard*, 24 May 2010.

13 *Metro*, 26 May 2011.

14 Yara Sharif, PhD thesis, University of Westminster.

15 Garrard, Her Majesty's jeweller is now using fair trade gold, *Metro*, 14 February 2011.

16 See www.adb.org/gender/practices/infrastructure/ind001.asp (accessed June 2011).

17 Efforts to replicate Grameen-style solidarity lending in developed countries have generally not succeeded. For example, the Calmeadow Foundation tested an analogous peer-lending model in three locations in Canada during the 1990s. It concluded that a variety of factors – including difficulties in reaching the target market, the high risk profile of clients, their general distaste for the joint liability requirement and high overhead costs – made solidarity lending unviable without subsidies.

18 See www.bbc.co.uk/worldservice/business/2009/07/090729_karlan_interview.shtml (accessed October 2010).

19 Williams, *50 Facts that Should Change the World*; see also http://en.wikipedia.org/wiki/List_of_countries_by_military_expenditures (accessed July 2011) which shows that the USA spends the most among countries in direct expenditure on its military – about 5 per cent of its GDP.

20 Williams, *50 Facts that Should Change the World*.

21 *Evening Standard*, 24 May 2010.

22 *Metro*, 8 February 2010.

23 *Metro*, 9 February 2010.

24 *Evening Standard*, 2 August 2010.

25 Quoted in Boyle, *The Little Money Book*.

26 The UK has announced a one billion pound climate fund for Africa after setting up the International Climate fund, ICF. See http://www.decc.gov.uk/en/content/cms/tackling/international/icf/icf.aspx.

27 Gita Verma, in Mike Davis, *Planet of Slums*, p. 78.

3 Gypsies, tramps and thieves: the story of cities and slums

1 Jonathan Raban, *The Soft City*, New York: Picador, 1974.

2 Doug Saunders, *Arrival City: How the largest migration in history is reshaping our world*, New York: Pantheon, 2011.

3 Robert Neuwirth, *Shadow Cities: A billion squatters, a new urban world*, New York: Routledge: 2006.

4 Roger Dixon and Stephen Muthesius, *Victorian Architecture*, London: Thames & Hudson, 1985, p. 10 say: 'Those who benefited from the unprecedented wealth created by the Industrial Revolution were in the main the owners of capital. But on the other end of the scale, although the standard of living of many of the working class improved, large numbers lived on incomes which provided them with only the bare necessities and sometimes not even that.' Middle classes were also not immune from poverty as shown by the poignant diary of Molly Hughes, in her book *A London Child of the 1870s*, London: Persephone Books, 2005, who lived not far from where I teach now in Islington and whose father committed suicide owing to shame from poverty and lack of a job. At that time, my own ancestors in India from Bengal were forced to grow indigo instead of rice, for the printed cotton (cotton from Indian and West Indian plantations) that was being processed and exported out of Britain's mills, even to India. Thousands of Bengali farmers paid with their lives for this practice that supported the economy of Britain. The lives of many British mill workers also continued to be miserable – which was highlighted by M. K. Gandhi during his visit in 1931 with his call for a boycott of British cotton.

5 See www.unhabitat.org/content.asp?typeid=19&catid=555&cid=5373 (accessed February 2010).

6 Charles Jencks and William Chaitkin, *Current Architecture*, London: Academy Editions, 1982, p. 222.

7 As a matter of interest, one of the slums in West Delhi is called Beadonpura/Bidonpura ('pura' instead of 'ville' as in Haiti).

8 See www.unhabitat.org/documents/media_centre/sowcr2006/SOWCR%205.pdf (accessed July 2010).

9 See www.timesonline.co.uk/tol/news/world/asia/article1805596.ece (accessed June 2011).

10 See www.adb.org/gender/practices/infrastructure/ind001.asp (acccessed July 2010). Much of the work I did at the Housing and Urban Development Corporation in Delhi in 1987–8 centred around low-income housing.

11 See www.adb.org/gender/practices/infrastructure/ind001.asp (accessed October 2010).

12 See http://1mundoreal.org/about/mundo-real-history (accessed July 2011) and also research carried out by Joao Wrobel, former student at London Metropolitan University, who continues to work there.

13 Alain Tarrius, 'Europe without borders: Migration networks, transnational territories and informal activities', in Barbara Drieskens, Franck Mermier and Heiko Wimmen (eds) *Cities of the South*, London: Saqi Books in association with Heinrich Böll Foundation, 2007.

14 Mike Davis, *Planet of Slums*, London: Verso, 2006.

15 See http://portalsostenibilidad.upc.edu/archivos/fichas/informes/huellaecol%F3gicadetoronto.pdf (accessed July 2011); also see Carolyn Steel, *Hungry Cities: How food shapes our lives*, London: Chatto & Windus, 2008, about food and the city.

16 See http://en.wikipedia.org/wiki/List_of_cities_proper_by_population (accessed June 2011). This list is about the city proper, not the Metropolitan area but even then Mumbai which is much smaller than Mexico city is not too far behind; see also http://en.wikipedia.org/wiki/List_of_metropolitan_areas_by_population (accessed June 2011).

17 See www.guardian.co.uk/world/2010/dec/28/jakarta-indonesia-capital-livable-move (accessed January 2011).

18 See www.unhabitat.org/content.asp?typeid=19&catid=555&cid=5373 (accessed February 2010).

19 Jyoti Hosagrahar, *Indigenous Modernities: Negotiating architecture and urbanism*, Abingdon: Routledge, 2005.

20 Sabine Bitter and Helmut Weber, *Caracas: Hecho En Venezuela*, Revolver Books, 2005. Interestingly, although these housing blocks were built, according to the authors and from an archival film I have seen, for the first time, *ranchos* began to be visible in the hills around the city too (the population of Caracas doubled between 1936 and 1952 owing to rural–urban migration).

21 See www.rainafoundation.com/slumhousing.asp (accessed March 2011).

22 See http://idsn.org/fileadmin/user_folder/pdf/New_files/India/Whose_Wealth_Whose_Commons.pdf (accessed January 2011).

23 See www.guardian.co.uk/world/2011/apr/26/favela-ghost-town-rio-world-cup (accessed April 2011) and www.guardian.co.uk/world/2010/dec/05/rio-de-janeiro-favelas-brazil (accessed January 2011).

24 See http://www.unhabitat.org/pmss/listItemDetails.aspx?publicationID=2101 (accessed April 2011).

25 Davis, *Planet of Slums*.

26 The *favelas* of Rio would form an exception to that as they are on prime land with good views and ventilation. However, they are built precariously on steep hills.

27 See www.independent.co.uk/news/world/americas/hurricane-katrina-the-storm-that-shamed-america-2057164.html (accessed November 2010).

28 See www.independent.co.uk/opinion/commentators/jon-snow-after-half-a-century-a-forgotten-scourge-is-back-2306273.html (accessed July 2011).

29 Sumita Sinha, original research, School of Planning and Architecture, 1985 and 2006.

30 Sumita Sinha, original research, School of Planning and Architecture, 1985.

31 There is a fascinating account called *Barcelonas*, by Manuel Vasquez Montalban, London: Verso, 1992.

32 Max Rodenbeck, journalist quoted in *Planet of Slums*.

33 Jencks and Chaitkin, *Current Architecture*, p. 222.

34 See www.bbc.co.uk/news/uk-england-bristol-13167041 (accessed April 2011).

35 See, for example, the thirteenth edition of the *Squatter's Handbook*, published by Advisory Service for Squatters, London, 2009, available for £1.50.

36 *Daily Mail*, 3 May 2010.

37 John Turner, 'Housing as a Verb', in Turner, John F. C. and Richter, R. (eds) *Freedom to Build: Dweller control of the housing*, New York: Macmillan, 1972, pp. 148–75.

38 See www.independent.co.uk/life-style/population-growth-spurs-surge-to-asias-cities-2300255.html (accessed July 2011).

39 Aldo Rossi, *Architecture of the City*, Cambridge, MA: MIT Press, 1984.

40 See http://en.wikipedia.org/wiki/Maurice_Halbwachs (accessed May 2011).

41 See http://de.wikipedia.org/wiki/Hans_Bernoulli (accessed May 2011).

42 Rossi, *Architecture of the City*.

43 See http://lang.sbsun.com/projects/fireflood/P3/bn29caracas.asp (accessed May 2010).

44 At one *barrio* where I worked, I was on higher ground than a twenty-storey block next to it and thankful for the metrocable that reached me there.

45 Gita Verma, 'Indore's Habitat Improvement Project: Success or failure?' *Habitat International*, 24, 2000, pp. 91–117.

46 See   www.guardian.co.uk/world/2011/mar/05/money-power-politics-battle-mumbai-slums (accessed July 2011).

47 This is just one of the references: http://bedouinjewishjustice.blogspot.com/2011/03/el-araqib-destroyed-for-21st-time-jnf.html (accessed July 2011) – there are many others.

48 Kenneth Frampton, *Contemporary Architecture and City Form: The South Asian paradigm*, Bombay: Marg Publications, 1997.

49 Marcus Fairs, *Icon Magazine*, June 2005, p. 111.

50 See   http://www.doorsofperception.com/mailinglist/archives/2005/02/doors_8_on_infr.php (accessed March 2008).

51 *Icon Magazine*, June 2005, p. 111. Here, 'North' means the rich Western countries.

52 Richard H. Robbins, *Global Problems and the Culture of Capitalism*, London: Allyn and Bacon, 1999, p. 354.

53 See www.globalissues.org/article/166/womens-rights (accessed March 2011).

4 Materials and technology

1 Marcus Fairs, *Icon Magazine*, June 2005, p. 10.

2 Inflation rate, Venezuela: 29.7 per cent, March 2011. See http://venezuelanalysis.com/news/5616 (accessed March 2011).

3 Paul Oliver (ed.), *Encyclopaedia of Vernacular Architecture of the World*, vol. 1, Cambridge: Cambridge University Press, 1997.

4 *Icon Magazine*, June 2005, p.109.

5 Sumita Sinha, *Encyclopedia of the Vernacular Architecture of the World*, vol. 2 (ed. Paul Oliver).

6 *Icon Magazine*, June 2005, p. 111.

7 Martin Pawley, *Garbage Housing*, London: Architectural Press, 1975; T. C Boyle, *Drop City*, New York: Viking Press, 2003.

8 Paul Oliver, *Built to Meet Needs: Cultural issues in vernacular architecture*, London: Architectural Press, 2006, p. 169.

9 See http://practicalaction.org/9262 (accessed March 2011).

10 Hassan Fathy, *Architecture for the Poor*, Chicago, IL: University of Chicago Press, 1973, p. 128.

11 Michael Braungart and William McDonough, *Cradle to Cradle*, London: Vintage, 2008, p. 58.

12 See www.bsigroup.co.uk/en/Assessment-and-Certification-services/Management-systems/Standards-and-Schemes/BES-6001 (accessed April 2011).

13 See   www.constructionproducts.org.uk/publications/dbfiles/Waste_Draft_Part%202_30-3-10%20V4.pdf (accessed March 2011).

14 See http://venezuelanalysis.com/analysis/797 (accessed May 2011).

15 Ibid.

16 See Thomas Lemken, 'New glory for old sites, re-new', *Daylight & Architecture*, Winter 2008, issue 10, p. 49.

17 Ibid.

18 Ibid.

19 From the publication *Energy Consumption in the United Kingdom*, Department of Trade and Industry and National Office of Statistics, 2002.

20 *Metro*, 13 May 2009.

21 *National Geographic*, October 2007.

22 Kingsley O. Dimuna, 'Incessant incidents of building collapse in Nigeria: A challenge to stakeholders', *Global Journal of Researches in Engineering*, 10(4), 2010, pp. 75–84. Online at: http://globaljournals.org/GJRE_Volume10/9-Incessant-Incidents-of-Building-Collapse-in-Nigeria.pdf (accessed March 2011).

23 See   www.indianexpress.com/news/in-2-yrs-35-buildings-collapsed-but-no-arr/743984 (accessed February 2011).

24   Ibid.
25   Kingsley O. Dimuna, p. 3.
26   Gita Verma, *Slumming India: A chronicle of slums and their saviors*, New Delhi: Penguin India, 2002.
27   Morna E. Gregory and Sian James, *Toilets of the World*, London: Merrell Publishers, 2006.
28   See http://lauriebaker.net (accessed January 2012).
29   Keith Hall (ed.), *Green Building Bible*, vol. 1, 3rd edn, Carmarthenshire: Green Building Press, 2006.
30   See   www.independent.co.uk/arts-entertainment/art/news/architecture-home-is-a-little-mud-hut-in-dagenham-dont-dismiss-it-as-primitive-says-sumita-sinha-earth-architec-ture-is-cheap-strong-and-ecologically-sound-1539914.html (article by author – accessed September 2011).
31   Sumita Sinha and Patrick Schuman, 'Earth building today: Technical paper', *Architects Journal*, 22 September 1994.
32   Keith Hall (ed.), *Green Building Bible*.
33   The Sustainability Statement of the Stone Federation Great Britain. Online at: http://www.stone-federationgb.org.uk/content.aspx?content=71.
34   Ibid.
35   See www.tufi.org.uk/news/july_2009_update.html#stone_unions (accessed July 2010).
36   Sumita Sinha, 'The ecology and ethics of brick kilns', *Basin News*, no. 11, March 1996.
37   See http://new.thebiggive.org.uk/projects/view/5327 (accessed September 2011).
38   Fathy Hassan, *Architecture for the Poor*, Chicago, IL: Chicago University Press, 1973.
39   Paul Oliver, *Built to Meet Needs: Cultural issues in vernacular architecture*, London: Architectural Press, 2006, p. 145.
40   Ibid.
41   Carole Ryan, *Traditional Construction for a Sustainable Future*, London: Spon Press, 2011.
42   Oliver, *Built to Meet Needs*.

5   Learning from tradition: sustainable cities

1   Robert Venturi, Denise Scott Brown and Steven Izenour, *Learning from Las Vegas*, Cambridge, MA: MIT Press, 1977, p. 3.
2   See   www.fig.net/pub/monthly_articles/august_2004/kotter_august_2004.htm   (accessed June 2011).
3   This is an interesting publication available online at: www04.abb.com/global/seitp/seitp202.nsf/c71c66c1f02e6575c125711f004660e6/64cee3203250d1b7c12572c8003b2b48/$FILE/Energy+efficiency+in+the+power+grid.pdf (accessed July 2011).
4   See http://news.bbc.co.uk/1/hi/business/4802248.stm (accessed June 2010).
5   Delhi Master Plan 2021, Ministry of Urban Development. See http://www.inrnews.com/indianrealestate/reports/delhi_master_plan_2021.pdf (accessed November 2009).
6   Heather Stuart, 'Water for healthy change: An exploration of water and sanitation development in urban India', MA thesis, London Metropolitan University, 2009.
7   See   www.newgeography.com/content/002170-the-problem-with-megacities   (accessed July 2011).
8   See   www.nationalatlas.gov/articles/people/a_international.html   (accessed   May   2010) and also see USA carbon emissions at: www.brookings.edu/papers/2011/0213_recovery_renewal.aspx (accessed July 2011).
9   See   http://greenanswers.com/q/63410/recycling-waste/garbage/what-countries-produce-most-trash (accessed June 2010).
10   'The Story of Stuff' on YouTube – there are several on different aspects.
11   See   http://thinkprogress.org/politics/2006/12/20/9281/bush-shopping   (accessed   June 2010).

12 Legal and General Market overview, 1 September 2009–28 February 2010 (note also that Japan is now in recession as a result of the impact of the 2011 tsunami).

13 See www.ft.com/cms/s/0/e66a3d7c-9073-11e0-9227-00144feab49a.html#axzz1Tb3lH9N6 (accessed June 2011).

14 See http://siteresources.worldbank.org/INTPAH/Resources/Publications/Dying-for-Change/dyifull2.pdf (accessed May 2010).

15 Jessica Williams, *50 Facts that Should Change the World*, London: Icon Books, 2004. I saw many obese people in the *barrios*, although not in the slums of India.

16 Craig Sams, *The Little Food Book*, Bristol: Alistair Sawday Publishing, 2003; Jules Pretty, *Agri-Culture: Reconnecting People, Land and Nature*, London: Earthscan, 2002.

17 Carolyn Steele, *Hungry City: How food shapes our lives*. London: Chatto & Windus, 2008.

18 Williams, *50 Facts that Should Change the World*; also see *The Little Food Book* by Craig Sam; the report on the 'Future of food and farming: Challenges and choices for global sustainability', available online at: www.bis.gov.uk/assets/bispartners/foresight/docs/food-and-farming/11-546-future-of-food-and-farming-report.pdf (accessed July 2011).

19 Bharati Mukherjee and Clark Blaise, in Simon Winchester (ed.) *Calcutta*, London: Lonely Planet Publications, 2004, p. 95.

20 It was common to find half burnt bodies thrown in the holy river by crematorium staff and attendants to save wood, probably in this belief.

21 See www.guardian.co.uk/news/blog/2008/jul/18/tenthingsivelearntaboutch?INTCMP=SRCH (accessed July 2011).

22 See Antony Clayton's book, *Subterranean City: Beneath the streets of London*, London: Historical Publications, 2000, for more description of the pollution problems.

23 See www.edie.net/news/news_story.asp?id=17705 (accessed December 2010).

24 Edo's sustainable credentials can be researched from many books and web references. Here are two which are particularly detailed: http://www.energybulletin.net/node/5140 (accessed July 2011) and http://www.japanfs.org/en/pages/009397.html (accessed July 2011). The second website contains the entire book *Japan in the Edo Period: An ecologically-conscious society* (*O-edo ecology jijo*, published in 2000, Kodansha Publishing Company) by Eisuke Ishikawa, who specializes in the environmental issues of the Edo period (1603–1867).

25 Daisaku Ikeda, *For the Sake of Peace: Seven paths to global harmony*, Santa Monica, CA: Middleway Press, 2002.

26 See *RIBA Journal*, August/September 2009 for more case studies.

27 Peter Droege, *The Renewable City: A comprehensive guide to an urban revolution*, Chichester: John Wiley & Sons, 2006, p. 105.

28 This particular webpage has many links to information about Curitiba: www.geography-pages.co.uk/curitiba.htm (accessed July 2011).

29 Jaime Lerner, 'Sustainable city', RIBA Trust Lecture, 4 November 2009.

30 See www.sustainablecitiesnet.com/models/sustainable-city-curitiba-brazil (accessed July 2011).

31 Revathi and Vasant Kamath, in Raj Rewal, Jean-Louis Veret and Ram Sharma (eds) *Architecure in India*, Paris: Electra France, 1985.

32 See Jennifer Elliott, *An Introduction to Sustainable Development*, London: Routledge, 1994 and Erika Cudworth, *Environment and Society*, London: Routledge, 2003.

33 Cudworth, *Environment and Society*.

34 See www.smithsonianmag.com/travel/Endangered-Cultural-Treasures-Jaisalmer-Fort-India.html (accessed July 2011).

35 See www.thehindu.com/todays-paper/tp-national/article2303973.ece (accessed July 2011).

36 See www.rainwaterharvesting.org/rural/manapia.htm (accessed September 2010).

37 James Bruges, *The Little Earth Book*, Bristol: Alistair Sawday Publishing, 2000.

38 See www.tarunbharatsangh.org (accessed July 2010). Also see Nitya Jacob's book, *Jalyatra: Exploring India's traditional water management systems*, London: Penguin, 2008 for more examples.
39 See www.tarunbharatsangh.org (accessed July 2010).
40 Ibid.
41 Droege, *The Renewable City*.
42 *Geography and You*, November–December 2008. Published in India in English and Hindi.
43 See report from Enercon here: https://climatefriendly.com/skins/files/file/pdf/project_page/Jaisalmer_Wind_Project_Profile.pdf?PHPSESSID=9eldhdq37f7vs2crul799es7m2 (accessed July 2011) which does not mention any of the problems.
44 Enercon was prohibited from exporting their wind turbines to the US until 2010 owing to alleged infringement of US Patent 5,083,039 (as of now, this dispute remains unresolved).
45 See http://www.gwec.net/index.php?id=13 (accessed May 2010).
46 Ibid.
47 Available in English online at www.geographyandyou.com/861.htm (accessed January 2011).
48 See www.mywindpowersystem.com/2009/07/wind-farm-or-solar-farm-land-for-sale-india/&usg= (accessed January 2010).
49 Quoted in *Middle East* magazine, April 2010. Also see www.desertec.org/en/concept/faq (accessed January 2010).
50 See www.dimts.in/pdf/Delhi_BRT_System_Lessons_Learnt.pdf (accessed July 2011).
51 Williams, *50 Facts that Should Change the World*.
52 A reed bed is used at the Centre for Alternate Technology, Wales, UK and the elephant enclosure at Chester zoo.
53 Presentation on Cuba's gardens, Venezuela Solidarity Conference, 16 April 2011. Also see Magdalena Morales, 'Cuba exports city farming "revolution" to Venezuela', *Reuters*, 22 April 2003.
54 See www.worldwatch.org/node/3912 (accessed January 2011).
55 Droege, *The Renewable City*.

6 Participatory design for scarce resources and rapid change

1 See David Gordon, 'Indicators of poverty and hunger', available at: www.un.org/esa/socdev/unyin/documents/ydiDavidGordon_poverty.pdf (accessed September 2011).
2 See http://lithgow-schmidt.dk/sherry-arnstein/ladder-of-citizen-participation.html (accessed January 2010), originally published as Sherry R. Arnstein, 'A ladder of citizen participation', *Journal of the American Institute of Planners*, 35, July 1969.
3 Lucien Kroll, 'Architecture of complexity', in Charles Jencks and Karl Kropf (eds) *Theories and Manifestoes of Contemporary Architecture*, London: Wiley-Academy, 1997, p. 101.
4 Participatory design workshop, London Metropolitan University, October 2010; Blundell-Jones, P., Petrescu, D. and Till, J. (eds) *Architecture and Participation*, London: Spon Press, 2005.
5 Gita Verma, *Slumming India: A chronicle of slums and their saviours*, New Delhi: Penguin India, 2002.
6 For an exhaustive description of how this works, see the 2006 ILO publication www.ilo.org/public/english/employment/recon/eiip/download/ratp/ratp07.pdf (accessed March 2011).
7 J.C. Nesbit, K. Belfer and J. Vargo, 'A convergent participation model for evaluation of learning objects', *Canadian Journal of Learning and Technology*, 28(3), 2002.
8 Participatory design workshop, London Metropolitan University, October 2010.
9 Sherry R. Arnstein, 'A Ladder of Citizen Participation', *JAIP*, 35(4), July 1969, pp. 216–24.
10 Blundell-Jones, P., Petrescu, D. and Till, J. (eds) *Architecture and Participation*.
11 Till, ibid.

12 Guy Bourgeault, *On Being Human*, Santa Monica, CA: Middleway Press, 2003.

13 See www.guardian.co.uk/environment/2011/may/25/nuclear-waste-kings-cliffe-landfill (accessed May 2011).

14 See http://pubs.iied.org/pdfs/G02826.pdf (accessed June 2011); also 'Reflections on practical ethics for participatory community-based adaptation' in *Participatory Learning and Action 60*, IIED, 2009, p. 175.

15 Participatory workshop, London Metropolitan University, 18 October 2010.

16 Verma, *Slumming India*. One of the projects is also described here – Habitat International 24 (2000) 91–117 which is downloadable from http://www.architexturez.net/+/subject-listing/000144.shtml (accessed November 2010).

17 Hugo Slim and Paul Thompson, *Listening for a Change: Oral testimony and development*, contributing editors Olivia Bennett and Nigel Cross, London: Panos, 1993.

18 See www.sasanet.org/documents/Tools/Participatory%20Planning.pdf (accessed March 2011).

7 Culture, ethics and other travelling discomforts

1 My response (said with a twinkle in the eye) to this was that if he could take off most of his clothes, then he would look like the Carib and Yanomami people. Perhaps because this student comes from an Islamic culture where men and women wade fully clothed into the sea, he looked rather puzzled.

2 As Chair of the Royal Institute of British Architects' Equality Forum, Architects For Change (2000–4), I was (and still am) amazed by the views expressed in emails and conversations that, for example, diversity and equal opportunities were not relevant issues for architects, along with other cultural issues.

3 Architecture and Design, 'The Everyday and Architecture', Profile 134, December 1998.

4 For details, see www.architecture.com/Files/RIBAProfessionalServices/Education/Validation/RIBAValidationCriteriafromSeptember2011Parts1,23.pdf (accessed November 2009). I am currently working on a research document for the Centre for Education in the Built Environment on how design methodologies incorporating social issues and participatory methods can be incorporated within the RIBA Part I and II.

5 Steen Elier Rasmussen, *Experiencing Architecture*, Cambridge, MA: MIT Press, 1959.

6 See also Paul Oliver's 'Necessity and sustainability: The impending crisis', Chapter 24 from *Built to Meet Needs: Cultural issues in vernacular architecture*, London: Architectural Press, 2006, pp. 421–4.

7 Paul Oliver (ed.) *Encyclopedia of Vernacular Architecture of the World*, vol. 1, Cambridge: Cambridge University Press, 1997, p. 499.

8 Thomas Friedman, *The World is Flat*, New York: Farrar, Straus & Giroux, 2005.

9 Oliver, *Built to Meet Needs*, p. 62.

10 Richard Wilson, *Don't Get Fooled Again: The sceptic's guide to life*, London: Icon Books, 2008.

11 Ben Goldacre, *Bad Science*, London: Harper Perennial, 2009.

12 Sumita Sinha, *Encyclopedia of Vernacular Architecture of the World*, vol. 1, (ed. Paul Oliver), 1997.

13 Oliver, *Built to Meet Needs*.

14 See http://portal.unesco.org/culture (accessed September 2010).

15 *The Courier Magazine*, April 2000, published by UNESCO.

16 *Art of Living magazine*, SGI-UK publication, November 2010.

17 India is a country with 1652 recorded languages (1961 census) and here the 'secondary official language', English, has become a unifying language.

18 Mahatma Gandhi, *Essential Writings*, Oxford: OUP, 2008, p. 291.

19 At the All-Party Parliamentary Group for International Development and the Environment conference, 'The view from streets: citizen-led contribution to urban poverty reduction', 17 October 2011, Houses of Parliament, London.

20 Mark Tully, *No Full Stops in India*, New Delhi: Penguin India, 1992, p. 7.

21 See www.geerthofstede.nl (accessed July 2010).

22 See www.geert-hofstede.com (accessed July 2010).

23 Raja Shehadeh, *Palestinian Walks: Notes on a vanishing landscape*, London: Profile Books, 2008, p. 47.

24 Clarissa Pinkola Estes, *Women Who Run with the Wolves: Myths and stories of the wild woman archetype*, London: Rider, 1992, p. 387. Followers of Freud call it 'projective identification'.

25 Jyoti Hosagrahar, *Indigenous Modernities: Negotiating architecture and urbanism*, Abingdon: Routledge, 2005, p. 163.

26 Michel Laguerre, *The Informal City*, New York: St Martin's Press, 1994.

27 Ibid.

28 Eduardo Porter, *The Price of Everything: The cost of birth, the price of death and the value of everything in between*, London: William Heineman, 2011.

29 Ibid.

30 Scott Carney, *The Red Market: On the trail of the world's organ brokers, bone thieves, blood farmers, and child traffickers*, New York: HarperCollins, 2011.

31 See www.guardian.co.uk/uk/2009/mar/02/westminster-cctv-system-privacy (accessed June 2009).

32 See www-05.ibm.com/innovation/uk/smartercity/index.html?csr=emuk_agspscit-20101108&cm=k&cr=google&ct=101AE02W&S_TACT=101AE02W&ck=smart_cities&cmp=101AE&mkwid=sjkhqQzue_7567491043_4328nk2971 (accessed December 2010).

33 Andrew Keen writing in *Wired* magazine, March 2011.

34 For an interesting view from the 'other side', read Mark Danner's review of Schlesinger's report for the New York Review, available at: www.nybooks.com/articles/archives/2004/oct/07/abu-ghraib-the-hidden-story (accessed September 2010).

35 Peter Singer, *Practical Ethics*, 3rd edn, Cambridge: Cambridge University Press, 2011, p. 11.

36 See http://www.sppsr.ucla.edu/up/webfiles/S11/229S11.pdf (accessed June 2011).

37 Robert Pirsig, *Lila: An Inquiry into morals*, London: Bantam Books, 1991.

38 See www.uxbooth.com/blog/using-lies-in-research (accessed April 2011).

39 Darrell Huff, *How to Lie with Statistics*, London: Penguin, 1991.

40 Chelsea Duke, *High Heels and a Head Torch: The essential guide for girls who backpack*, London: Pan, 2009.

41 Watching a gang robbing a woman in the lobby of a hospital in West London in April 2011 was a stark reminder of that.

42 Jerry Hirshberg, *The Creative Priority: Putting innovation to work in your business*, London: HarperCollins, 1999.

43 See www.homeoffice.gov.uk/agencies-public-bodies/crb (accessed September 2011).

44 Padmasiri de Silva, *A Dialogue of Cultures for Sustainable Development*, London: Commonwealth Ecology Council, Calverts Press, 1992.

45 Ethics Workshop, Graduate School, London Metropolitan University, June 2010.

46 Quoted in Alan Fletcher, *The Art of Looking Sideways*, London: Phaidon, 2001.

47 Wallace Stevens, 'Man Carrying Thing', *The Collected Poems of Wallace Stevens*, London: Vintage Books, 1954.

48 UNFPA, *Working from Within: 24 tips for culturally sensitive programming*. Available at: www.unfpa.org/culture/tips.htm (accessed September 2011) (a downloadable training manual has also been produced for development activists).

8 Observing and recording the 'soft' city: tools and (cautionary) tales

1 Jonathan Raban, *The Soft City*, New York: Picador, 1974, p. 163.

2 For a humorous account of this, see Darrell Huff, *How to Lie with Statistics*, London: Penguin, 1991.

3   *Slumming it*, *Channel 4*, January 14–15, 2010.

4   Habraken, N.J., *The Structure of the Ordinary: Form and control in the built environment*, Cambridge, MA: MIT Press, 2000, p. 3 (prologue).

5   A group of artists and designers in London have come together to document such spaces. See www.walkwalkwalk.org for more information (accessed June 2010).

6   Tali Hatuka and Rachel Kallus, 'The myth of informal place-making: Stitching and unstitching Atarim Square in Tel Aviv', *Journal of Architecture*, 12(2), April 2007, pp. 147–64. (Stitching is used in the paper to denote the coming together of the complex web of informal relationships in informal spaces.)

7   Sabine Bitter and Helmut Weber, *Caracas: Hecho En Venezuela*, London: Revolver Books, 2005, p. 12.

8   Robert Venturi, Stephen Izenour and Denise Scott Brown, *Learning from Las Vegas: The forgotten symbolism of architectural form*, Cambridge, MA: MIT Press, 1972.

9   Peter C. Bosselmann, *Representation of Places: Reality and realism in city design*, Berkeley, CA: University of California Press, 1998.

10 Juliet Davis, *Touching the City*, Canterbury: Canterbury School of Architecture, 2009.

11 For example, Kevin Lynch, 1960; Kaplan and Kaplan, 1982; Cullen, 1961; Von Meiss, 1990.

12 Michel Laguerre, *The Informal City*, New York: St Martin's Press, 1994.

13 Edward De Bono, *Simplicity*, London: Penguin, 1998.

14 See www.bbc.co.uk/news/world-latin-america-13193503 (accessed May 2011).

15 Roger Trancik, *Finding Lost Space: Theories of urban design*, New York: John Wiley & Sons, 1986.

16 Clarissa Pinkola Estes, *Women Who Run with the Wolves: Myths and stories of the wild woman archetype*, London: Rider, 1992.

17 Oscar Newman, *Defensible Space: People and design in a violent city*, London: Architectural Press, 1973. The concept of defensible space is not without criticism. In Hatford, Connecticut, USA, streets were closed and assigned to police teams but Hartford did not show a dramatic drop in crime. Yet, privately accessed areas of St Louis, USA, have much lower crime than public streets. It is possible that in St Louis people had the capacity and incentives to defend their defensible spaces. For example, residents had the right to ask an unwelcome individual to leave the space.

18 Steve Edwards, *Photography: A very short introduction*, Oxford: Oxford University Press, 2006, pp. 5–6.

19 Viet Hoai Nguyen, MA design thesis, London Metropolitan University, 2009.

20 V. Johnson, E. Ivan Smith, G. Gordon, P. Pridmore and P. Scott (eds) *Stepping Forward: Children and young people's participation in the development process*, London: Intermediate Technology, 1998.

21 Lorraine Farrelly, *Basics Architecture: Representational techniques*, Lausanne: AVA Publishers, 2007.

22 Viet Hoai Nguyen, MA design thesis, London Metropolitan University, 2009.

23 Clarissa Pinkola Estes, *Women Who Run with the Wolves*, London: Rider, 1992.

24 Desmond Morris, *The Human Animal*, London: BBC Books, 1994, p. 191.

25 Aboriginal moiety refers to the system of law governing social interaction, particularly marriage, in traditional Aboriginal culture.

26 W. Caruana, *Aboriginal Art*, London: Thames & Hudson, 1993.

27 Steen Eiler Rasmussen, *Experiencing Architecture*, Cambridge, MA: MIT Press, 1959.

28 See http://festivalbrazil.southbankcentre.co.uk/project-morrihno (accessed July 2010).

29 Banksy, *Wall and Piece*, London: Century Books, 2005, p. 8. The book comes with its ironic warning: 'the book shows the creative/artistic element of graffiti art and is not meant to encourage or induce graffiti where it is illegal or inappropriate'.

30 Ikeda, *A new Humanism: The University addresses of Daisaku Ikeda*, New York: Weatherhill, 1996, p. 156.
31 Quoted in Hugo Slim and Paul Thompson, *Listening for a Change: Oral testimony and community development*, London: Panos Publications, 1993.
32 From *Geography and You* magazine, December 2008 – article about wind farms in Jaisalmer, India.
33 Hatuka and Kallus, 'The myth of informal place-making'.
34 Nelson Mandela, *Long Walk to Freedom*, Boston and New York: Little Brown, 1994.
35 Che Guevara, *The Motorcycle Diaries: Notes on a Latin American journey*, London: Harper Perennial, 2003.
36 See http://www.eltiuna.org (accessed January 2010).
37 Juliet Davis, *Touching the City*.
38 Alain de Botton, *The Art of Travel*, London: Penguin, 2003.
39 Blaise Pascal, *Pensées*, London: Penguin, 2003, p. 37.

9 The development activist and new ways of working

1 Ziauddin Sardar, *Introducing Chaos: A graphic guide*, London: Icon Books, 2008, pp. 156–7.
2 *Building Design*, Life Class, March 11, 2011.
3 Nabeel Hamdi, *Small Change*, London: Earthscan, p. 45.
4 Ian Collins, *RIBA Journal*, March 2011.
5 Ibid.
6 Stephen Levitt and Steven Dubner, *Freakonomics: A rogue economist explores the hidden side of everything*, London: Penguin, 2007.
7 Nabeel Hamdi, 'Inspire2Aspire' conference, 4–5 March 2008, London Metropolitan University.
8 Ben Addy, *Building Design*, 11 March 2011. See http://www.bdonline.co.uk/comment/debate/are-schools-of-architecture-letting-students-down?/5014816.article (accessed March 2011).
9 *Building Design*, letters from Jake Ireland and Keir Alexander, 11 March 2011.
10 See http://apps.cadc.auburn.edu/rural-studio/Default.aspx?path=Gallery%2fPurpose%2f Objective%2f (accessed June 2011).
11 Paul Hyett, *In Practice*, London: Emap Construct Publishers, p. 119.
12 See http://rectoversoblog.com/2009/11/22/letters-to-a-young-architect (accessed June 2011).
13 See www.urbanouveau.com/index.php?/ihs/interviews (accessed September 2011).
14 Alan Fletcher, *The Art of Thinking Sideways*, London: Phaidon, 2007, p. 76.
15 Bremner, Lindsay, *Writing the City into Being: Essays on Johannesburg*, Johannesburg: Fourthwall Books, 2010, p.208.
16 Ibid., p. 217.
17 See http://en.wikipedia.org/wiki/Colonia_(United_States) (accessed September 2010).
18 Tsunesaburo Makiguchi, *Zenshu*, vol. 10, p. 146.

Suggested reading

Chapter 1

Dorling, D., Newman, M. and Barford, A., *The Atlas of the Real World: Mapping the way we live*, London: Thames & Hudson, 2010.

Hamdi, Nabeel, *Small Change: About the art of practice and the limits of planning in cities*, London: Earthscan, 2004.

Henderson, H. and Ikeda, D., *Planetary Citizenship*, Santa Monica, CA: Middleway Press, 2004.

Juniper, Tony, *How Many Light Bulbs Does It Take to Change a Planet? 95 ways to save the planet*, London: Quercus, 2007.

Norton, Michael, *365 Ways to Change the World*, London: Harper Perennial, 2006.

Williams, Jessica, *50 Facts that Should Change the World*, London: Icon Books, 2004.

Chapter 2

Black, Maggie, *The No-Nonsense Guide to International development*, Oxford: New Internationalist Publications/Verso, 2002.

Boyle, David, *The Little Money Book*, Bristol: Alastair Sawday's Fragile Earth Books, 2003.

Porter, Eduardo, *The Price of Everything: The cost of birth, the price of death and the value of everything in between*, London: William Heinemann, 2011.

Schumacher, E.F., *Small is Beautiful: A study of economics as if people mattered*, New York: Vintage, 1993.

Stalker, Peter, *The No-Nonsense Guide to Global Finance*, Oxford: New Internationalist Publications, 2009.

Wheen, Francis, *How Mumbo-Jumbo Conquered the World: A short history of modern delusions*, London: Fourth Estate, 2004.

Chapter 3

Dreiskens, B., Mermier, F. and Wimmen, H. (eds), *Cities of the South*, Saqi Books with Heinrich Boll Foundation, 2007.

Hosagrahar, Jyoti, *Indigenous Modernities: Negotiating architecture and urbanism*, Abingdon: Routledge, 2005.

Mitlin, Diana and Satterthwaite, David, *Empowering the Squatter Citizen: Local government, civil society and urban poverty reduction*, London: Earthscan, 2004.

Sainath, P., *Everyone Loves a Good Drought*, New Delhi: Penguin India, 1996 (reprinted 2002).

Swift, Richard (ed.), Squatter Town: the South's urban explosion, *New Internationalist*, special edition, January/February 2006.

UN-HABITAT, *The Challenge of Slums: Global report on human settlements*, 2003, available at: www.unhabitat.org/content.asp?typeid=19&catid=555&cid=5373 (accessed September 2011).

Verma, Gita, *Slumming India: A chronicle of slums and their saviors*, New Delhi: Penguin India, 2002.

Chapter 4

Fathy, Hassan, *Architecture for the Poor*, Chicago, IL: Chicago University Press, 1973.

Guzowski, Mary, *Towards Zero Energy Architecture: New solar design*, London: Laurence King Publishing, 2010.

Horning, Jonathan, *Simple Shelters*, Glastonbury: Wooden Books, 2009.

Jencks, Charles and Chaitkin, William, *Current Architecture*, London: Academy Editions, 1982.

Oliver, Paul (ed.), *Encyclopedia of Vernacular Architecture of the World*, Cambridge: Cambridge University Press, 1997.

Oliver, Paul, *Built to Meet Needs: Cultural issues in vernacular architecture*, London: Architectural Press, 2006.

Pearson, David, *The New Natural House Book*, London: Conran Octopus, 1998.

Stulz, Roland and Mukerji, Kiran, *Appropriate Building Materials*, Switzerland: SKAT Publications, 1993.

Chapter 5

Black, Maggie, *The No-Nonsense Guide to International Development*, Oxford: New Internationalist Publications/Verso, 2002.

Cudworth, Erika, *Environment and Society*, London: Routledge, 2002.

DfID (Department for International Development), *Developments Magazine*, Issue 46, 2009 (available at: http://webarchive.nationalarchives.gov.uk/+/http://www.dfid.gov.uk/Get-Involved/Developments-magazine/Back-Issues/Developments-magazine-issue-46/).

Droege, Peter, *The Renewable City: A comprehensive guide to an urban revolution*, Chichester: John Wiley & Sons, 2006.

Godrej, Dinyar, *The No-Nonsense Guide to Climate Change*, Oxford: New Internationalist Publications, 2007.

Steele, Carolyn, *Hungry Cities: How food shapes our lives*, London: Chatto & Windus, 2008.

Thomas, Derek, *Architecture and Urban Environment: A vision for the New Age*, London: Architectural Press, 2002.

Chapter 6

Blundell-Jones, P., Petrescu, D. and Till, J. (eds), *Architecture and Participation*, London: Routledge, 2005.

Chambers, Robert, *Participation Workshops: A sourcebook of 21 sets of ideas and activities*, London: Earthscan, 2002.

Fisher, Roger and Ury, William, *Getting to Yes*, New York: Random House Business Books, 1981.

Hamdi, Nabeel, *The Placemakers Guide to Building Community*, London: Earthscan, 2010.

Johnson, V., Ivan-Smith, E., Gordon, G., Pridmore, P. and Scott, P. (eds) *Stepping Forward: Children and young people's participation in the development process*, London: Intermediate Technology Publications, 1998.

Chapter 7

Carmona, M., Heath, T., Oc, T. and Tiesdell, S., *Public Places, Urban Spaces: Dimensions of urban design*, London: Architectural Press, 2003.

Conefrey, Mike, *The Adventurer's Handbook: Life's lessons from history's great explorers*, London: Collins, 2005.

Dupre, Ben, *50 Big Ideas You Really Need to Know*, London: Quercus, 2009.

Ikeda, D., Simard, R. and Bourgeault, G., *On Being Human: Where ethics, medicine and spirituality converge*, Santa Monica, CA: Middleway Press, 2003.

McGreal, Ian P., *Great Thinkers of the Eastern World*, HarperCollins, 1995.

Robinson, Dave and Garratt, Chris, *Ethics: A graphic guide*, London: Icon Books, 2008 (note – this book is only about Western ethics).

Sennett, Richard, *The Uses of Disorder: Personal identity and city life*, London: Penguin, 1970.

Singer, Peter, *Practical Ethics* (3rd edn), Cambridge: Cambridge University Press, 1993.

Websites

IRAS (the Integrated Application System): www.myresearchproject.org.uk.

National Research Ethics Service: www.nres.npsa.nhs.uk.

Social Care Research Ethics: www.screc.org.uk.

Chapter 8

Berger, John, *Ways of Seeing*, London: BBC and Penguin, 1972.

Farrelly, Lorraine, *Basics Architecture: Representational Techniques*, Lausanne: AVA Publishers, 2007.

Farrelly, Lorraine, *Drawing for Urban Design*, London: Laurence King, 2011.

Frederick, Matthew, *101 Things I learnt in Architecture School*, Cambridge, MA: MIT Press, 2007.

Habraken, N.J., *The Structure of the Ordinary: Form and control in the built environment*, new edn, Cambridge, MA: MIT Press, 2000.

Jacobs, Jane, *Death and Life of Great American Cities*, New York: Random House, 1997.

Mayall, W.H., *Principles in Design*, London: Design Council, 1978.

Rasmussen, Steen Elier, *Experiencing Architecture*, Cambridge, MA: MIT Press, 1959.

Chapter 9

Baderman, James and Law, Justine, *Everyday Legends: Ordinary people changing our world*, York: WW Publishing, 2006.

Bethel, Dayle M. (ed.), *Education for Creative Living: Ideas and Proposals of Tsunesaburo Makiguchi*, trans. Alfred Birnbaum, Ames, IA: Iowa State University Press, 1989.

Branson, Richard, *Screw It, Lets Do It: Lessons in life and business*, London: Virgin Books, 2010.

Gladwell, Malcolm, *The Tipping Point: How Little Things Can Make a Big Difference*, New York: Little Brown, 2000.

Levitt, Steven and Dubner, Stephen, *Freakonomics: A Rogue Economist Explores the Hidden Side of Everything*, London: Penguin, 2007.

Miller, Anne, *How to Get Your Ideas Adopted: And change the world*, London: Marshall Cavendish Business, 2009.

Wilson, Richard, *Don't Get Fooled Again: The sceptic's guide to life*, London: Icon Books, 2008.

Website

http://www.spatialagency.net (inspirational accounts of opportunities in which architects and non-architects can operate and suggests 'other ways of doing architecture').

Further references

Bitter, Sabine and Weber, Helmut, *Caracas: Hecho En Venezuela*, London: Revolver Books, 2005.

Bosselmann, Peter C., *Representation of Places: Reality and realism in city design*, Berkeley, CA: University of California Press, 1998.

Boyle, T.C., *Drop City*, New York: Viking Press, 2003.

Braungart, Michael and McDonough, William, *Cradle to Cradle*, London: Vintage, 2008.

Bremner, Lindsay, *Writing the City into Being: Essays on Johannesburg*, Johannesburg: Fourthwall Books, 2010.

Carney, Scott, *The Red Market: On the trail of the world's organ brokers, bone thieves, blood farmers, and child traffickers*, New York: HarperCollins, 2011.

Caruana, W., *Aboriginal Art*, London: Thames & Hudson, 1993.

Clayton, Antony, *Subterranean City: Beneath the streets of London*, London: Historical Publications, 2000.

Cullen, Gordon, *Concise Landscape*, London: Architectural Press, 1961.

Davis, Mike, *Planet of Slums*, London: Verso, 2006.

De Bono, Edward, *Simplicity*, London: Penguin, 1998.

De Botton, Alain, *The Art of Travel*, London: Penguin, 2003.

De Rosney, Joel, *The Macroscope*, trans. Robert Edwards, New York: Harper & Sons, 1977.

De Silva, Padmasiri, *A Dialogue of Cultures for Sustainable Development*, London: Commonwealth Ecology Council/Calverts Press, 1992.

Dixon, Roger and Muthesius, Stephen, *Victorian Architecture*, London: Thames & Hudson, 1985.

Edwards, Steve, *Photography: A very short introduction*, Oxford: Oxford University Press, 2006.

Elliott, Jennifer, *An Introduction to Sustainable Development*, London: Routledge, 1994.

Fletcher, Alan, *The Art of Looking Sideways*, London: Phaidon, 2001.

Foucault, Michel, *Discipline and Punishment: The Birth of Prison*, trans. Alan Sheridan, New York: Vintage Books, 1995.

Frampton, Kenneth, *Contemporary Architecture and City Form: The South Asian paradigm*, Bombay: Marg Publications, 1997.

Friedman, Thomas, *The World is Flat*, New York: Farrar, Straus & Giroux, 2005.

Goldacre, Ben, *Bad Science*, London: Harper Perennial, 2008.

Hall, Keith (ed.), *Green Building Bible*, vol. 1, 3rd edn, Carmarthenshire: Green Building Press, 2006.

Hamdi, Nabeel, *Small Change*, London: Earthscan, 2004.

Huff, Darrell, *How to Lie with Statistics*, London: Penguin, 1991.

Ikeda, Daisaku, *For the Sake of Peace: Seven paths to global harmony*, Santa Monica, CA: Middleway Press, 2002.

Jacob, Nitya, *Jalyatra: Exploring India's traditional water management systems*, London: Penguin, 2008.

Jencks, Charles and Kropf, Karl (eds), *Theories and Manifestoes of Contemporary Architecture*, London: Academy Editions, 1997.

Kaplan, S. and Kaplan, R., *Cognition and Environment: Functioning in an uncertain world*, New York: Praeger, 1982.

Laguerre, Michel, *The Informal City*, New York: St Martin's Press, 1994.

Lévi-Strauss, Claude, *Tristes Tropiques*, trans. John Russell, New York: Criterion Books, 1961.

Lynch, Kevin, *Image of the City*, Cambridge, MA: MIT Press, 1960.

Martin Pawley, *Garbage Housing*, London: Architectural Press, 1975.

Morris, Desmond, *The Human Animal*, London: BBC Books, 1994.

Neuwirth, Robert, *Shadow Cities: A billion squatters, a new urban world*, new edn, New York: Routledge, 2006.

Pawley, Martin, *Garbage Housing*, London: Architectural Press, 1975.

Perec, Georges, *Species of Spaces and Other Pieces*, London: Penguin, 1974.

Raban, Jonathan, *The Soft City*, New York: Picador, 1974.

Rewal, Raj, Veret, Jean-Louis and Sharma, Ram (eds), *Architecure in India*, Paris: Electra France, 1985.

Rossi, Aldo, *Architecture of the City*, Cambridge, MA: MIT Press, 1984.

Rowe, Dorothy, *The Real Meaning of Money*, London: HarperCollins, 1998.

Ryan, Carole, *Traditional Construction for a Sustainable Future*, London: Spon Press, 2011.

Sardar, Ziauddin, *Introducing Chaos: A graphic guide*, London: Icon Books, 2008.

Saunders, Doug, *Arrival City: How the largest migration in history is changing our world*, New York: Pantheon, 2011.

Shehadeh, Raja, *Palestinian Walks: Notes on a vanishing landscape*, London: Profile Books, 2008.

Slim, Hugo and Thompson, Paul, *Listening for a Change: Oral testimony and community development*, London: Panos Publications, 1993.

Taleb, Nassim Nicholas, *The Black Swan: The impact of the highly improbable*, New York: Random House, 2010.

Trancik, Roger, *Finding Lost Space: Theories of urban design*, New York: John Wiley & Sons, 1986.

Vasquez Montalban, Manuel, *Barcelonas*, London: Verso, 1992.

Venturi, Robert, Izenour, Stephen and Scott Brown, Denise, *Learning from Las Vegas: The forgotten symbolism of architectural form*, Cambridge, MA: MIT Press, 1972.

Von Meiss, P., *Elements of Architecture: From Form to Place*, London: E&F Spon, 1990.

Wright, Alex, *Glut: Mastering information through the ages*, Washington, DC: Joseph Henry Press, 2007.

Index

Page numbers ending in 'f' refer to figures and ending in 'n' refer to notes.